DOING BUSINESS IN RUSSIA

DOING BUSINESS IN RUSSIA

Basic Facts for the Pioneering Entrepreneur

Tankred G. Golenpolsky
Robert M. Johnstone
Vladimir A. Kashin

Edited by Linda Pinkham

The Oasis Press® / PSI Research
Grants Pass, Oregon

04/21/95

Table of Contents
Содержание

Tables

Russian Foreword
Предисловие Русское

Has the collapse of the Soviet Union led to the disintegration of the promising development of trade and economic relations between the United States and the USSR? To what extent has the political instability in the Commonwealth of Independent States that has sprung up on the ruins of a former superpower served as a major handicap for American businesspeople, who are looking for possible investment variants and patterns in our part of the world? Will relations with Moscow, Kiev, Alma-Ati and other capitals of the former Soviet Union become simpler or more complicated because the old, centralized, bureaucratic system has become extinct? In a situation of general instability, shakiness, and unsteadiness, how do you get reliable information on possibilities to make profitable investments? Whom can you deal with and are there any pilots who can take you to a safe haven through the roaring and stormy sea of endless change, which, when looking from abroad, may seem a manifestation of boundless anarchy?

These and other questions I am sure worry American business and political circles. And that is quite natural, for much of what happened came as a surprise for the United States, as well as for many of us in the USSR Depending to a great extent upon the answers, are the chances for a fast and profound progress in trade, finances, and other spheres of economic cooperation with the United States on the one hand and Russia and other countries of the post-Soviet zone on the other.

It is also important from the point of view of continuing the development of political cooperation between our two countries. Particularly, because of the corridors of power in Russia — and I have reason to believe this refers to other states of the Commonwealth — political priorities today are being built in a way that depends on the readiness of these states to help the economic revival of this country, help it "warm up" in every possible way the national economy with the help of investments, credits, and other forms of business involvement.

As someone who has dedicated the greater part of his professional life to Soviet-American relations and their comprehensive partnership, as a person who sincerely and emotionally feels for the future of Russia and its neighboring countries, I would want to share with the readers of this book some of my thoughts.

I am sure that doing business with Russia, Ukraine, Kazakhstan, Byelorussia, and other parts of the former Soviet Union can be most profitable for American corporations, as well as for middle-size and small businesses. The untapped wealth of these countries, the high level of education of the population, the cheap labor, and particularly the thriving and unprecedented in scale markets exist as realities. The crash of the old totalitarian system and the formation of a democratic country and a democratic society have created a certain type of discomfort.

Instead of one highly centralized partner, American businesses shall have to deal with a multitude of yet unknown partners, with often no experience in international commerce. But this is only a seeming discomfort. In reality, the possibilities of profitable investments for foreign businesses have grown immensely. This has occurred as the result of decentralization and the growing independence of the nongovernmental, privatized economy.

In no way do I want to diminish the difficulties that exist in reality. I am referring to the insufficiently developed constitutional and legal framework for the activity of foreign capital in Russia. All sorts of contradictory laws are still in existence, though people are already working on doing away with them. Other problems include: the lack of experience of many of the new CEOs in the new firms and companies that are today taking their first steps in foreign trade, our undeveloped banking system, the mish-mash of taxation laws, and the unclear situation in land ownership.

To those Western corporations that are capable of risk taking, today is the day to begin and quickly accomplish the strategy for interaction with Russia. I would think that it would be worthwhile to establish a presence in the region by opening up representations or starting up joint ventures here. Those who will be able to secure for themselves positions in the economies of the Commonwealth may be sure that they shall retain the privileged position in the future boundless market that is being conceived now.

The economic system of the USSR operated on principles different from the United States, but had a built-in manageability necessary for joint decision making when faced with world problems. As a result of the processes that are taking place today, the transition to free enterprise have upset this system of manageability without simultaneously starting off the new mechanism at the appropriate speed for market regulated economic and social processes.

A dangerous pause has occurred that is dramatically slowing down the process of democratic change so necessary for Russia. The consequences may be dangerous both for the people of Russia and for the general international situation.

The experience of my whole life in the practical aspects of international politics and the conclusions of historic analyses testify that this sort of development should be and can be opposed. In this sense, partnership with the United States is especially beneficial, not only in the sense of borrowing some of its experience, but also in the form of mutual development of the industrial raw materials and intellectual potential. Cooperation of this sort cannot be unproductive. Moreover, it shall have a positive impact upon other countries whose economic well-being depends upon the situation in Russia.

The authors of the book you are about to read do not try to conceal the existing difficulties in Russia, but they invite you to overcome them jointly. And the many examples they give, confirm that this can be done and with a good profit for foreign investors, too. I think it is an honest and timely book.

Of course, there are difficulties, but do not forget that Russia today has to cover a similar distance that took the West many decades to travel. And Russia has an essential imperative for the sake of its people to do it in several years and months. And, yes, one should not think that everything is starting from scratch in Russia. What in reality is happening could be called the restoration of an economic system that put Russia in certain sectors in the forefront of the economically developed countries in the beginning of the twentieth century.

Russia will not be able to achieve success without including businesspeople from both our countries in the orbit of mutual cooperation. Many of my American friends are already actively involved. I wish them success. I also wish both success and prosperity to the American readers of this book. I am sure they shall find it a necessary and useful guide into the world of Russian business. Others will get interested in the booming Russian market. The authors have performed a positive service for their countries in an example of cooperation based upon shared values and goals in an honest presentation.

ALEXANDER A. BESSMERTNYKH
President, Foreign Policy Association
Former USSR Ambassador to the United States

Moscow, Russia, 1995

American Foreword

Предисловие Американское

Even the casual follower of events in the post-Soviet era understands that "Doing Business in Russia" is not for the faint-hearted or the risk-averse. But it is doable, and for the pioneering entrepreneur, this book of the same name makes patently clear how to do it.

Written in a style designed for the business reader considering an investment in Russia but with little or no Russian experience, the book lays out its thesis on the feasibility of successful investment in Russia and then proceeds to a no-holds-barred analysis of how to make it happen.

Doing business in Russia requires all of the careful analysis of doing business in the United States and elsewhere in the developed world. In addition, Russia offers the full gamut of challenges of doing business in a developing country with economic, legal, social, political, and other uncertainties. What is unique in Russia is this: those many environmental factors that make doing business in the developing world difficult manifest themselves in Russia in ways that are often more complex, intense, and changing. The foreign investor must make special efforts to track these changes on a real time basis, whether it is the vagaries of tax and customs laws or the key bureaucrats and politicians or the reliability of sources of raw materials for your operations. That is where this book comes in.

This book takes on the challenges of doing business in Russia chapter by chapter and pulls no punches. Each chapter reviews the background aspect of the subject, whether it is banking, taxes, or crime; highlights the special problem areas; and then proceeds to give you solid advice on how to resolve them.

While no book could hope to answer all the questions regarding doing business in Russia or solve all the problems, this book takes you far enough in your understanding that you should be able to handle new, unanticipated problems when they arise. And the authors are not afraid to make recommendations in key areas, not just provide a useful background and leave you to make your own way.

From the opening chapter they lay out their argument that Russia is the "new Klondike" to the tearout cards in the back on how to ask for a taxi, toilet, or police officer, the authors have the practicing businessperson, on the ground in Russia, constantly in mind. Even for those who have explored doing business in Russia since it opened for Western investment in the early 1990s, this book represents the best up-to-date treatment of what is happening there and the direction the country is going in areas of direct relevance for business.

No book can hope to define a successful path to doing business in Russia into the future, but this is as good a road map as you can find today. Equally important, the book will leave you with the necessary tools to find your way in the future when the road map ends.

EARL A. MOLANDER
Board of Directors

Russian-American Enterprise Fund
Portland, Oregon, 1995

Acknowledgments

От авторов

The authors wish to express their special appreciation for the dedication, talent, and loyalty of Maria George (Masha).

The book in its present form would not have been possible without the extraordinary editing skills of managing editor Linda Pinkham of The Oasis Press, the editorial assistance of Vickie Reierson, the book's design and typography by Constance C. Dickinson, typographic assistance of Jan Olsson and Melanie Whalon, and the cover creation by Debra Ross. A great debt of gratitude is owed to our publishers Ardella and Emmett Ramey for their faith, patience, and support in making this project a reality.

We are also indebted to *The Moscow Times*, *The Moscow Tribune*, and the U.S. Foreign Commercial Service of the American Embassy.

We acknowledge the kindness, generosity, and extraordinary efforts of Jerry and Helen Stern.

For his wisdom and advice, we thank Charles G. Botsford (Charlie), Chairman and Director of Rusam, Inc., Washington, D.C.

We also wish to acknowledge the support and criticisms of Dr. Earl A. Molander, Board Member of the Russian-American Enterprise Fund and Executive Director of the Free Market Business Development Institute, School of Business Administration, at Portland State

University. Further acknowledgments go to Alexander Bessmertnykh, former Foreign Minister of the U.S.S.R, former Ambassador of the U.S.S.R. to the United States, Chairman of the World Council of Former Foreign Ministers, and Chairman of the Foreign Policy Association of Russia.

A special debt of appreciation is also owed to Joseph S. Johnstone and Catherine I. Johnstone; Stephen J. Aragon; Health Trust, Inc.; Jeb Bladine, publisher and editor of the *News-Register*, McMinnville, Oregon; Gayle Anderson, Chief of the Orange County Office of Protocol; Dr. Larissa Nezhinskaya; Wade Miller; Bruce G. Bryant, President of Valley Community Bank; Delford M. Smith, Chairman of the Board of Evergreen International Aviation; Murl Anderson, Ph.D.; Gene Carlson, M.Ed.; Frank Nelson, Ph.D., Richard F. Emery, M.A., and President Vivian Bull, Ph.D. of Linfield College, McMinnville, Oregon; and Allan De Sarran and Eric Weaver of the Foreign Commercial Service, U.S. Department of Commerce.

Chapter 1

Russia at the Crossroads
Россия на распутье

Russia today

Ten years have elapsed since the time Mikhail Gorbachev came to power in the Soviet Union — ten years that have shaken Russia and changed the map of Europe and the history of the modern world. Of course, when economic reforms were first introduced by Gorbachev's regime, many Soviet and world leaders theorized about what these reforms would mean to the country and world.

Few leaders at the time could have envisioned the extent of the changes those reforms have brought. From the collapse of the Berlin Wall and break up of the Soviet Union to the free market in Russia and the end of the Cold War, the consequences of these reforms are significant and surprising. The democratic and economic reforms led the country from the plains of a strict, centrally directed, unitary state, with a single economic plan, into the wilderness of a controversial but extremely active market economy.

That market has moved Russia from an all state-owned economy to one million, privately owned small businesses that today employ almost nine million people. Seventy percent of former state-controlled industries have been turned over to private owners within just the last three years. More than half of Russia's workers are now employed in the private sector. The total number of employed in Russia today totals 70.7 million people of the 148 million citizens living in the country as of March 1994. However, another major consequence those in power never envisioned was a country with well over six percent of the workforce unemployed, whereas before the changes, unemployment was virtually unknown.

With all of the radical changes that have occurred and that are still going on, you will want to acquaint yourself with today's Russia before you decide to do business there. In this book, you will find many reports and facts on the difficulties of doing business in Russia, but you will not find any recommendations on whether you should do business in Russia or not. Rather, you will find recommendations and information you can use if you do decide to go. That is what this book is about.

Dynamics of change

A survey on the change in dynamics of the situation, conducted from 1992 to 1994 by the Russian Independent Institute for Social Problems, shows that economic reforms have had a different effect on the various sections of the population. The winners are those who have become entrepreneurs or who were formerly the heads of private and state-owned enterprises. The losers, those who have been hit especially hard, are the pensioners and the rural population. And yet, in the summer of 1993, 76.8 percent of workers complained about their declining living standards. A year later, this figure was 18 percent lower. While 71.7 percent of the engineers and technicians were expressing their dissatisfaction in the summer of 1993, a year later, the figure dropped to 54.9 percent, even though the situation in the industry was getting drastically worse. Since the economic situation is hardly improving greatly, but dissatisfaction is decreasing, you can only conclude that Russians are adapting to the new economic conditions.

According to calculations made by the Russian government's Economic Trends Center in March 1994, compared to March 1993, the real average income per capita of the wealthiest part of the population (20 percent) has increased by 50 percent. Meanwhile, income remained practically unchanged in the lowest income group, which is as large as the wealthiest income group.

In March 1994, the very richest of the wealthiest part of the population (10 percent) accounted for nearly 30 percent of all incomes, with the very poorest of the lowest income group (10 percent) accounting for only 2 percent of all incomes. The gap between these two income groups is seriously increasing.

The majority of the population, falling between the extremes of wealth and poverty, are in a state of transition due to the major changes in the economic structure. Meanwhile, salaries of public health service workers, artists, scientists, and teachers are 20 percent below an average salary in the national economy.

Social tensions

In an economy like Russia has today with the income gap growing and the economy struggling to meet the demand for more jobs, if Russia did not have some social tensions, you would certainly be surprised. While social tensions are evident today in much wealthier countries, the extent of social tensions in Russia has been very much played up in the media — both Russian and foreign — with attention-grabbing articles.

For almost 70 years, Russia had both the wealthy and the poor, and both were invisible. The rich lived in government-provided DACHAS — suburban houses behind tall, green fences — and shopped in canteens designated only for them, which even in those days, were as well stocked as any foreign supermarket.

These privileged people were members of the Communist Party and government elite, their children, and their relatives. Their children studied in prestigious universities that guaranteed them long-term jobs abroad. True, they were afraid to demonstrate the extent of their wealth, even to each other for fear of being demoted: demonstrating richness was like demonstrating dirt. For example, Brezhnev's granddaughter would be taken to work in a state-owned car, but she would get out and walk the remaining two blocks to her workplace.

The poor lived in villages, and the crippled, sick, and homeless had to stay out of the streets of large cities. They were taken care of in special residences, sometimes more than 100 kilometers outside large towns.

As for the 'average' citizen, the gap between his or her salary and that of the head of a ministry was immense. Roughly speaking, $30 a month was the usual wage for the average citizen, while for the head of the ministry, this figure was $150. Today, the lower income bracket makes around $15 a month and the average income is $30, thus the two have not changed, but the upper bracket is around $3,000. Both wealth and poverty have insultingly poured out into the streets of towns and cities. The fact that modern Russian supermarkets are full of imported products and drinks can be a source of irritation because they are unavailable to perhaps a third of the population. Psychologically, quite a number of people would prefer to stand in lines the way 'it was then' and buy the available, rather than gaze at the unavailable. Such were the moods in the beginning, when the reforms just started.

As time has gone by, moods have tended to change somewhat. As polls showed in June 1994, 25 percent of the population said they do not feel social tensions. In provinces, which are worse off than in the center, 32 percent of the respondents seemed calm and untroubled. In heavily populated areas like Moscow or St. Petersburg, the indicator was worse, with only 11 percent untroubled. People between the ages of 40 and 50 showed higher sensitivity, nervousness, and a tendency to talk of politics.

Tensions were felt by both unprofessional workers and elderly persons with higher education. In the public sector, these indicators are 30 to 80 percent higher than in the private sector. In Moscow, 12 percent of those surveyed mentioned participating in meetings and demonstrations. The aggression factor was twice as high for Moscow and St. Petersburg compared to the Russian average. Major city residents feel that people are ready for violence and clashes with police.

The table below indicates the results of a survey of 1,100 people from various communities all over Russia in answer to the question, "How do social tensions show up in your community?"

Table 1: Social Tensions

Behaviors indicating tension	Percent (%)
Increasingly irritated people	52
Angry talk in queues and transport	41
Conversations with friends	32
Graffiti and vandalism	6
Meetings and demonstrations	2
Strikes	2

Source: All Russian Center for Public Opinion Studies.

A changing lifestyle

However, one reason for irritation could be the diet in Russia. A poll conducted by the Medical Academy's Institute for Dietetic Studies offered the following table:

Table 2: Russian Diet*

Foodstuffs	1989	1991	1992	1993
Wheat bread	68.66	73.03	71.46	70.48
Rye bread	23.62	24.70	26.69	26.68
Potatoes	93.83	98.10	106.65	117.58
Vegetables, watermelons, melons and gourds	91.00	87.00	83.00	74.00
Fruit and berries	41.00	37.00	34.00	37.00
Sugar and confectionery	33.00	29.00	28.00	33.00
Meat and meat products (total)	75.00	65.00	54.00	58.00
Beef	18.90	15.60	14.10	16.60
Mutton	2.23	1.50	1.39	1.22
Pork	10.35	9.50	10.29	10.98
Poultry	13.65	12.60	10.31	8.70
Sausage	14.40	13.00	10.37	10.54
Fish and fish products	16.10	14.10	11.60	12.00
Milk and dairy products (total)	397.00	348.00	299.00	298.00
Unskimmed milk	116.60	118.00	106.40	99.50
Sour cream and crecm	14.05	13.30	6.48	6.48
Butter	7.14	5.51	5.57	5.84
Eggs (pieces)	237.00	229.00	243.00	255.00
Vegetable oil, margarine	6.90	6.10	6.50	7.20

* Reported as kilograms (kg) consumed by each member of a family.

As you can see from the table, the average Russian's intake of potatoes and bread has increased substantially, with a corresponding reduction occurring in consumption of meats, fresh produce, and dairy products. An interesting comparison is to the annual diet of the average American, which consists of 1,650 pounds (748 kg) of meat, eggs, and dairy products and 150 pounds (68 kg) of grain. Forty-three percent of the total diet of the average American consists of vegetables and fruits.

Traditional Russian foods

By comparative standards, Russia is not known for its cuisine. The Russian diet does not have the variety of Asian dishes or Southern European cooking. In sum, the traditional Russian diet is simple and predictable. The problem is they apparently learned their cooking from the Norwegians!

The traditional meal of peasants consists primarily of boiled or fried vegetables, such as potatoes (KARTOSHKA), turnips (REPA), onions (LUK), cucumbers (OGURTSY), beets (SVYOKLA), and cabbage (KAPUSTA). These vegetables are often pickled for preservation and use in winter. Cabbage and cucumbers are used as garnishes. Strawberries (KLUBNI-KA) and raspberries (MALINA) and during the months of August and September, melon (DYNYA) and watermelon (ARBOOZ) are seasonal supplements to the diet. In the winter, cranberries (KLYUKVA) are also available, as well as apples (YABLOKA), tangerines (MANDARINY), and persimmons (KHURMA).

Mushrooms (GRIBY) are widely used and popular. For lunches, soup is a main staple. Most Russians believe that eating lunch without soup will upset your stomach. The common soup is borscht, which has a deep red color derived from beets, which is its main ingredient.

Milk products, including yogurt, are available. Kefir is a very common, drinkable yogurt and is known by many as a wonderful nonprescription remedy for the morning after a night of too much toasting.

Bread, including black rye bread (RZHANOY KHLEB), is eaten with every meal. White bread is available in Moscow and the populated areas but is less available in rural areas. Cereals, such as wheat, barley, and oats, are a staple in rural areas and are usually found in a preparation called kasha, prepared by boiling the grain in water with salt and butter.

Meat was a rarity in old Russia; however, fish has always been a common menu item since the rivers provide bountiful yields of fish, including herring, red salmon, and black sturgeon. Red caviar is derived from salmon (KRASNAYA IKRA), and black caviar (CHORNAYA IKRA) is derived from sturgeon. Most frequently used appetizers include raw and smoked fish. In modern Russia, meat of all kinds — beef, pork, and lamb — is established as a main source of protein. Sausages (KOLBASA) are also much in demand. Vegetarianism is not common in

Russia. Particular meat dishes include ravioli or dumplings (PELMENI), a hotpot dish covered in dough (ZHARKOYE), cutlets (KOTLETY), and shish kebabs (SHASHLYK).

Russians normally drink tea (CHAY) and coffee (KOFYE) at the end of a meal. They tend not to use milk with coffee or tea, but saturate both with sugar.

To provide you with a broader view of Russian lifestyles, the article, "Everyday Life in Russia 1990–1994: 'Elusive' Routine," by Yelena Jaginova has been reprinted from *Business World Weekly* (No. 42/135) and is located at the end of this chapter.

Moving towards recovery

Poverty of the country amidst its naturally abundant resources has always been a problem for Russia. To overcome this problem, everything done previously was based on extensive farming methods, as opposed to intensive farming methods. Hence, the territorial expansion of the past: in four centuries, Russia increased its size four times.

The best age of Russia's national economy — the turn of the century — was based upon ideas, technology, and direct financing from the West. That was how new industries came into being. But richness of space and resources have played against Russia's interest, creating an illusion that these resources would never end. This lulled the initiative of the people — along with the 70-year-long experiment in creating a society of triumphant have-nots — the proletariat.

But time has passed, no curtain surrounds Russia anymore, and the country's leaders are out to find the best road to the country's future. These are the same leaders who once formulated the economic policy of the Central Committee of the Communist Party. After the fall of the Soviet Union, they enthusiastically embraced the other extreme in their attempt to transplant the Western model onto Russian soil. They named the remedy 'shock therapy.' The nation experienced the shock and is still expecting the therapy.

East meets West

Many Western economists have urged and continue to urge Russia to take the economic road that mirrors the one in the West. Attempts to deviate or take local conditions into account often call forth criticism from the West, verging on accusations of attempting to restore Soviet imperialism.

As a result of this pressure, in a country with almost no experience in genuine democracy or capitalism, things have gone out of control. Today, after all possible errors have been made, it is apparent that Russia needs its own path of development, which takes into account its history and traditions, geography, climate, level of culture and education, and multi-national character.

As for Russia's economic decline — isn't a decline universal for all countries with transitional economies? However, in its development, Russia has to consider the country's relationship to the world economy, taking into account the various aspects of French, Chinese, Spanish, and American economic realities; however, keeping in mind that after the end of the Cold War, the West's economy is also by far not in its best shape.

In mid-1994, commenting on the possibilities of cooperation between Russia and the West, Mr. Arkady Volsky, president of the Union of Industrialists and Entrepreneurs of Russia, wrote the following article, which appeared in *Business World* in connection with an industrial exhibit.

The rendering of financial and economic assistance to Russia and the various attitudes towards this have recently become the subject of wide discussion in many countries. Numerous publications in the mass media obviously tend to accuse the new Russian government of departing from the course of radical economic reforms and thus justify world financial institutions, which seek to slow down economic stabilization in Russia by holding back their assistance.

Such a position testifies that the West is obviously uncertain of Russia's capabilities for using the resources precisely for promoting economic and social reforms in the country. However, it was the imposition by the International Monetary Fund (on the initial stage of the reform) of abstract macroeconomic patterns completely disregarding the production structure and historical specifics of Russia that brought about the crisis of the Russian economy, fraught with escalating political extremism and growing social tension in the country.

Attempts are presently being made to explain to Western countries who claim that the necessary political and economic conditions have not been created in Russia.

Some elements of tension are still preserved, but this is connected, primarily, not with political, but rather with social and economic

*difficulties predetermined by grave miscalculations of monetary ro-
manticists who headed the reforms.*

*The Russian government is currently seeking to rectify the economy,
eliminate social tension, and create conditions necessary for attracting Western capital, which is badly needed to continue the reforms. It
would be wrong and even dangerous to raise the regulating role of the
state in production and foreign economic spheres, carry out structural changes in industry, ensure an uninterrupted functioning of key
branches, and create a system of social protection of the population
with the departure from market-oriented transformations.*

*In the past few years, Russia has been actively striving to enter the
General Agreement on Tariffs and Trade (GATT) by holding negotiations with foreign partners. It is fully understood that the admission
to GATT implies Russia's concessions to the partners. However, these
concessions should be bilateral and well-considered with due account
of Russia's economic potential, role in the world community, interests,
as well as the transition character of the Russian economic system.*

*Regrettably, Western countries still conduct the tactics of dual stan-
dards with respect to Russia, while their proclaimed course of cooperation, not infrequently, boils down to 'one-way traffic.' Russian exports of advanced technologies are invariably hampered. Their
creators, scientists, and specialists, are welcomed in the West. Moreover, no obstacles have been created in Russia to prevent Russian scientific and technical personnel from sharing their talent for the sake
of the world community.*

*Russian industrialists and entrepreneurs call upon Western politi-
cians and businessmen to recognize the existing political realities and
give up all verbiage about international assistance to Russia, replac-
ing it by real, mutually advantageous and constructive cooperation.
Only in this case will everybody profit, including rank-and-file citizens, businessmen, politicians, and the world community as a whole.*

As though in reply to Mr. Volsky's appeal, the *New York Times* came
out with an article written by a person well known among former
Sovietologists: Marshall Goldman, director of the Russian Research
Center at Harvard University. The former supporter of Russia's swift
transformation into a market economy, evidently disappointed at the
fact that his prescriptions didn't work, now urges Americans to stop
investing in the Russian economy. You should familiarize yourself
with Mr. Goldman's article. At the end of the chapter, the story is
reprinted as narrated by Dmitry Radyshevsky, the Moscow-New
York correspondent.

Making generalizations is always risky business, particularly when they concern not just one person, but a whole nation. In medicine, scientists first try experiments out on guinea pigs. Unless they take another nation for guinea pigs, perhaps scholars should be less categoric in their statements.

No one denies that the events Mr. Goldman describes could have taken place. There were cases when planes did not take off — five, six a year. And certain entrepreneurs lost money on inflation, an American accountant was killed, and yes, the legal system is just being formed. This is no secret that Russia has always been known as a country that writes beautiful plans and comprehensive laws only to violate them. After all, the 'great Stalin Constitution' had all that a democratic country can dream of in it: freedom of speech, travel, even cessation rights for republics of the USSR — so what? It never worked. There are many other countries, even democratic countries, where certain laws are not observed now and then. But are separate occurrences enough to generalize and say to all foreign businesspeople that these events are what happen in Russia every day? Soviet Cold War style propaganda seems to be contagious for people, such as Goldman, who have been working with it for an extended period of time.

Russians, too, have had their share of disappointments. Stories like: "One grade of products was paid for, and a lower grade was delivered in containers," or "Contracts were signed, and American businesspeople did not honor them." Scores of other cases are known of in the Russian business environment. Does that mean, "Don't do business with the Yankees?"

Furthermore, the Mafia seems to have found a comfortable *modus vivendi* — way of life — with their U.S. colleagues. Can anyone explain how the movies *Jurassic Park* and *Cliffhanger* could appear in Russia as pirated videos before they appeared on the movie screens — not as video — in the United States, unless the 'bad guys' on both sides found each other?

The new Klondike

The Russian market today is indeed the new Klondike. And even if you haven't reread your Jack London stories, you may remember that down there you could find the good guys and the bad guys. And some of the bad ones later became known as the robber barons and still later, founded some of America's best universities. Most people would agree with Mr. Goldman that doing business in Russia today is not for people with weak nerves. That is why this tough breed of people are called entrepreneurs and are not professors of history or prima donnas.

Increasing foreign investments

Most Russians realize that if Russia wants to obtain increased foreign investments, the country must, without any delays, introduce a number of major changes to the tax and customs regulations. "The amount of investments in Russia is dozens of times smaller than it could be in view of the size of the country," said the First Deputy Prime Minister of Russia, Anatoly Chubais, in his speech to foreign investors during the summer of 1994. Chubais also acknowledged, "There is a tough competitive struggle going on between a number of countries for foreign investment."

According to Economics Minister Yevgeny Yasin in another speech to foreign investors in November 1994, the most important solutions to questions on the government's agenda today are those that have been a bane to foreign investors. Some suggested solutions are to:

- Clarify banking regulations, particularly in relation to hard currency transactions;
- Abandon the value-added tax (VAT) on capital investments and equipment brought in from abroad;
- Exempt foreign companies from paying the excess wages tax; and
- Reform the profit tax.

Earlier in June, Prime Minister Victor Chernomyrdin told a conference designed to promote foreign investment and reassure investors about legal uncertainties, that the government plans to exempt foreign businesses from paying profit tax for five years and provide a three-year exemption from detrimental changes in legislation. However, neither measure has been implemented yet.

On the subject of reform, Mr. Chubais adds:

The current reform has already changed the institutional foundations of society and the form of ownership .... Financial stabilization has been achieved and if we solve the investment problem today, tomorrow everyone will talk about an economic miracle .... I very well understand that the success of reforms can hardly be tied in with the everyday feelings of people who have found themselves in an extremely difficult situation at the factories and mills that stand idle today. For someone who doesn't get his wage for three months, my discourses about portfolio investments going to Russia are something like tales about life on Mars.

When a top statesman has to confess about such things, it is a sad event. At the same time, Chubais' statement shows a major change in the level of frankness that exists between the Russian government and the people, something that was unheard of under Communist rule.

An ambiguity will always exist when the fate of a country at the crossroads is defined in terms of the next century, while the fate of that country's people — who are alive today and wanting a decent life — remains undefined. Of course, you cannot have your cake and eat it at the same time. The year 1995 could be a breakthrough for foreign investments in Russia, but financial stabilization certainly does not depend only on foreigners.

Bringing home Russian profits

"If the expatriated money comes back, we won't have to worry about loans," said one official close to the Prime Minister. And the expatriot Russian investors are gradually beginning to bring their money back home. For example, Andrei Pannikov, the first independent Russian oil trader whose company is registered in Belgium, will invest $70 million in a project that has lured him back to Russia. Pannikov has already invested the first $1.5 million. Another example is Mr. Farkhad Akhmetov, who owns a company in London. His company intends to work with the U.S. firm Bechtel in Russia's gas-producing fields. Akhmetov has already made a fortune exporting Russian oil.

Another sphere for repatriating dollars is in the securities market. By the beginning of September 1994, the total volume of portfolio investments — money collected by professional investment and stock brokerage companies — amounted to $2 billion. Two hundred million, or ten percent of this sum, has been brought back by Russian entrepreneurs abroad.

Examples of foreign investment activities

Fortunately, foreign investors also tend to turn a blind eye to the alarming figures of official Russian statistics relating to the national economy. Many of them believe, according to press reports, that statistics are unable to reflect the true dimensions of the market being developed in Russia. Foreign investment managers coming to Moscow are apt to believe that political chaos screens out the real progress of economic reforms.

According to the Moscow office of the Grant Financial Center, a private business, more than 90 percent of deals closed by Russian investment companies involve foreign clients. Some of the most successful examples of such joint cooperation between Russian enterprises and foreign investors are:

- The Kaluzhsky Turbine Factory, in which the Siemens Company — a German business — owns 10 percent of the stock. The German investor allocated DM 2 million (2 million deutsche marks equals approximately $1.4 million) to replenish the Russian company's circulating capital and supplied the factory with new equipment worth an additional DM 2 million.
- The British-American company, BAT, bought a package of stocks from the Saratov Tobacco Plant and is planning to invest $40 million for the plant's reconstruction.
- Proctor & Gamble owns 14 percent of the stock in the joint-stock company, Novomoskovskbythim, and plans to invest $50 million into that enterprise.
- The German firm, Zellstoffund Papier, recently purchased 30 percent of the Zhukovski Cooling Works' stock, as well as provided the works with $2 million in orders — enough to raise production by 32 percent. This type of Western investment helps Russia's privatized enterprises to overcome the production slump.
- The project between the logging enterprise Troitski-Pechersk in the Komi Region and the French firm, Yuet Holdings, is one of the largest collaborative efforts. Foreign investments in this project have reached $300 million.
- Credit Swiss First Boston Ltd. of the United States is the leading foreign investor with $500 million invested in Russian securities. B. Jordan of Credit Swiss' management team estimates the sum at about 70 percent of total foreign investment on the Russian securities market.

Analyzing the results of the first half of 1994, *Business Week* magazine states that Russia today is in the front line as the most attractive investment target. By March 1994, businesses from the United States established 953 joint ventures in Russia. In addition, they set up 327 that were 100 percent U.S. owned enterprises.

The top ten industries that were particularly attractive for foreign investments by 1994 are shown in Table 3 below.

Table 3: Top Ten Industries

Industry	1st quarter 1994 $ million
Fuel industry	61.5
Trade and restaurant business	14.0
Woodworking, cellulose, and paper	13.3
Machine building and metal working	10.3
Other manufacturing sectors	8.0
Construction	6.1
Science and research services	3.6
Transport and communications	3.6
Finance, credit, insurance, pension plans	3.3
Forestry	2.4

Table 4: Investments by Region

Region	1st quarter 1994 $ million
Moscow.	42.00
Arkhangelsk Region	41.00
Tomsk Region	16.30
Novosibirsk Region	5.00
Moscow Region	4.20
Irkutsk Region	3.30
St. Petersburg	3.10
Sakhalin Region	2.60
Republic of Karellya	2.15
Vladimir Region	2.13

Table 4 shows those regions with the largest investment volumes. As is seen in the table, Russia's best successes are indicated by the combined totals — exclusive of Moscow — of the provinces, where industries have been delegated broad authority and have established extensive connections with foreign investors, very often bypassing Moscow.

As one Reuter's report from Moscow put it, "Investment funds in Russia's independent-minded regions, frustrated by political and legal chaos in Moscow are talking independently to Western investors to sell them blocks of shares (in industries from aluminum to oil)."

One company countered the Moscow-centered economic approach when it created a holding company that represents 60 percent of Russia's gold — according to official data, Russia produces annually 146.8 tons of gold and exports 6.6 tons — and 70 percent of its oil. The Siberian Holding Company formed eleven different investment funds all the way to Kamchatka.

Similar regional alliances are being formed in and around the Urals and in the Far East. In Fall 1994 as Boris Yeltsin's Chief Economic Adviser, Alexander Livshits, puts it: "Reform in Russia cannot come from the power base, it must come from the masses."

When you are contemplating a deal or investment in Russia, advises Robert Wad-Gery, Vice-Chairman of British-based Barclays Bank investment banking division, known as BZW, "You've got to think pragmatically about what is the real power balance between a region and Moscow. The answer might be completely different from one area to another."

According to an unusually optimistic prognosis made by Russian and foreign economists voiced at a recent conference in Moscow, Russia's economic decline is bottoming out and there are signs of stabilization. "The economy has hit the bottom and is drifting there, getting ready to rise to the surface," said Sergei Pavlenko, Director of the Center for Economic Reform. However, Russia's Prime Minister Victor Chernomyrdin is more careful in his evaluation of the situation:

We face today the following scenario: either the production slump will become a sluggish depression or the economic mechanisms, designed to ensure economic improvements in 1995 and lay the groundwork for positive development in 1996–97, will begin to work. The key aspects of this movement are: a major decline in the federal budget deficit and suppression of inflation to a level which will improve the investment environment, production, and living standards.

Summary

The radical changes that have occurred in Russia have had an impact on the government, the economy, and even the social fabric. Converting to a market economy has created opportunities for business and, at the same time, an onslaught of eager investors, for which the government and the economic structure are not equipped.

In later chapters, as you learn how business is done in Russia, you will better understand how laws in the areas of business registration and regulation, taxes, currency and banking, and property ownership and rights, are lagging behind the economic boom — to the point of crisis — in the new Klondike, Russia. Learning as much as possible about your Russian colleagues and their culture will help you immensely. For this reason, interesting articles, documents, and statistics have been reprinted and included at the end of many chapters in this book.

The article, "Pulling Out of the Crisis," appearing on the next several pages is somewhat shortened from the version that appeared in the Moscow English-language paper, *Business World*, in Fall 1994. The article provides an analysis of the situation in Russia and proposes solutions. The author, Abel Aganbegyan, is one of Russia's top economists and is the scholar traditionally considered to be one of the masterminds behind the concept of Mikhail Gorbachev's perestroika — the name given to the Soviet policy for economic and political reform. Aganbegyan is a member of the Academy of Sciences of the Russian Federation and director of the Academy of National Economy under the Council of Ministers of the Russian Federation.

Pulling Out of the Crisis
by Abel Aganbegyan

Russia's economy entered a new phase in mid-1993. Prior to that period, it was possible to check the production slump through monetary injections into the economy. Since the middle of 1993, however, the production slump has steepened. Even budgetary subsidies have had little effect on production dynamics.

What is to be done?

World experience has shown that economic crisis can be overcome through boosting investments. To step up investment activity, it's necessary to bridle inflation ....

A fall in the inflation rate will make Russian banks lower interest rates. The Central Bank of Russia (CBR) has already announced its decision to cut interest on the credit. Lowering inflation and interest rates will stabilize the ruble/dollar exchange rate and encourage savings, while lowering interest on capital will extend the term of credit .... To accelerate the process, it's necessary to create a favorable environment for attracting foreign capital.

There is money in Russia

... Currently, there are over $20 billion on currency accounts in Russia, another $18 billion are stashed abroad. Some R1 trillion [1 trillion rubles] are exchanged for dollars and marks daily. The population displays much activity in buying up various shares and securities. There is money in Russia, but, just as in other market economies, it has mostly sunk into the pockets of the population. The Russian economy, which has developed under a totalitarian regime and central planning, is mostly geared to satisfy the needs of the military-industrial complex and heavy industry rather than consumer demand, which lead to a structural crisis and a sharp production decline in defense and heavy industries.

So, the population or, to be more precise, its well-to-do brackets, have accumulated a lot of money, as have some enterprises and organizations, but are unwilling to spend it for the purchase of costly domestic goods of poor quality. High import tariffs push up prices for foreign-made goods, which restricts purchasing power. So, the consumers wait for better times to arrive ....

Who will go bust?

A drop in the inflation rate will entail bankruptcies. The potential bankruptcies are:

• Banks, which won't be able to return credits due to the insolvency of their clients — enterprises and organizations. The latter hoped to cash in through selling goods at inflated prices. According to estimates, over 50 percent of the banks may go broke. So, the people and organizations, which deposited their money in these banks, will also suffer losses. This primarily refers to investment funds, various credit and financial institutions. The process has already taken hold and is sure to pick up speed;

• Intermediary trading outlets, which gamble on a rise in prices. Nearly all small firms, which have capitalized on sugar sales, have now collapsed. This is due to a fall in wholesale sugar prices;

• Enterprises, whose products find no demand on the market since high production costs push up prices. Bankruptcy does not always mean the liquidation of an enterprise. It can be swallowed up by some larger commercial entity, which undertakes repaying its debts and organizing more efficient production.

Learning to survive

During the transition to a market economy, the majority of enterprises will manage to survive if they cut production costs .... The easiest way to reduce costs is to cut personnel, phase out ineffective production, and switch to a tight financial policy.

All these measures will trigger a growth in unemployment. The number of unemployed in Russia has now reached one percent of the labor force. However, West European experts in unemployment believe the jobless account for five percent to six percent of the labor force, including part-time employment and unpaid leaves.

The insolvency of enterprises is closely related to all the above problems. The total debts of enterprises run at R 32 trillion, overdue payments at R 16 trillion. Indebtedness accounts for some ten percent of the GDP (Gross Domestic Product).

Is there a panacea?

... The time is ripe for taking radical measures. Making due payments is of paramount importance. Currently, many enterprises have enough funds at their disposal, but, nevertheless, are in no hurry to pay for the delivered products. In a number of cases, the suppliers can't cancel the delivery of their goods as they are under obligation to the states (for example, oil deliveries to certain refineries). At that, neither the state nor the consumer answer for payment period. This situation needs to be rectified. Introducing promissory notes could help settle the nonpayment crisis.

Small business – it's serious

One of the ways to overcome the crisis, to check the growth of unemployment and enhance the living standards is to develop small business. It seems that Russia is the only country which holds back from granting privileges to small business .... Thousands of firms went into small business illegally to avoid taxes. The development of small business will help expand employment and ensure additional income. Moreover, small business is the most dynamic sector of the economy; it quickly adapts to the rapidly changing situation and more fully meets social requirements.

Where is the real owner?

By now, the bulk of Russian enterprises have gone through the first stage of privatization — a closed allotment of shares and voucher auctions, which were selling approximately 20 percent of the block of shares .... The majority of privatized enterprises has not received a proper market assessment of their value and failed to find a real owner, though this is precisely what the privatization drive was conceived for.

The entire post-privatization activity of an enterprise will aim at assessing its market value and finding a real owner, at restructuring and, quite possibly, switching over to more effective production.

First, it's essential to develop marketing systems. Learning to market goods is more important than producing them. Large firms should have their own trading outlets and dealers in order to successfully market goods. The firms with a vertical set up prove more successful on the market. Their activity is not limited to mining raw materials, it covers the whole production cycle, up to the consumer. Vivid examples of that are oil companies, which stake on oil refining and production of petrochemicals, rather than on oil extraction. In addition, they have their own network of gas pumps.

Second, enterprises should develop their own financial services. In some cases, special financial corporations are to be set up and industrial enterprises are to be transformed into the industrial-financial groups.

And lastly, legal advice bureaus need to be created.

❄

The New Klondike Myth is Dispelled
by Dmitry Radyshevsky

Instead of optimistic essays about American businessmen who success-fully invested capital in Russia, The New York Times *has printed an article "Business in Russia? Not for the Time Being."*

Moscow Bureau, New York

Why Americans won't do business in Russia

Ordinary Americans' enthusiasm for Russian reforms has been replaced by apathy. American citizens are as tired of hearing about Russia's great difficulties and small successes as about the war in Bosnia and tribal massacres in Africa. Under Congressional pressure, President Clinton strives to stress that he is not biased by his friendship with President Yeltsin and intends to pay more attention to other CIS countries.

Marshall Goldman, author of the *New York Times* article and Director of the Russian Research Center at Harvard University, was initially a supporter of Russia's swift transformation into a market economy. He is now preparing to publish the book entitled, *A Missed Opportunity: Why Economic Reform in Russia Hasn't Worked.* He has also published an article urging Americans to stop investing money in the Russian economy.

Obviously the widespread Russian view — "we are in a muddle, but we are a Klondike for investors" — is not shared by Americans. The descendants of cowboys are not at all inspired by the idea that we have a wild West in Russia. Moreover, rapacious investors did not plan to rob Russia but, on the contrary, dream of getting out.

The first reason why Marshall Goldman does not advise Americans to invest money in Russian business is obviously organized crime: "About 80% of businesses in Russia are controlled by criminal groups who have already begun to demand tributes from and even partnership with foreign companies in Russia. Those who refuse are threatened with bombings, attacks on employees and even murders, as was recently the case with an American accountant in Moscow."

The second reason is "ordinary" crime, particularly thefts. Goldman notes that the time has passed when a foreigner felt safe in Russia under the wing of the KGB; big Western businessmen now need to take a rope with them on trains so that they can tie their compartment doors and not have to worry about thieves.

The third reason is the absence of elementary conditions needed for business. Air transport is practically impossible, writes Goldman, since planes don't usually take off for lack of fuel and if they do, soon crash because of negligence.

The fourth reason is the banking system. No Western businessman can get used to the Russian system, whereby cashing a check takes at least a month. "Foreign entrepreneurs sometimes lose a third of their income because of inflation," writes the author, "one oil company was forced to charter a plane to deliver several tons of rubles to suppliers."

The fifth reason is the absence or nonobservance of the law. Goldman writes about several American businessmen who found themselves on Moscow streets despite rental agreements, because the landlord found another more profitable tenant. (Goldman notes that Moscow rents are already more expensive than in Tokyo.) "Civil authorities behave equally unceremoniously. Several years ago, Yeltsin's government cancelled the state monopoly on vodka. It was suddenly reinstated this spring, destroying the businesses and investments of many Western entrepreneurs."

But Goldman believes the greatest problem is the Russian tax system, which, besides changing regularly, is the most gouging in the world. Tax police imposes monstrous fines on the most preposterous grounds. Goldman cites the example of Grand Hotel Europa in St. Petersburg that was fined 28 million dollars for keeping money in foreign banks instead of Russian ones.

Goldman calculates that Russia has a 39% tax on wages, 35–38% tax on profit, 2% tax on property and 23% tax on goods sold and foreign investments. There are also export taxes, motor vehicle taxes and even a tax on the commercial use of the word "Russia"!

Goldman writes that many Western oil companies decided not to do business in Russia having calculated that all the taxes demanded by the Russians would amount to 120% of profits.

"And these are only federal Russian taxes!" the author exclaims. "There are also local taxes. Instead of considering advertising as a business expenditure, Moscow authorities levy a 5% tax."

The seventh reason is the unreliability of Russian partners. Goldman notes that any American businessman, aware that each month Russian businessmen transfer abroad a billion dollars, may suspect that their Russian partners are more preoccupied with sending profits abroad than working in their joint businesses.

For the sake of justice, the author notes that Western businessmen who supply Russia with foods, perfumes, cigarettes, polaroid cameras, computers and expensive cards have indeed gotten rich. But most serious foreign investors curtailed their businesses after the first successful post-perestroika years and returned home; Russia became much too dangerous and unprofitable.

In conclusion Marshall Goldman advises Western businessmen: "Keep away from Russia, at least for the time being."

❊

Everyday Life in Russia 1990–1994:
"Elusive" Routine
by Yelena Jaginova

It is only recently that the attention of scientists has turned to everyday life. At the end of the 1960s and the early 1970s a new branch of social science sprung up and gained rapid momentum. It is called 'sociology' and its roots are ethnic methodology and phenomenology.

Some time later this science roused the interest of historians, cultural scientists, teachers, psychologists, and others. By the end of the 1970s not only social ritual, but everyday economic relations, food ratios, clothing, use of household appliances and machines, behavior at schools, hospitals and every imaginable element of everyday life was becoming the topic of scientific investigation, study and statistical analysis. Today, sociology of everyday life is one of the most influential branches of social science.

from *Business World Weekly*

The sphere of everyday life is made up of trivial events and happenings in the family, at the workplace, between relatives, friends and acquaintances. These habitual and outstanding events and relationships form our everyday life.

The recurrence, rhythm and routine of everyday life determines the stability of entire societies and countries. Everyday life is the foundation of human existence because no social layer can escape from the daily routine. Scientific analysis of the tendencies in everyday life reveals social transformations. Everyday life links different aspects of social activity (economics, politics, morals, culture and leisure) and is an indicator of the physical condition of the society. Through everyday life we make our judgment of other countries and civilizations.

This analysis is an attempt to determine (at least statistically) different types of everyday behavior in Russia and to isolate the most stable and characteristic time-spending activities.

Major pastimes

The All-Russia Public Opinion Research Centre repeated the public opinion poll in May 1994 which was conducted in 1990 under the headline "Social Activities and Consumption". 1600 Russian citizens over 15 answered the questionnaire. The aim of the poll was to determine the frequency of the following activities: reading of newspapers, books, magazines; shopping, childcare, entertainment, communication, gardening and other routine occupations beside work.

Beside pastimes, typical of both sexes, Table 1 below illustrates the current breakdown of male and female activities in Russian society. Men and women spend almost equal time watching TV and listening to the radio and to music; both read newspapers, do the shopping and work in their gardens. Women, however, devote more time to childcare (28% more than men), shop twice as much, and knit and sew 12 times more than men.

Men, for their part, do three times as much repairing around the house and engaging in "do it yourself" projects.

	Men		Women	
Table 1: Recurrence of Various Pastimes In a Year (Days or Times a Year)*				
Variants of pastimes	1990	1994	1990	1994
TV	220	223	224	225
Radio	183	188	213	185
Provisioning	146	112	209	169
Childbearing	107	84	132	132
Gardening	71	96	82	108
Newspapers	200	109	167	95
Books	65	88	62	75
Music records	78	73	64	75
Shopping	61	37	108	60
Love-making**	—	33	—	33
Outings with friends	78	58	44	59
Parties (at home and out)	35	29	42	38
Knitting, sewing	3	4	46	48
Home repairs	41	40	10	12
Sports	40	37	18	23
Professional development	28	24	17	17
Magazines	81	22	75	19
Games: cards, chess, etc.	36	27	18	14
Sports competitions	5	11	2	4
Playing musical instruments	19	6	4	9
Movies	17	6	18	5
Bars, disco clubs	10	5	4	5
Photography, filming, painting	5	2	2	2
Theatre, concert	3	2	2	2
Restaurants	2	2	1.5	2
Tourist trips	6	3	3	3
Political meetings	3	0.3	1	1

* Actually the questionnaire had it as "How often do you go shopping?" Variants of answers were "every day," "2–3 times a week," "once a week," "once or twice a month," "more seldom," "never." The results were obtained by setting a rating to each answer and averaging the scale.

** In 1990 this question was not asked.

Marriage brings interests together

Daily routine not only differs depending on the gender of the respondent, but also on his or her marital status. Marital status: married, divorced, widowed, or never been married illustrates a number of established and predictable scenarios of daily routine and behavior.

For example, bachelors are the greatest readers of magazines, but practically ignore newspapers (they read fewer newspapers than any other category of respondents). On the other hand, unmarried women indulge in fiction, while bachelors appear not to; this attitude compares with that of married men. Time devoted to favorite TV programs in the group is the same as in other categories, although bachelors do not favor radio as much as an "average" Russian.

Unmarried women are avid readers of fiction and magazines, love music and listen to records as much as unmarried men. In all other pastimes: movies, parties, bars and disco clubs, sports, professional development, unmarried women are as active as unmarried men, and in some spheres such as music lessons, tourism and social contacts they are the leading group. Unmarried women are large purchasers of ready-made clothes; their visits to department stores are 5 times the average, but, unfortunately, because they are not the most prosperous group, actual buying lags far behind visiting stores.

Divorced men (young for the most part) resume their bachelor habits and acquire new ones, such as attending political meetings. It is seven times more likely to encounter a divorcee at a political meeting than anyone else. They also favor sports and exercising.

The life of divorced women with children combines the daily family routine with elements of independence. They become ardent concert and theatre-goers.

Table 2: Influence of Urbanization On Everyday Life Routine
(Days or Times a Year)

1	2	3	4	5
Read books	91	90	89	55
Listen to records	76	63	73	57
Do gardening	24	60	109	181
Participate in sports	44	28	20	24

1 - Variants of answers
2 - Moscow, St. Petersburg
3 - Large cities
4 - Mid-sized and small towns
5 - Villages

Three ages of Russian men

Men under 30. This group enjoys maximum independence and, apart from money-making, try to make the most of their lives. TV and radio rank first among pastimes, then comes music, and outings with friends once in three days on average. One out of four days they buy food for the family. Books and newspapers are not favored as much as

Table 3: Influence of Education On Everyday Life Routine (Days or Times a Year)			
1	2	3	4
Read books	122	86	59
Go shopping	54	55	37
Participate in sports	36	26	21

1 - Variants of answers
2 - H gher education
3 - College education
4 - College dropout

older men. One out of five said they take care of their children, if any, and one in six days will be spent helping their parents with the garden. They hold parties and attend parties once a week, the same frequency with which they play sports, play cards or chess, or have sex.

Men between 30 and 50. Men of this group are active TV and radio fans, they take care of their children more frequently (one of three days), read more newspapers and do more shopping (as often as they play with the kids). The garden or suburban cottage takes one more day a week. Pop music is gradually ousted by books (they read once in 3–4 days), love and sex retain their frequency, but friendly meetings are much more scarce (only once a week), to say nothing of going-out which is a mere once in three weeks. A man of that age is a "stay-at-home", buried in a "do-it-yourself" magazine or mounted on a ladder with eternal hammer in hand.

Men over 50. Men over fifty still watch TV but prefer radio and, especially, newspapers. Shopping takes one third of their spare time, while another third is devoted to their gardens or summer cottages. All other activities begin to decrease. Books remain popular (once in 5 days on the average), looking after children and grandchilds — once in six days, household repairs — once a week, and sex — only once in a fortnight. Outings with friends become a rare treat (once in three weeks), and friendly parties are an exceptional occasion — only once a month. Magazines and sport are neglected — once in three weeks, on the average.

Three groups of Russian women

Women under 30. Major pastimes are TV, radio and shopping. Childcare takes as much time as listening to pop music (once in 3 days). Young women in Russia read a great deal: 1.5 times more fiction and newspapers than men of the same age. Compared to men under 30, young women have fewer outings with friends, but love to host home parties. Judging by the frequency of their visits to clothing stores, fashion is twice as important to them as to young men. Young women work at their gardens as much as one of four days. Knitting and sewing is once in 8 days, and the same is true of sport activities.

Women between 30 and 50. Shopping, cooking and childbearing are the heaviest burdens on the shoulders of middle-aged Russian women and take most of their time. They still have some time for TV and radio. Fiction is gradually replaced by newspapers, although music is still a pastime; middle-aged women are ardent music fans. Friendly outings are a little less frequent (once in 5 days); and the same applies to clothing shopping (one visit to a department store every six days), sex — once a week, knitting and sewing — once in 8 days. Guests are invited once every 12 days, and once in a fortnight all Russian women are engaged in professional development.

Women over 50. Women over 50 still watch TV, but develop a liking for the radio. Finally, shopping takes less of their time, but they do as much gardening as men of their age. Newspapers, fiction and children take less of their time compared to middle-aged women, and instead they indulge in knitting and sewing. Love-making is rare — once every 9 days and so are department store visits — once every 10 days. Outings are almost as infrequent as visits with friends — only once every 3 weeks.

Impact of education

The average daily routine described above is surprisingly different depending on the education of the respondents or their habitat. Large cities attract educated people. For example, reading at least once very four days, a total of 90 days per year, is common for any city-dweller, whereas in rural areas this pastime occupies half as much time (see Table 2). On the other hand, gardening in the rural population occupies 8 times the number of days as in large cities such as Moscow or St. Petersburg. Villagers spend half of their lives toiling the land (or statistically, every other day). In Moscow, gardeners visit their suburban cottages once in a fortnight, on average. In mid-sized and small towns people garden (or farm) 109 days annually; compared to 60 days in large cities and 181 days in villages. Sports are largely a privilege of the capital, and, to

a lesser degree, of town-dwellers. Statistics cite 44 days annually of exercise in Moscow and St. Petersburg, 28 days — in other cities and only 20 days in small towns, although in villages people enjoy 24 days of physical exercise.

Changes, tendencies and forecasts

Food shopping. Since 1990 time spent on buying food decreased 1.25 times. We owe this welcome shrinkage to fewer shortage and the consequent absence of shop lines. Unfortunately, men over 50 benefit from this the most, while women spend as much time in food shops as four years ago. On the whole, food shopping is the domain of women.

Children. On the whole, the time that Russians devote to child rearing remained unchanged. Women under 30 now devote more time to their kids, while men under 30 and over 50 spend much less time with children.

Gardening. In comparison with 1990 an average Russian citizen devotes 1.13 times more hours to gardening. Men under 30 help their parents with the garden twice as often as four years ago; women of the same age spend 1.6 times more hours working in the garden. One possible explanation for this trend is the impact of the federal program that provided many town-dwellers with their own plots of land in suburban areas.

Newspapers. Average interest in newspapers has decreased 1.75 times compared with 1990, particularly among men under 50 and among women over 50. This is another indicator of declining political activity.

Books. The general level of fiction reading has grown 1.35 times, and 1.7 times among women over 30. One of the explanations of this phenomenon is the abundant choice of literature for women.

Magazines. Research showed a four-fold decrease in magazine since 1990. Such a rapid reduction of subscribers may be accounted for by an unprecedented loss of interest in magazines by people over 50. Nowadays they leaf through a magazine 5 times less often than 4 years ago.

Shopping has decreased 1.8 times primarily among the low-income category of people over 50. The spending ability of women in this category dropped three times and twice among men of the same age.

Household chores. In 1994 women do a bit more knitting and sewing than in 1990, especially women under 30 and over 50. Men practice home repairs as often as in 1990, with the only difference that presently men under 30 do 1.3 times less of handiwork.

Sports. Sport competitions are as popular now as in 1990. However, young women now attend 3.3 times more sport events than in 1990, men over 50 — 3 times more and men between 30 and 50 — 2.5 times more.

Professional development. In 1994 the time devoted to professional development has decreased overall by 1.7 times compared with 1990. The category least interested in professional development are men under 50, while men over 50 and women between 30 and 50 have spent 1.4 and 1.6 times more of their free hours on professional development, respectively. Possibly, these changes stem from the breakdown of the Russian state system of free professional development which was replaced by very expensive and disorganized professional training.

Conclusions

The general character and scheme of the daily routine has undergone few changes in 4 years. Nevertheless, some evident qualitative changes point to some general conclusions and predictions.

1. The most notable tendency is that of increased demand for quality information. TV, radio programs and newspaper articles are carefully selected. The value placed on personal free time is increasing, especially among the young generation.

2. Young men under 30 do not fit wholly into the daily routine scheme. They are acquiring new roles: of money-making businessman, breadwinner for the family and, therefore require different activities for relaxation to rejuvenate them. Hence, the selective approach to anything has developed, information included.

3. The creation in contemporary society of a new young generation consumer group parallels the decrease in spending ability and the rapid decline in income among the older generation, particularly among women over 50. The monotony of their lives, absence of relaxation, limited consumer capacity and social security, lack of such resources as health, energy, etc., are fostering an anger and alienation that has no outlet. At the present stage of development, society lacks the means and resources to cushion the shock of reform on this social group.

4. The male and female roles in contemporary society are becoming more disparate. Women take care of the household, family and children, whereas men spend most of their time outside of the home: in business, in bread-winning and with friends.

❄

Yelena Jaginova is an officer of the Federal Public Opinion Research Centre.

Chapter 2

Such Is Business Life
Такова деловая жизнь

Your most important and basic questions

So, you are thinking about starting your business in Russia. You are probably aware by now that doing business in Russia is apt to be a very different experience than doing business elsewhere. This chapter will help you answer your most important and basic start-up questions. Topics covered include Russian partners and where, when, and how much to invest. In addition, more information is given about specific sectors of investment and included is a discussion of how privatization — where state-run businesses and property are turned over to private enterprise — affects doing business in Russia and market conditions. More specific questions you may have — such as about taxes, real estate, and banking — will be answered in later chapters. For now, you need to consider the most important decision you will make. Usually, as an investor you start by asking yourself three questions:

- Where should you invest your money?
- When should you invest your money?
- How much money should you invest?

Answering these questions correctly can assure success elsewhere, but not so in Russia.

In Russia, everything begins with the selection of the right person to work for you.

Choosing your Russian partner

If you find someone to be your genuine Russian partner for years to come, your path to success is open. If you fail to choose the right person, no analysts from Harvard or Yale can help.

Naturally, you will find exceptions to this rule. But eventually, a foreigner who succeeds in doing business in Russia will have to turn to Russians. You might even consider moving to Russia, marrying a Russian, and growing into the community. But since most readers are not prepared for so drastic a move, remember: Look carefully for your Russian partner and consider it your main task. Everything depends on this choice, and mistakes here are irreparable. You would do better to start your business in another country rather than face the consequences of making a mistake in this all-important first step.

In practice, the person you find may be an administrator, a former party or state leader, an industrial engineer, a science fellow from a research institute, or a businessperson — the 'new Russians' type. A new Russian is the equivalent of a yuppie in the United States. The important thing is that this person must be eager to work, competent, and fairly ambitious. Furthermore, your future partner must have a commanding spirit, be without fear of risk, and be absolutely honest. Naturally, these qualities can be tested only in long-term and fairly close contact, so do not hurry your final choice. Give a number of candidates a chance.

A number of recommendations are offered on the pages that follow. While these recommendations may seem questionable from certain points of view, they are fully warranted considering the actual experiences of those who have been there. These recommendations may be considered part of a certain "Code of Rules for Safe Business in Russia." Of course, by following these recommendations, you are not completely risk free. But hopefully, this information will help protect you from mistakes that have destroyed many efforts by foreigners to succeed economically in Russia.

Don't rely on word of mouth

To find a Russian partner, the U.S. Department of Commerce recommends that you start by placing an advertisement in one of the business periodicals. You can also inquire and recruit at Russian business schools or enlist the help of a placement firm. To find a corporate partner, several agencies specialize in matching Russian partners with foreign firms. The U.S. Department of Commerce also publishes investment opportunities — see Chapter 13 for more information.

When contacting a private person, conduct a personal interview. Don't rely on word of mouth or a general inquiry. Determine what other business involvement the person has had with Westerners or with Russians. Observe the way the potential partner handles him or herself in business situations.

Involve your partner as a team member

Make your Russian partner a member of your team. He or she should not be the head of your Russian enterprise, as opposed to you as the owner. But your partner should be a member of your group of investors, with more or less full authority, and should be included in your business' general training and promotion system. At least every two or three years, give him or her at least three-to-six month training and testing periods in other branches of your business outside Russia.

Methods of achieving this recommendation are well tested in many business systems, using incentives like profit-sharing, ownership options, or management authority. Simply stated, you want your Russian partner to feel a sense of involvement in decisions affecting the business enterprise.

Remember, however, that it is not desirable to parade this involvement. On the contrary, on the outside your partner should look like an executive or at least no more than an adviser to you, the foreign investor who makes the decisions. This protects your partner from direct pressure by other Russian colleagues since he or she can claim to be following the orders received from abroad. Any sharing of profits or stock should come not from the capital fund of the Russian enterprise, but from the foreign investor enterprise. This makes it clear to your partner that he or she is dependent on you personally, and not the Russian business, for bonuses. The same policy applies to social security and pension fund payments, assistance in getting apartments, or other fringe benefits and expenses.

Naturally, your candidate must meet some basic requirements such as fluency in English and an education comparable to his or her

Western colleagues. He or she preferably should be married since this indicates a degree of stability and seriousness, and the spouse must be ready to fit into a new system of relationships — relationships that did not exist in the former Soviet Russia.

Pay attention to connections

Pay particular attention to your candidate's connections with local authorities and members of the state administration, or to his or her ability to make such connections. In Russia, success in business depends considerably on your relationship with today's authorities. Your method of maintaining these relationships may range from friendly talks, to polite tug-of-wars, or to blunt payoffs. Of extreme importance is that your Russian partner behaves in a way that causes no ill-feelings from bureaucrats.

A closely related idea is that of your reinvestment plans. Many disputes between Russian and foreign partners concern investment and profit repatriation alternatives. Russian partners not only consider reinvestments to be a guarantee of their better life in Russia in the future, but as a means of maintaining good relations.

A feasible reinvestment scheme presented at the initial stages of setting up a foreign business is a trump card in the course of negotiations with the federal and local authorities. The correct approach can promote the quick overcoming of red tape barriers hindering the establishment of your business, as well as secure administrative support in the future.

Russia is still a country where business can't exist independently of those in power. No one can point out a single case of successful foreign capital investment in Russia that prospered without direct or indirect participation of local authorities or state administration bureaucrats in one way or another.

Gather information and make inquiries

Get as much information as possible about your Russian partner. As in any country, there is a possibility that your partner may deceive you or provide questionable information that you cannot validate. Try to make inquiries at his or her former places of work and with law enforcement agencies. What you don't know may hurt you. In the West, you can use firms like Dun and Bradstreet, which now has an office in Moscow, to sift though financial and business data so you can determine economic history and creditworthiness. Russia's new market economy lacks much of this infrastructure, however, and the process is a bit different. Some small firms that purport to provide background checks use former KGB agents, or have informal access to selected databases. You have several other options, however.

Also examine the Register of Russian Partners for Effective Business and Foreign Economic Activity. This was established in February 1993 as a service of the Russian Chamber of Commerce and Industry (RCCI). Inclusion in the register indicates that the RCCI has investigated the reliability of the subject firm.

Besides, the U.S. and Foreign Commercial Service at the American Embassy and its consulates in St. Petersburg and Vladivostok can provide some background of Russian firms. This service is called the World Traders Data Report, and a nominal fee is charged.

While some information you receive naturally will alarm you, don't let a previous conviction scare you off if it was not connected with a crime against a person. Work with party organizations, army political departments, KGB, or state organizations, should not be considered negative — in fact, many foreign businesspeople prefer to choose their people out of this contingent.

Sign a long-term contract

After a reasonable probation period, sign a long-term contract of at least three to five years with your Russian partner. In wages, stress fringe benefits and delayed payment rather than the base salary. You should have in store an effective program for your partner's participation in profits. However, direct payments in the form of high wages and salaries can hardly be assessed as an effective way of stimulating productivity, at least from your business' point of view. This is due to the total fund of wages and salaries in Russia being subject to heavy tax withholding, especially if those wages exceed six times the official minimum wage per employee.

Actually, only a small part of each dollar of net profit can be transformed into wage payment due to the taxation burden and the obligatory exchange to rubles of a portion of hard currency revenues at the Central Bank's rate. Another form of compensation has proven to be effective in Russia — providing home appliances, consumer electronics, a car, a flat, or tourist trips abroad, in addition to wage or salary compensation. Naturally, your partner's working conditions should be the same as for his or her Western colleagues.

Send your partner on trips outside Russia

Be generous with trips outside Russia for your partner. The sooner he or she comes to know how business is run by your head office and the rules by which business is done in the West, the sooner your partner can assume full charge of your Russian enterprise. This means fewer trips to Russia for your top officers — trips that in most cases produce surprisingly few results even if the officers understand the language and have experience working in Russia. As suggested in the second recommendation, at least every two to three years, give your Russian partner a three-to-six month stint in some branch of your business outside Russia.

Look for flexibility

Lack of flexibility can mean problems, or at least lost opportunities, in the Russian world of business. Under current conditions, you will want to always be ready to:

- Change fields;
- Master adjacent fields; and
- Promptly make use of unexpected opportunities.

Diversification is a key to success in Russian commercial activities. In contrast with international practices, Russian partners insist on the diversification of a business' activity, involving many branches of business. Although many examples exist demonstrating that the internationally accepted practice of specialization is correct in Russia too, the diversification of business activities is an effective method of survival under the unstable business environment in Russia. Actual examples of flexibility and diversification include: a publishing agency investment that became a successful theater business, a restaurant that was turned into a bank, and a consulting firm that developed into a major industrial financial concern.

Of course, dealing with things you know best is always better. But you will be unwise to miss the opportunity to start a new business if the old one is falling apart. When those opportunities arise, Russian specialists can be found easily and for relatively small money. These situations, where you must make quick changes, are quite apt to arise nowadays in the period of privatization, with large enterprises splitting into smaller ones, old business connections breaking, and production stoppages occurring when changes in state borders close off access to old markets.

Ideally, when you come to Russia, you will know exactly what you are going to do, and you can choose your partner based on those objectives. Following the recommendations above should be helpful to you in forging a successful business relationship with your Russian partner for many years to come.

Where you should invest

Now, that you understand your most important task — that of finding your Russian partner — you can return to your original questions of: Where to invest? When? How much?

Where should the money be invested in Russia? No one can pretend to be a prophet or make infallible judgments. The situation in Russia is changing continuously, and the advantages of investments in many fields depend on government policies that are difficult to predict today. However, examining the Russian stock market can help answer the question of where to invest.

Investing in privatized enterprises

Russia's privatization program is a major source of stock market activity. In an effort to facilitate the transition to a market economy and attract foreign investment, the Russian government has initiated a broad-scale privatization program of its former state and municipal-owned enterprises and properties. The first phase of the program was based on the use of vouchers issued free to every citizen. The second phase of privatization sells the remaining shares for cash.

The Russian Federation State Property Management Committee supervises and controls the privatization process, in which the local authorities and the labor staff of the enterprise also have significant influence.

Various methods are used for carrying out the privatization of a state-owned enterprise, and although some criteria on the choice of the privatization method have been determined by fundamental provisions of the law, such choices remain at the discretion of the State Property Management Committee. The methods for privatization are:

- The sale of shares of enterprises that are being transformed into joint stock companies;
- The sale of enterprises at auctions;
- The sale of enterprises through competitive bidding;

- The sale of enterprises through noncommercial investment tenders;
- The sale of property and other assets of acting enterprises, enterprises in the process of being liquidated, or enterprises that have been liquidated; and
- The redemption of property belonging to an enterprise that was leased to the labor collective of the enterprise before the *Privatization Law* of July 1991 was adopted.

The privatization legislation gives the employees of an enterprise the right to purchase shares of their enterprise on preferential terms. It also allows foreign parties to participate in the privatization of certain facilities and enterprises, although some restrictions remain in place. Despite this provision, in practice, no concrete steps have been taken to facilitate the active participation of foreigners in the privatization process.

However, no further restrictions have been placed on the ability of foreigners to invest in the enterprises being privatized. Foreign investors, who take part in the privatization of state and municipal property, have the right to privatize a plot of land belonging to that enterprise. Furthermore, the given enterprise has the right to buy more land if it is planning to extend production.

Marketing shares of privatized enterprises unexpectedly has become the most extensive segment of the Russian securities market due to the interest of foreign investors, though focused on a limited number of enterprises: oil wells and production facilities, telephone communications, nonferrous metals, and production of mineral fertilizers. The market turnover on shares of these enterprises reaches $200 million per month, and the profit on transactions is up to 1,000 percent in 1994.

Naturally, foreign investors, such as investment companies and banks that have taken the risk of investing their money in the Russian stock market, have received considerable shares of participation in very attractive Russian enterprises, and now have extremely favorable conditions. For example, a control package of shares — 30 percent and more — of such giants as the Magnitogorsk Metallurgic Plant, car plants AutoVaz and GAZ, and Lukoil Petroleum Company could be purchased for $3–9 million.

Foreign investors in 1994 bought considerable shares of participation in enterprises of oil wells and refineries, the gas industry, and nonferrous metallurgy. Brokers received big foreign orders to purchase shares of such Russian monopolistic enterprises as United Power Systems of Russia Joint Stock Company, Gazprom, and Russian Nickel.

The Russian government has decided to continue the process of privatization. Today, shares of newly privatized enterprises appear on the market in the areas of machine building and defense, and with many private companies that are trying to attract new money resources by going public.

Meanwhile, stock market investors should be cautious, making sure they get the latest information concerning any prospective enterprise. At privatized companies, conflicts occur sometimes during sales of stocks between inside and outside shareholders, and between the administration and worker-shareholders. Cases of interference by the State Property Management Committee have occurred in the procedures of privatization, not always with predicted consequences. For example, there was a scandal in the GAZ Car Factory, where company directors violated laws by trying to distribute all shares at artificial low prices without offering them at auction.

In another example, managers of a car plant on the Volga — the AutoVaz — tried to remove undesirable outside investors from participating in the auction. In the case of an oil and gas company, Yuganskneftegaz, an arbitrary decision by the State Property Management Committee increased the assigned capital — the amount set aside for creditors of the enterprise — on the last day before the auction, so auction participants received a smaller than expected number of shares for the same money.

Direct investments

Considering all that, direct investments, as opposed to purchasing stock, seem to be safer since they are done through direct agreement with the administration of the enterprise. Listed below are some common areas for direct investments and a brief assessment of the reliability of each.

- Raw materials. Investments in raw materials are justified, although each single investment in this field is very large as a rule. The primary advantage is that these industries are oriented toward export, and as a source of foreign currency, they provide additional insurance against inflation of the national currency.

- Services. Investments in the services sector — telephone and radio communications, restaurants and fast-food outlets, three star hotels and motels — are second in reliability.
- Construction. Investments in construction, especially of living quarters, and construction materials are a promising field for direct investments, but they are cyclical industries and, thus, depend heavily on the general economic climate and the dynamics of personal income growth.
- Agriculture. Investments in agriculture are quite reliable, but only after agrarian land reform is carried out and in regions with a developed road network.
- Food industries. Investments in food industries are usually risky, but government protectionist measures can make these investments rather attractive. You can find profitable investment opportunities in this field if they are linked or if you have a way of linking them with orders from abroad.
- Machine building and long-term consumer goods. Investments in machine building and production of long-term consumer goods are fairly risky.
- Chemical industry. Investment situations with the chemical industry remain uncertain. As a whole, chemicals remain one of the most modern sectors capable of attracting large investments, but ecological considerations call for being very careful in choosing this field for investment.
- Other fields. Investments in health care, education, entertainment, and tourism may be very attractive, though again, they depend entirely on the rate of personal income growth. And while banking and insurance investments are extremely risky, shares of the largest banks are among the most reliable securities in the Russian stock market.

To find out more about locating investment opportunities, refer to Chapter 13.

When you should invest

Answering the question of when to invest is easy. The answer is: Today! Tomorrow may be too late. "What's the rush?" you may ask. "There hardly are too many competitors so far." That is true, when considering only competitors from the West, but that tunnel vision may cause you to miss your chief competitor: Russian capital repatriated from abroad.

Russian capital makes pointedly conservative investments abroad, mostly in real estate and the most reliable banking and investment companies. But at home, that capital is much more aggressive and tough. Today, it is looking for partners and is ready to cooperate with Western capital. However, by the time Western capital reaches a common language with the Russian government, most profitable investments may be out of reach for Western capital.

Of course, those who already have come to the Russian marketplace most probably will stay there. But in order to stay, you've got to come!

This section of the chapter explores and analyzes some of the trends and underlying facts that show the current direction of Russia's economic climate. After you have gained insight into the inner workings of the Russian marketplace, you may agree that now is the time to invest.

Suggestions from the Russian government

The fact that the Russian government whole-heartedly approves of foreigners making investments in the country is very encouraging. Mr. Yakov Urinson, First Deputy Economics Minister of Russia, in a Fall 1994 speech, cites five directions for investments that are desirable among Russian authorities:

The development of Russia's scientific and technical potential is considered the first and most important direction for foreign investment, and that potential is quite ample, especially at converted defense enterprises.

The second direction is the promotion of foreign investment in broadening and diversifying Russia's export potential.

The third is the creation of import-substituting production facilities, [where production is done in Russia of products that are now being imported] and, development for the production of consumer goods. Here we have a whole range of interesting examples, including the assembly of household appliances, the production of footwear, the construction of the Mars' factories outside Moscow. But their number is certainly insufficient.

The fourth direction calls for the promotion of foreign investment in transport and communications, in the development of infrastructure.

And the fifth, promoting foreign investment in regions with labor surplus, primarily in Russia's central and north-western regions, as well as in eastern areas rich in mineral resources.

In connection with these priorities, Mr. Urinson makes an important point:

The problem of desired correlation between investment in production and in services is often debated in Russia. I believe that we should consider it normal if investment activity began with the launching of companies focusing on import and marketing of their own products in Russia. Then, after they have accumulated the resultant financial resources, they begin investing in production. In other words, foreign investors first create demand for their products and only after that, provided that demand is stable, they invest in launching a corresponding production facility.

Draft laws have been prepared concerning amendments to the laws on foreign investment, on free economic zones, and on concession agreements.

The law on the tax on profits of enterprises ... will be supplemented with provisions that will considerably improve the investment climate.

... Other planned measures include speeding up talks with interested foreign countries with a view toward the signing of agreements calling for mutual protection of and creating the incentives for investment. Plans also call for the drafting of a Russian governmental ordinance concerning application of the difference of exchange when implementing agreements on the setting up of enterprises with foreign investment.

The year of 1995 will be the year of wide-scale and severe stock-jobbing.

The opportunities and challenges of privatization

The process of privatizing Russian businesses has presented many opportunities to make a very high return on investments. However, two major drawbacks have become apparent with the process of privatization — a suffering Russian economy due to the practice of stock-jobbing and a lapse in common business ethics because of incomplete or conflictive legislation regarding the relationship between business and government. Briefly, stock-jobbing, which is explained in greater detail below, is the repeated selling and reselling of shares purchased at a low price and resold almost immediately for a high profit.

The basic scenario of 1994 may be repeated — shares of enterprises to be privatized may be purchased at fabulously low prices arranged by artificially lowering the estimates of the initial capital figures. Usually this is done by:

- Evaluating enterprise assets by their initial balance cost;
- Distributing shares behind the scenes;
- Limiting access of potential customers to primary sales; or
- Buying up shares from enterprise workers to whom they were sold on favorable conditions.

The resulting price for initial purchases of shares is so low that their resale, practically at any price, brings high profits. In some cases, foreign investors can participate in a chain of several resales, but as a rule they buy shares through second or even third hands.

Foreign investment companies tried this scheme out in 1994, with major success. Most stock-jobbing that year involved shares of oil and gas companies, with prices of shares going up tens or even hundreds of times just during the first half of the year. Resulting profits, of course, were astronomical for both investors and middlepersons.

In the second half of 1994, the stock market saw a revival of interest in enterprises of nonferrous metallurgy, such as aluminum and nickel, and harbor management companies.

The same scheme continued, with the result, perhaps, holding back development of the investment cycle. Privatization 'for a song,' having opened the field for stock-jobbing, shut down the access of new investments into production. Only initial stockholders and middlepersons receive profits from shares, and for as long as stock-jobbing is upwards, enterprises have no chance to get a single dollar (or ruble) of new investment. This makes investments in reselling shares for high, short-term income more profitable than investments in long-term production programs. The greatest risk is becoming the last owner of shares at the end of the stock market boom.

While people are making this kind of money at the stock exchange, production facilities receive no new capital for reconstruction and development and are progressively falling to pieces. Those 'last day' investors may have to focus not on further development, but on restoration or even complete replacement of obsolete technology. As a rule, stock-jobbers don't think of such consequences, but for those interested in long-term investments, the consequences may be disastrous.

The second built-in drawback to the suffering caused by the Russian capitalism is explained next. To survive in Russia, any private businessperson either Russian or foreign, continuously must break the law. Many reports have described those who tried to do business 'in accordance with the law' instead of actually doing business. They wasted their time 'begging' for various registrations, licenses, and permissions, giving endless accountings and explanations. As a result, some just dropped the whole thing, while others managed to bribe their way through by creating unaccountable 'black funds' — funds not shown on the books and hidden from the tax collector.

Those who succeeded went further, learning to fiddle with taxes, either bribing them off, conducting unreported cash transactions, or making arrangements with racketeers who, for a certain 'tax,' took care of their unscrupulous partners residing within government structures. Thus, an originally honest and law-abiding Russian businessperson is forced to learn ways not too different from the early days of American capitalism.

Thus, you can conclude that investing in Russia is a financial risk. Financial lobbies and investors in exporter countries are well aware of that fact, and by today's measures are right not to get excited about investing in Russia. But they are missing the main point: They are bound to invest in Russia in the very near future if they hope to maintain the same position in the world market exporting capital they hold today.

Russia's exportation of capital

Tomorrow, two things are expected in the world of business, and you don't have to be a prophet to predict this scenario. Russia will become one of the biggest exporters of money, and Russian capital exporters will be far more prepared to compete in that arena than Western investors. Exporting capital is the process of using capital to conduct business abroad.

The export of capital reflects the growth of Russia's domestic savings, which are being transferred abroad to safe havens, thus avoiding taxes, inflation, and instability. When those earnings are brought home as hard currency for investment or savings, Russian capital increases.

Already, Russia is becoming a major exporter of capital, and this tendency is growing despite any change in the Russian situation. Internal hardships only speed up the growth of Russia's internal savings being moved abroad.

If the Russian political and economic situations improve, the growth of this capital exportation will slow or even stop, but the absolute value of investments transferred abroad will continue to grow for many years due to their diversified character. Thus, the relative poverty of Russia is not an obstacle. On the contrary, this circumstance may favor the growth of the portion of savings in the national income and a desire to place a greater part of these savings abroad. Japan and the Arab countries already have demonstrated this phenomenon to the whole world.

Will Russia be able to earn enough hard currency to support its export of capital? Some experts have no doubt about it, and here are at least three sectors that provide examples.

Raw materials, oil, and gas carriers. The position of Russia in these markets looks quite reliable, and when Russian authorities can provide a minimum amount of organization for the export of these commodities, the profits from this sector will grow solidly, even with a decrease in the absolute value of the exports. What is needed is the elimination of competition among Russian exporters themselves, putting an end to the chaotic invasion of Russian outsiders into the world markets, which undermines the established price system.

Most likely, monopolistic structures will be formed in this sector in the near future, with support from the state. The market will be rigidly organized, thus eliminating price competition. This already has begun in oil, gas, nonferrous metals, and diamonds, and next will come ferrous metals and, possibly, timber and chemical fertilizers.

The arms sector. Russia, with its huge military-industrial complex, maintains a favorable starting position in this sector, and the industry can reliably occupy the entire niche of medium-technology arms. True, high-tech American arms can punch holes in the upper, left-side window of the enemy's headquarters, while Russian missiles will only tear the entire building to pieces. But, will the customer pay an extra $10 million for this delicate nuance?

Russia is capable of supplying the world with reliable, medium-class weapons, and no Western producer can compete in terms of price. And Russian quality is good enough, as demonstrated by the

70 million KALASHNIKOVS — AK-47 assault rifles — that are wandering about in 80 countries of the world. Russia is forming military-industrial monopolies that already have started winning world markets, even in such highly competitive fields as fighter planes.

The food sector. This will surprise many, but Russia very soon may become a food exporter with whom Western farmers will have difficulty competing. This process is just waiting for the start of an agrarian reform that will introduce full-scale, private property rights on Russian land. The process will be accelerated as soon as Western Europe realizes the harm of maintaining agricultural subsidies.

Realistically, Western Europe can be expected to maintain production of crops that require very special cultivating conditions — such as flowers and exotic vegetables — while basic agricultural produce will be shifted to the endless lands of Russia and Siberia. This tendency already was evident in the beginning of this century, but two factors intervened: The world agricultural market was taken over by the United States, where land remained unaffected by combat during both world wars, and the destructive Communist 'experiments' with the land and the people. Experiments, such as the collective farms, demonstrably diminished Russian farming.

All three economic sectors — raw materials, oil, and gas carriers; arms; and food — are oriented to export, and Russia has few serious competitors in the same rank or that can compete in terms of price. As soon as the government lifts the excess tax burden from these sectors, they will start bringing in major income in rubles and dollars.

Where will the money go?

Once earned, where will the money go? Since this will not be capital directly controlled by the government, hopefully, it will not be used for the support of 'friendly' regimes abroad. Nor will it directly increase the income of the Russian people, since money will remain under the control of monopolistic structures, rather than being dissipated through government channels or because of trade union pressure. This money will not go to cover Russian state debts unless the government and its creditors provide particularly favorable conditions for such capital movement.

Thus, the money will be free for investment. Where to? Anywhere, so long as the investment is reliable and profitable. With the present political and economic instability in Russia, this money most likely will be looking for a niche in the West. This stage already is underway.

However, in the next stage, investments will return to Russia — in part justified by stabilization of the country's political and economic scene. Russia is now on the verge of this stage. First will come economic and psychological adaptation of Russia, as a whole, to new and strange realities; then comes political stabilization. In a country where people were brainwashed for 70 years to believe that private wealth is a dirty concept, psychological factors may be no less important than economic ones.

Finally will come the third stage: Russian capital will begin a wide-scale immersion into the world market, backed by a Russian economy rich in resources and developing vigorously. Few countries will be able to combine such a favorable combination of resources and development when competing with Russian capital.

Is this scenario too fantastic? Not really, considering that such almost was the situation for Russia at the turn of the century — the world financial market, with its center in Paris in those days, believed in that. Later, the present might of the United States was built in exactly the same sequence of stages.

What or who can prevent such development of events? Will it be competition among local investors? In reality, within the Russian financial market supply steadily is ahead of demand, which provides for relatively cheap acquisition of various objects of investment.

Russian capital, when it enters the Western market, has an important advantage over local investors, due to its flexibility compared to 'oil dollars' from the Middle East, because Russian capital can be invested both in the West and in the domestic market.

The additional advantage of Russian capital over Middle East 'hot' (fast) money is that Russian investors have the powerful potential of the Russian economy behind them, allowing them to buy depressed enterprises in the West at the price of an 'ugly duckling' and convert those businesses into 'beautiful swans.' The Russian investor can link those businesses to a cheap Russian source of raw materials or lead them to some closed segment of the Russian internal market.

Russian capital, if properly controlled, will be directed at capturing key sectors and enterprises, providing for increasing profits not only today but in the future. As the volume of investment grows, an understanding of how to best accomplish this inevitably will come. Another advantage of the Russian export of capital is in the fact that it is concentrated in the hands of super monopolies — gas and oil companies — that can easily coordinate their activities in one or another direction. When Russian capital starts returning to its home markets, it shall have the advantage of coming to a familiar market, familiar people and habits, well-established contacts with government structures, and access to sources of confidential information — and these are only the legal avenues of contacts and information.

When Russian 'hot' money is combined with Russia's huge markets, it surely will create a great power on the world stage. These prospects are comparable to the Japanese expansion since World War II. After all, possibilities not yet accounted for include the possibility of profitable transit through Russian territory between East and West; Russia's huge scientific and technological potential; the advantage of the ruble becoming one of the world's reserve currencies, which is not only possible but inevitable; or for Russia's practically untapped tourist potential.

The time is now

All of the information presented above simply reflects today's reality, and to disregard this information is to forego an unparalleled economic opportunity. So far, the West is passively watching Russian events. But soon, the time will come to make choices about how to enter this market.

One way is to stay out of the Russian pot and wait until Russian capital gains power, then try to push those investors off the positions they achieve. The second course is to waste no time in acting on the principle: "If you can't get rid of your competitors, join them and win with them." The second course of action is recommended. Moreover, now is the most convenient time to penetrate and get settled into the Russian market, while competitors are still few and the market's chaotic state allows such high return on the risk. Those entering the Russian market today have to compete with domestic and foreign investors in this market. Tomorrow, after Russian capital is enriched by its experience in the West and returns to domestic markets, not much space will be left for strangers.

Remember, only recently the Russian market was absolutely closed to foreign hard liquor. Today, in contrast, liquor stores are full of even foreign-made brands of vodka — talk about taking coal to Manchester! Now is exactly the time for you to put up a distillery, for example. Join forces with the Russians, and the market is all yours. Tomorrow, the Russian producer, though strangled by taxes, will succeed in repatriating Russian capital, and together can put pressure on the Russian government to get protectionist laws for the industry. Then the opportunity for investment will be closed, perhaps for decades.

If a Western whisky manufacturer took the risk today and opened a distillery in Russia, he or she might very well remain alone in the Russian market, pushing all other foreign competitors to the lines of duty-free shops at the airports. By the way, Western monopolies already have purchased a lion's share of the Russian tobacco industry.

How much to invest

To say how much money you should invest in Russia is difficult. Profitable portfolio investments may begin at several thousand dollars, but the risk does not depend upon the sum. An enterprise in Russia may be reliable with an investment of less than $10,000, but extremely risky even with an investment of hundreds of millions of dollars.

Opinions vary widely on the question of how much to invest. The former U.S. ambassador to Moscow, Robert Strauss, in a 1993 interview, recommends, "If I were a young person with $100,000 to invest and I wanted to run it to $10 million, I would take it to Russia. But if I had $10 million, I would still only take $100,000 to Russia."

At the other end of the spectrum, the U.S. Department of Commerce recommends using your expertise and not your money at the initial stages of doing business in Russia. Furthermore, the commerce department asserts that know-how is in shorter supply than capital in Russia. Whatever anyone may say on the subject, you will need to decide for yourself. However, it is no secret that major investment activities are going on in Russia, as you will see in the next chapter, which describes the spheres and scope of foreign investments in Russia.

A final comment on risk

The weak inflow of foreign capital into Russia is explained in great measure by the absolute risk value; however, the risks in Russia are no greater than those in other countries. The difference is that Russian risks are unusual to the Western business mentality. Indeed, investing, say, in an electronic industry, you have a greater chance of losing your money in Japan than in Russia. The advantage of the Russian market is that you can start your business with one-tenth —

or even one-hundredth — of the money required to open your enterprise in Europe or Japan. This factor reduces the degree of risk.

Russian risks may look frightening because they are not found or hardly noticed in the developed, civilized markets of Western countries. The risk of confiscation, interference by authorities, monetary reform, tyranny of fiscal agencies, and racketeering were all but eliminated long ago in the West because of its relatively stable political life and developed legal system. But as a whole, these risks in Russia do not exceed Western risks normally involved with the same level of profit potential as is found in Russia.

For example, what risks must you take in the West if the expected profit is 50 percent per year? Quite high ones is the answer any professional in the American securities market will tell you. Place Russian risks in the same category and say, "What risks are you ready to accept if the expected profit is 10 to 50 percent per month, or 100 to 500 percent per year?" These are profit levels made in the Russian security market in 1994 in full-weight dollars — not inflated rubles! And this estimate does not include the potential value of direct foreign investments in Russian enterprises in the course of privatization, when for some $10,000, it is possible to obtain controlling shares in the capital of major enterprises.

Of course, it isn't all just pennies from heaven, but the result is worth the trouble.

Summary

Here is where you must come full-circle to where this chapter began. Find your person in Russia. Make him or her your friend and partner, build a qualified and reliable team together, and you may be sure your risks in Russia will be no higher than in Brazil or Turkey. Don't run everything yourself — your power lies with your place in the Western business world, and this power will be doubled if combined with the Russian human factor.

If you are not looking for such links, you might as well forget about the Russian market. Forget the Russian market until it reminds you of itself. But by then, it might be too late.

Chapter 3

Foreign Direct Investment
Инвестиции

Major trends and statistics

Even though many negative tendencies are present in Russia's business environment, foreign investment is growing by leaps and bounds. The information in this chapter has been excerpted or paraphrased, with permission, from the U.S. Department of Commerce's publication, *U.S. Firms in Russia: A Handbook for Doing Business in Russia.*

The statistics on the next several pages provide both an informative and objective look at investment activities going on in Russia. You will be encouraged by the numbers of U.S. enterprises already doing business in Russia. The sizes of the investments range from more than 100 million rubles to less than 1 million rubles — in fact, the vast majority of businesses are in this smaller investment category. So, even though the prospects for doing business in Russia appear somewhat daunting, be aware that many businesses have already proven that success is not only possible, but can be extremely profitable.

The State Committee on Statistics (GOSKOMSTAT) reported that in 1993, foreign investment totaled $2.9 billion (in U.S. dollars), with 90 percent of the capital in direct investments, which gave the right of controlling stakes in the Russian companies to the investors. Presently, the total volume of accumulated foreign direct investment is $7.0–7.2 billion. If you count the amounts invested in all of the Commonwealth of Independent States (CIS), including Russia, the total rises to $10–11 billion. Nevertheless, conservative estimates place the current level of foreign investment, even with the noticeable increase over the past two years, far below Russia's potential demand, which could easily handle $15–17 billion annually.

As of July 1, 1993, between $6.8–7.0 billion was invested in Russia. Table 5 below shows the percentage share of the total investment belonging to each of eight countries or regions making the largest investments.

Table 5: Registered Foreign Investments by Country

Country	Volume of investments (%)
East European countries	14.5
United States	10.6
Finland	9.0
Germany	8.3
Italy	7.8
Great Britain	4.5
Austria	4.0
France	3.4

Source: Association of Joint Ventures and International Amalgamations and Organizations.

As you can see, U.S. businesses are making substantial dollar investments. Table 6 below shows that U.S. businesses, as of July 1, 1993, also account for the largest number of joint ventures in Russia.

The current total number of registered enterprises with foreign participation is approximately 12 thousand. That is a two-fold increase in comparison with late 1992. In 1993, the inflow of foreign investment fluctuated. A rush of foreign investment registrations in the summer was followed by a considerable decline in October, due to growing political instability in Russia. In October, the volume of foreign investment was ten times below the September level — $13.8 million and $115.7 million, respectively.

Table 6: Registered Joint Ventures by Country

Country	Number of enterprises	Percent (%)
United States	1,433	15.7
Germany	1,141	12.4
Great Britain	557	6.1
Italy	511	5.6
Austria	475	5.2
Poland	438	4.8
Finland	429	4.7
China (PR)	347	3.8
Switzerland	319	3.5
France	283	3.1
Sweden	238	2.6
Bulgaria	237	2.6
Canada	209	2.3
Japan	173	1.9
Hungary	164	1.8
Total	9,128	100.0

Source: State Register of Enterprises with Foreign Participation.

While the sum of foreign investments and the number of enterprises with foreign share holdings grew, this growth was accompanied by a decline in the amount of the average foreign share in the charter capital of enterprises with foreign participation from 75–80 percent in mid-1993 to 35–36 percent in early 1994. The overwhelming majority of joint ventures involve minor investments by foreigners — see Table 7.

Table 7: Registered Joint Ventures by Charter Capital

Charter capital	Percent of enterprises (%)
Above R 100 million	0.4
R 10 – R 100 million	3.8
R 1 – R 10 million	19.8
Below R 1 million	76.0

Source: State Register of Enterprises with Foreign Participation as of July 1, 1993.

The bulk of joint ventures in Russia (76 percent) begin with charter capital below R1 million each — in May 1994, R1 million was equal to approximately $540–550. Predominately, joint ventures stick to a foreign market pattern, not an import-substituting one. As pointed out in Chapter 2, the Russian government foresees import-substituting industries as the next phase of foreign investment. According to GOSKOMSTAT, the share of enterprises with foreign participation in the total industrial output was approximately 2.4 percent — including 3 percent of the oil output — while their share in Russia's exports and imports exceeded 6 percent and 13 percent, respectively.

Even with the growth of foreign investments, employment by the new boom of joint ventures remains insignificant. The number of persons employed by these enterprises equals 300 thousand as of November 1, 1993 — which is still insignificant even though this represents a 110 thousand job increase compared with December 1992.

Sectors preferred by foreign investors are determined by specifics of Russia's business environment and have little in common with the real needs of structural adjustment to the Russian economy. In general, the sectors in which foreign capital is being invested have not changed during the last two years.

Table 8: Sectoral Distribution of Registered Joint Ventures

Sector	Percent of enterprises (%)*
Intermediary services and consulting	80.0
Production of consumer goods	58.0
Construction	51.0
Services	48.0
Advertising and publishing	46.0
Trade	44.0
Tourism and hotels	36.0
Production of technological equipment	20.0
Medicine	18.0
Chemicals and petrochemicals	10.0
Ferrous and nonferrous metallurgy	6.0

* Sectoral distribution as percentage of the total number of enterprises with foreign participation was calculated in accordance with the information on types of activity declared in the charter documents of these enterprises.

Source: State Register of Enterprises with Foreign Participation.

Evidently, the investment choices made by foreigners do not correspond with the sectoral priorities as defined by Russia's government — as discussed in Chapter 2. As before, foreign investors prefer involvement in the service sector, thus avoiding large-scale investments into Russia's basic industries. Table 8 shows the distribution by sector for the 12,294 joint ventures registered as of January 1, 1994.

Table 9 shows the percentage of the total amount of investment — $7.0–7.2 billion — as invested in various sectors of the economy as of January 1, 1994.

Table 9: Sectoral Distribution of Accumulated Foreign Investment

Sector	Volume of foreign investment (%)
Production of consumer goods, consumer and business services	35.5
Basic industries — oil and gas, chemicals and petro-chemicals, metallurgy, machinery building, and timber	32.2
Construction and production of construction materials	13.5
Production and trade in computer hardware and software	8.3
Agro-industrial complex	8.3
Other	2.2

Source: Association of Joint Ventures and International Amalgamations and Organizations.

Although the investments made by foreigners are not exactly as the Russian government would like, certain positive shifts have been noticed lately. Contrary to the assertions by the press that foreigners prefer the fuel and energy sector, as much as $678 million went to the machine building and metal industries last year. Foreign capital in these sectors actually reached 23.2 percent of the total investment in 1993. Foreigners put $475 million into the fuel and energy sector. The other sectors receiving a large share of investments included:

- Trade at $443 million;
- Construction at $156 million;
- Timber processing and pulp industry at $132 million; and
- Construction materials industry at $111 million.

Furthermore, foreign investments were increased in the spheres of conversion of defense enterprises — especially aviation plants — as well as production of communication and medical equipment. Table 10 shows the distribution by sector of the $2.9 billion of foreign direct investments accomplished in 1993.

Table 10: Sectoral Distribution of Foreign Direct Investment (FDI)

Industry	FDI volume (U.S. $ million)	Share (%)
Machinery building and metal working	678.0	23.2
Fuel Industry	475.0	16.3
Trade and public catering	443.0	15.2
Civil engineering	156.0	5.3
Timber processing and pulp and paper industry	132.0	4.5
Construction materials	111.0	3.8

Source: State Committee on Statistics.

Complete data on the regional distribution of foreign investments is not available. But according to estimates, over a quarter of all investments — 26.2 percent or $766 million — were channeled into the Moscow region, while $414 million went to the Krasnoyarsk Territory, and the Omsk and Arkhangelsk regions received $238 million and $231 million respectively.

Estimates show that the Jewish autonomous area received $173 million of foreign investments, the Belgorod region received $119 million, the Mari Republic received $145 million, and the Komi Republic received $105 million. Tables 11 and 12 illustrate the distribution of joint ventures and foreign investments by region.

Table 11: Regional Distribution of Joint Ventures

Region	Volume of joint ventures (%)	Volume of investments (%)
Moscow and Moscow region	55.0	44.0
St. Petersburg and Leningrad region	15.0	10.0
Central economic region	10.0	15.0
West Siberia region	8.0	13.0
Far East region	8.0	12.0
Other regions	4.0	6.0

Source: Association of Joint Ventures and International Amalgamations and Organizations.

In Table 11 the figures represent the percentage of the total number of joint ventures (12,294) and the percentage of the total amount of investment ($7.0–7.2 billion) as of January 1, 1994.

Table 12 represents the volume in dollars for each region and the share by percentage of each region of the total volume of foreign direct investments, totaling $2.9 billion during 1993.

Table 12: Regional Distribution of Foreign Direct Investment (FDI)

Region	FDI volume (U.S. $ million)	Share (%)
Moscow	766.0	26.2
Krasnoyarsk territory	414.0	14.2
Omsk region	238.0	8.1
Arkhangelsk region	231.0	7.9
Jewish autonomous area	173.0	5.9
Mari Republic	145.0	5.0
Belgorod region	119.0	4.1
Komi Republic	105.0	3.6

Source: State Committee on Statistics.

Foreign investments in privatization

In the second half of 1993, foreign investors turned their attention to the privatization process in Russia's economy.

Approximately $1.2–1.4 billion of foreign investment was used for privatizing Russian enterprises in 1993 and the first half of 1994. However, the Russian economy's potential for absorbing foreign investments is considerably greater. For more information about privatization, refer to Chapter 2.

The state program for the privatization of state and municipal enterprises, which became effective by *Presidential Decree No. 2284* of December 24, 1993, granted foreign businesspeople the right to make transactions with privatization vouchers. This enabled them to participate in voucher auctions, which offer 29 percent of shares of enterprises under privatization.

The largest privatization transactions with participation of foreign investors have taken place in the tobacco, foodstuffs, and apparel industries. As a rule, the most attractive factor for the Russian side is the readiness of foreign companies to invest in the modernization of Russian enterprises.

In 1993, the most important joint venture deals were:

- Siemens bought a ten percent share of the Kaluzhsky Turbine Enterprise. In August, 1993, the company signed an agreement on cooperation for producing and selling power turbines with a capacity of 35 megawatts and lower, in Russia and in other countries.
- Some 49 percent of shares of the biggest Russian garment producer, Bolshevichka, were bought by Illinguard Morris (Great Britain). The British company will invest 3.64 million pounds sterling into technology, personnel training, and licensing.
- Nordwest AG from Switzerland bought 20 percent of the Cherepovetsky joint stock company, Amophos. Eight million dollars will be invested in a joint venture project.

Investment auctions will be a priority form of sales now that voucher privatization has ended. Portfolios of shares of enterprises subject to privatization will increase. Such auctions are already being held and yielding good results. For instance:

- Proctor & Gamble bought blocks of shares of the Novomoskovskbytkhim company with a charter capital of R 276 million. Proctor & Gamble will invest $50 million in developing production over the next five years and $1 million for satisfying the social requirements of the cities of Novomoskovsk (the Tula region) and Tula.
- The Baltic Beverage Holding Company of Sweden bought 13.5 percent of the shares of St. Petersburg-based Baltika brewery. In addition, the company will invest 150 million kronas for developing production within the joint-stock company.
- The Huet Holdings Company of France won the investment bid in the Troitsko-Pechersk region of the Republic of Komi. The holding company bought shares in a timber enterprise and will invest close to $100 million over the next ten years.

A slowdown of foreign investments

Despite upward dynamics in several sectors, joint ventures have not become an important sector in the Russian economy, neither from the viewpoint of the investment volume, nor from the viewpoint for the output share in separate branches.

However, in the first through third quarters of 1993, enterprises with foreign participation managed to increase their output in comparison with the corresponding period of 1992 in the following manner:

- Oil and condensate by 210 percent
- Aluminum by 200 percent
- Paints and varnishes by 300 percent
- Steel by 43 percent

The output of construction materials, sewn and knitwear, meat and meat products, sausage, fish and fish products, personal computers, refrigerators, and tape recorders increased as well. At the same time, the production of footwear, cloth, and telephone equipment declined. In early 1994, the downward tendencies in the inflow of foreign direct investment have continued.

Joint venture entrepreneurship in manufacturing in the Russian Federation has been less successful that originally envisaged by the Russian government. The shares of basic industries with foreign capital — machinery, fuel and energy complex, chemicals, and timber complex — are equal to only 18 percent of the total number of enterprises with foreign investments and 32 percent of the total investment capital of these enterprises. Only ten percent of the machine-building joint ventures actually produce machinery and equipment, and the sales carried out by a handful of machinery-building joint ventures account for 75 percent of the total volume of machinery-building sales by enterprises with foreign investments. And while sales are decreasing, the share of imported consumer goods, computers and office equipment, and cars is growing.

The investment environment in Russia remains problematic for large-scaled schemes involving foreign participation. Experts of the Ministry of Economy are reporting a considerable slowdown in foreign investment in the Russian economy.

In January 1994, 397 enterprises with foreign investments announced their aggregate foreign deposits to charter funds at $16.4 million. This is compared to 504 such enterprises and $244.1 million in December 1993.

As before, mainly smaller-sized enterprises are being formed. In comparison with R 245.2 million and $123.4 thousand in 1993, the average volume of the these enterprises' charter funds and foreign deposits registered in January 1994, fell by roughly three times — to R 80.3 million and $41.3 thousand, respectively.

The downward trend in the inflow of foreign investment becomes more obvious if you know that the total volume of the charter funds of the enterprises with foreign investments registered in January, and the aggregate volume to foreign deposits, 26.6 percent and 36.6 percent respectively belonged to one enterprise created with participation of the well-known firm, Procter & Gamble. With the deduction of this investment, each of the remaining 396 enterprises accounted for an average of only R 59 million and $26.5 thousand.

A major factor contributing to the decline is the fact that providing mutually acceptable conditions for Russian and foreign investors is not at all simple. The Russian enterprises want to be matched with a foreign partner and investor willing to invest financial resources in Russian enterprises. However, foreign investors prefer not to invest money, but offer new technologies and equipment. Nonetheless, most Russian enterprises, especially in the provinces, want to work independently, without having any foreigners on their board of directors. As far as financial resources, which the Russian enterprises desire, many firms with respectable reputations that want to make a name in Russia offer funding, but all of them want suitable guarantees as well.

Patterns of foreign investors

Foreign investors are interested in legally establishing their presence in Russia's market. However, as a rule, they have avoided the risk of large-scale investments into the manufacturing sector, including high-tech industries. Most of the joint ventures prefer to operate in spheres with low investment barriers and speedy returns, such as commercial — intermediary or consulting — activities and services.

A major factor for businesses is the establishment of confidential relations in Russia's corridors of power as a generally recognized way of doing business. The most active and successful companies are those that have established long-term informal relations with the former Soviet bureaucracy during the Soviet Union era. Many U.S., German, Italian, Finnish, as well as East European businesses, have done this very well. Newcomers, such as South Korean companies, who have invested in establishing such relations, have also been rather successful. Because most foreign businesspeople are eager to be closer to traditional centers of decision making, the bulk of joint ventures are registered in Moscow and St. Petersburg — amounting to more than 70 percent of the total number of registered joint ventures.

The characteristic pattern for foreign investors is to use a step-by-step approach. The first step, usually, is making sporadic trade deals with the same partners. This step is then followed by long-term export and import contracts, and later by joining together for wholesale and retail trade networks. The final step of this approach, provided all has gone well with the partners, is to make joint investments into the production sphere. This approach is particularly favored by investors from Taiwan.

The organizational form of the traditional joint venture is becoming less attractive for foreign companies in comparison with a 100 percent foreign-owned company or a minority joint venture having formal foreign participation equal to a sufficient percentage necessary for legalization in Russia. See Chapter 4 for more about organizational forms.

The traditional joint venture has been plagued by the inevitable disputes among the participants, which are caused by the lack of reliable methods of assessing the foreign investor's investment into the charter capital. As a result of this problem, the largest share of successful enterprises are either 100 percent foreign-owned companies or minority joint ventures.

Patterns of specific countries

At the same time, investors from individual foreign countries have specific behavior patterns.

United States. Currently, U.S. businesses are the most active in Russia's private sector. They prefer to deal with Russian entities that are risking their own money and are ready to share the responsibility for profitable exploitation of a joint venture.

Great Britain. British firms are the most conservative investors. With rare exclusions, they invest in the Russian economy only on obtaining guarantees from the British government, which are strengthened by corresponding intergovernmental agreements.

Canada. Canadian companies offer an example of generally being well prepared for business. Most Canadian businesses engaged in Russia start their activity with comprehensive feasibility studies, prepared in close cooperation with Russian experts. As a result, 71 percent of registered joint ventures with Canadian capital are successful — compared with the average 35 percent of the total that are functioning joint ventures.

South Korea. South Korean companies have been firm in implementing a set of consecutive measures to establish themselves in a limited number of strategically important industrial branches — namely the oil and gas industry, chemicals, electronic industry, timber processing industry, as well as participating in the conversion of defense enterprises.

Overview of making foreign investments

As is well known, practical ways of carrying out business activities in any sphere of Russia's economy differ substantially from the corresponding laws and regulations governing those business activities. The most glaring difficulties faced by foreign investors are connected with Russia's rapidly changing and unstable legal environment and the inability to effectively evaluate potential Russian partners. See Chapter 2 for tips on choosing your Russian partner.

Solving the practical issues

As far as legislation relating to foreign investments is concerned, it should be stressed that there are no practical mechanisms for putting investments into practice. That is why a foreign investor is compelled to solve many practical issues concerning an investment project. In the course of informal negotiations, the investor must resolve issues on three levels:

- With a potential partner, whether an individual or an enterprise;
- With federal governmental bodies responsible for regulating foreign investments; and
- With local authorities in a region — area, district, territory, or all three — where the investment will be made.

Obviously, this situation leads to numerous legal and financial problems. Establishing a manufacturing enterprise needs substantial initial investment, while there are no guarantees of regular supplies of equipment, components, and raw materials, and no clear prospects for marketing your future products — especially for hard currency. While being oriented to Russia's internal market, such businesses need to import the bulk of components used for the production of final articles in order to guarantee their quality.

Hard currency settlements are forbidden in Russia — the ruble is the only legal tender — so import-substituting manufacturers face a pressing problem with the use of their ruble profits because of the extreme fluctuation in their value. In other words, your contracts are negotiated based on rubles, for which no quantifiable guarantee can be given for what that amount will eventually translate into as dollars later on when the contract is fulfilled. In any case, would-be manufacturers are in urgent need for substantial legal benefits nonexistent in the present version of the Russian hard currency regulation.

The next big problem is that the present foreign investment legislation provides foreign investors with no tax holidays. Nevertheless, you can obtain corresponding exclusive benefits through personal contacts with authorized officials. However, you have no guarantee that such benefits will not be terminated in the future. Profits reinvested in the development of the technical and productive base of your business are not exempt from taxation.

The Russian government's definition of profit — as any income — differs substantially from the Western definition. See Chapter 7 for more information about Russian taxes. The good news is that experts predict a package of benefits, including a three-year taxation holiday, may be restored in the near future.

Profits of Russian enterprises resulting from participation in an enterprise with foreign investment are levied three times:

- By the value-added tax (VAT) — 20 percent, plus 3 percent tax designated for promoting Russia's vital industries;
- By the profit tax — 38 percent, or 45 percent for several types of activity; and
- By the dividends withholding tax — 15 percent.

The present situation provides Russian counterparts with no tax stimulus to cooperate with you as a foreign investor.

Foreigners who come to Russia will face a lot of problems, mostly due to incomplete legislation for regulating activities of foreign investors, including registration, taxation, currency, and customs controls. For your undertaking in Russia to be successful, you will need reliable information and qualified advice from lawyers and consulting firms about the most complicated and sensitive, legal and economic aspects of doing business.

Below are some of the commonly agreed upon interpretations of fundamental provisions of the current legislation regulating foreign investments.

Spheres for foreign investment

Generally, other than following the registration procedures for the relevant enterprise, no special permission is required for a foreign person or entity to make an investment in the Russian Federation. The *Law on Foreign Investment* (dated July 4, 1991) allows foreign investors to make almost any type of investment in the Russian Federation, though some activities — including mining, oil and gas, banking, insurance, and brokerage connected with the circulation of securities — require licenses from the appropriate Russian ministry.

Setting up businesses with foreign investments

According to current legislation, the following legal entities may make foreign investments in the Russian Federation:

- Foreign legal entities, including for example, any firms, companies, enterprises, organizations, and associations created and authorized to make investments in accordance with the legislation of their countries of origin;
- Foreign citizens, persons without a citizenship, and Russian citizens that reside permanently abroad, on the condition that they are registered to carry out economic activities in the country of their citizenship or permanent residence;
- Foreign states; and
- International organizations.

The legislation provides further that foreign investments can be made with all kinds of material and intellectual properties, deposited by foreign investors into objects of entrepreneurial and other activities in order to receive profit (income). As a foreign investor, you have the right to make investments in the Russian territory by:

- Holding shares in joint ventures with the legal entities and citizens of the Russian Federation and other ex-Union republics;
- Creating enterprises that completely belong to foreign investors, as well as branches of foreign legal entities;
- Acquiring buildings, property complexes, enterprises, constructions, shares, stocks, bonds, and other securities, as well as other property, which in accordance with the current Russian legislation can belong to foreign investors;
- Acquiring the rights to use land and other natural resources;
- Acquiring other proprietors' rights; and

- Carrying on other investment activities that are not forbidden by the current legislation on the territory of the Russian Federation, including supplying loans, credits, property and proprietors' rights.

The Russian currency, the ruble, is used by foreign investors to carry out investments under the conditions defined by the current legislation on the Russian Federation territory. Foreign investments on the Russian Federation territory can be deposited into any objects not forbidden for such investments by the legislation. Those objects can include:

- Newly created and modernized fixed assets and floating, or circulating, assets in all spheres and branches of the economy;
- Securities;
- Designated monetary deposits;
- Intellectual property rights; and
- Other property rights.

As you can see, few enough restrictions exist so that anyone wanting to invest in Russia can find the opportunity and venue to do so.

Summary

While major investment activities have been carried out successfully in Russia, keep in mind that most investments risk very small amounts of money. The route to accomplishing any of these investments has not been easy for foreign investors, since Russia's newly formed market economy has many glitches to be worked out. A government document, demonstrating the work going on within the government to make foreign investments more attractive to foreigners, is reprinted at the end of this chapter.

Meanwhile, those entrepreneurs who are persistent will continue to find ways to work with the government and solve the problems. To gain more insight into how things work — or in many cases, don't work — in Russia, keep reading. The next chapter explains how to legally register your business enterprise in Russia. Remember, you will need qualified legal advice at every step.

Document: The Russian Government's Ordinance #1108
On Spurring the Work on Attracting Foreign Investment
in the Russian Economy

In a bid to stimulate the work on drawing foreign investment in the Russian economy and to ensure the relevant consistent and well-balanced state policy, the government of the Russian Federations decrees:

1. To consider the work, which is carried out by the federal executive bodies of state power on attracting foreign investment in the Russian economy and creating a favorable legal, taxation and customs regime for foreign investors, to be a vitally important task.

2. To establish a Consultative Council for Foreign Investment in Russia (hereafter referred to as the Consultative Council) headed by the Russian Prime Minister.

To approve the appointment of Alexander Shokhin, deputy Prime Minister, as deputy chairman of the Consultative Council and Yakov Urinson, first deputy of the Russian Economics Minister — as the Chief Executive Officer of the Consultative Council.

The Council's Chief Executive Officer shall submit proposals for the council's personal composition and the activity program to the Russian government within a month.

To approve the appointment of the heads of the following working groups of the Consultative Council:

- *a group for drawing up proposals for improving the investment climate in Russia and the mechanism of cooperation between foreign investors, and federal executive bodies of state power and executive bodies of the Russian Federation subjects shall be headed by Yakov Urinson, first deputy Economics Minister and Yevgeny Yasin, head of the Presidential Analytical Center (as agreed upon);*

- *a group for working out proposals for the taxation, customs and currency policy in Russia shall be headed by Sergei Dubinin, acting Minister of Finance;*

- *a group for drawing up proposals for making Russia more attractive for foreign investors shall be headed by Oleg Davydov, Minister for Foreign Economic Relations.*

The heads of the working groups shall coordinate and submit the personal composition and work plans to the Council's Chief Executive Officer before November 1, 1994.

To entrust the Russian Economics Ministry with ensuring the activity of the Consultative Council and coordination of the working groups' activity.

3. *The Economics Ministry shall ensure the formulation and implementation of the state policy on attracting foreign investment in the Russian economy, coordination of the activity of federal executive bodies of state power and executive bodies of the Russian Federation subjects on the problems of cooperation with foreign investors, including the establishment of free economic zones and organization and holding of international biddings, the elaboration of concession agreements and contracts on the division of products, the organization of work on using the credits extended by international financial organizations and foreign states to Russia for implementing specific investment projects.*

4. *The Economics Ministry, the Ministry for Foreign Economic Relations, the Ministry of Finance, the Ministry of Foreign Affairs, the State Committee for Construction, The State Committee for Industrial Policy, the State Committee for Defense Industries, the State Committee for State Property Management, the State Customs Committee, the State Committee for Anti-monopoly Policy and Support of New Economic Structures, other interested executive bodies of state power, the Central Bank of Russia and the Russian Chamber of Commerce and Industry shall draw up a draft* Comprehensive Program for Encouraging Domestic and Foreign Investments in the Russian Economy *and submit the draft program and proposals for its implementation to the Russian government in the first quarter of 1995.*

5. *The Economics Ministry, the Ministry for Foreign Economic Relations, the State Customs Committee, the Ministry of Finance, the Ministry of Justice and other interested federal executive bodies of state power shall put finishing touches to the draft federal laws* On Making Changes and Additions to the Russian Federation Law 'On Foreign Investments in Russia', On Free Economic Zones and On Concession Agreements and Contracts for Provision of Services and Agreements on Division of Products Concluded with Foreign Investors, *taking into account the critical remarks, within two months.*

While putting together the above drafts the following shall be done:

- *the draft law* On Making Changes and Additions to the Russian Federation Law 'On Foreign Investment in Russia' *shall envision the ensuring of necessary conditions for attracting foreign investment in the Russian economy, including in the field of taxation, export/import tariffs and currency regulation;*
- *the draft law* On Free Economic Zones *shall envision the establishment of a privileged regime of economic activity, including the foreign economic one, on the territory of those zones;*

- *the draft law* On Concession Agreements and Contracts for Provision of Services and Agreements on Division of Products Concluded with Foreign Investors *shall envision the preservation of terms and conditions of the division of products during the term of validity of those agreements and contracts and a possibility of making changes in them provided the parties to them have no objections.*

6. *The Economics Ministry, the State Committee for Defense Industries and the State Committee for State Property Management shall elaborate a program for drawing foreign investment for conversion of defense enterprises, provided they are guaranteed state orders and fulfill their obligations not to divulge state secrets and accomplish mobilization preparation tasks, within three months and submit it to the Russian government.*

7. *The State Committee for Anti-monopoly Policy and Support of New Economic Structures shall devise proposals for taking into account anti-monopoly requirements in the process of drawing foreign investment in the Russian economy and submit it to the Russian government.*

8. *The Economics Ministry, the Ministry of Finance, other interested federal executive bodies of state power and the Central Bank of Russia shall submit proposals for establishing the system of insuring and guaranteeing direct foreign investment to the Russian government within three months.*

9. *The State Committee for State Property Management, the Ministry of Finance, the Economics Ministry, other interested federal executive bodies of state power and the Central Bank of Russia shall draw up proposals for the mechanism of using mortgage forms of drawing foreign investment within three months and submit them to the Russian government.*

10. *The Economics Ministry, the State Committee for State Property Management, other interested federal executive bodies of state power, the Central Bank of Russia and the Russian Chamber of Commerce and Industry shall compile a list of the types of activity and territories on which it is expedient to impose restrictions and bans regarding foreign investment within three months and submit it to the Russian government.*

11. *The Economics Ministry, the Ministry for Foreign Economic Relations, the Ministry of Finance and other interested federal executive bodies of state power shall speed up the holding of negotiations with foreign states on concluding agreements on mutual protection and encouragement of investment. Alexander Shokhin, deputy Prime Minister, shall approve the negotiations' schedule.*

12. *The Economics Ministry, the Ministry for Foreign Economic Relations, the Ministry of Foreign Affairs, the State Committee for State Property Management and other interested federal executive bodies of power shall*

*draw up proposals for improving the system of providing information to for-
eign investors about Russian legislation, branch and regional programs and
projects proposed to be implemented with foreign investor's participation
within three months and submit them to the Russian government.*

*To reorganize the State Information Center for Encouraging Investment,
which was set up under Russian government ordinance #908* On Measures
to Organize Provision of Information to Russian and Foreign Investors
About Privatization of State-run Enterprises *of November 24, 1992
(Collection of the acts of the President of the Russian Federation, 1992, #22,
Article 1914) into the State Information Center for Encouraging Investment
of the Economics Ministry and the State Committee for State Property
Management. The above departments shall submit proposals on the center's
activity within a month.*

*13. The Economics Ministry, the Ministry for Foreign Economic Rela-
tions and the Ministry of Justice shall work out proposals for improving the
system of registration of enterprises with foreign investment on the territory
of the Russian Federation within two months and submit them to the Russian
government.*

*14. The State Statistics Committee and interested federal executive bod-
ies of state power shall draw up proposals for improving the system of statistics accounts regarding foreign investment drawn to Russia within two
months and submit them to the Russian government.*

*15. The Economics Ministry, the Ministry of Finance, the Central Bank
of Russia and the Russian government agents engaged in the work with
domestic and foreign investments — the State Investment Corporation, the
Russian Financial Corporation, the Russian Joint-stock Investment-Com-
mercial Industrial and Construction Bank (Promstroibank), the Russian
Bank for Reconstruction and Development and the Entrepreneurship Development Bank shall submit proposals for defining those agents' specialization,
coordination of their activity and cooperation with federal executive bodies of
state power within two months.*

*16. Alexander Shokhin, deputy Prime Minister, shall hear the progress
reports of representatives of the Russian Federation in international financial organizations on a quarterly basis as well as submit proposals for enhancing the efficiency of using the possibilities of the above organizations for
developing the Russian economy to the Russian government in the first
quarter of 1995.*

*17. The Economics Ministry shall hold a meeting with representatives of
the corresponding executive bodies of the Russian Federation subjects in
1995 on the problems pertaining to drawing foreign investment in Russia's*

regions, generalize and analyze the proposals of its participants, elaborate specific recommendations for improving the work with foreign investment in regions.

Victor Chernomyrdin
Russian Prime Minister

September 29, 1994

Chapter 4

Legal Entities
Типы юридические формы

Advice about Russian laws

Unless you wish to offend bureaucrats in Russia, avoid using the word 'law' in their presence. There seems to be an idiosyncrasy towards it. Moreover, by using it, you are making two grave mistakes: first, you are infringing on the sacred right of a bureaucrat to unilaterally interpret law and, second, you are shutting yourself out of any future possibility to establish a mutually beneficial, friendly relationship with that representative of power. If, before uttering that awful word, you are addressed as 'old man,' 'my lad' or even 'pal,' after saying that word you immediately become 'Mister' if not 'suspect.'

Recently, two reporters from a popular newspaper made a test of this premise about how bureaucrats feel about law. As part of the experiment, they had a glass of vodka each and went out in search of adventure in the evening city. Both had their pockets empty, though one purposely had with him the *Criminal Code of the Russian Federation*.

The first of the two was calling his wife from a police station in about an hour. In another 30 minutes, somewhat crumpled and with a substantial blow to his family budget, he was home. The second one was found only on the third day, thanks to the joint effort of the paper and the highest ranks in the Ministry of Internal Affairs. The

District Police Station he was held in had been reluctant to let him go, insisting that he was already identified as a long-wanted sexual maniac and that they already possessed his voluntary confession of taking part in six apartment burglaries and nine car thefts. Over and above that, the bouquet of accusations also included insolent safe-breaking in the police station itself, resulting in the theft of a long list of valuable evidence and a large sum of money which he hid — exactly, you guessed it — in the volume of the *Criminal Code of the Russian Federation*, that supposedly belonged to the chief of the police station himself.

After being let out, the reporter applied for a two-week leave of absence. No one could get a word out of him. When he finally broke the story, he confessed that the criminal code book was 'borrowed' from the desk of his acquaintance in the Chief Military Prosecutor's Department. Naturally, he was going to return it after the experiment.

The only thing that saved him was the fact that the book came from a library, so he finally managed to convince the police detective to phone the library and find out in whose name the book was provided. "I tried to throw the book [across the desk] at the cop. That's when it all started."

So, laws exist in Russia, but you are recommended to use them only after consulting with an appropriate authorized official. However, something told you by one official may very well be refuted by another and not necessarily of higher rank. Therefore, after any new law is issued in Russia, you are better off waiting for an 'instruction' — a departmental document explaining the rights and powers of various state institutions in applying and interpreting the law. In the long run, the instruction is what matters.

Is it possible to defend the rights established by the law in court? Theoretically, yes, but successfully only after the instruction that clarifies the law in question is issued. Otherwise, the judge will simply not understand you in most cases. When conducting your business, you cannot refer to the law exclusively in substantiation of your rights and ignore the instructions, especially since the instructions have the tendency to interpret law exclusively in the interests of departmental officials.

The best way out of this situation is to acknowledge the rules of the game and keep up with the instructions. For a foreign investor, this advice is even more important because the basic rules with regard to investment and business activities in Russia are still regulated either by temporary governmental orders or by amendments and supplements to the federal or republican legislation of the now-extinct Union of the Soviet Socialist Republics. Such is the situation you have to face when confronted with the decision to open and register a business.

The same state of affairs applies to regulations on activities, such as conducting commercial transactions, marketing securities, and making real estate transactions. While the Russian government understands that success for economic reforms depends on the improvement of both the legal and tax regimes for foreign investors, plans for changes in the laws on businesses, trusts, securities, the stock exchange, and land and property legislation, are only in the making to be discussed in the Parliament.

Legal forms of enterprises in Russia

Naturally, this situation makes the orientation difficult for the investor entering the Russian market for the first time. As a rule, you will need to conduct a special investigation in order to provide for a solid approach on how to implement each actual project you undertake. At the same time, a certain practice exists already, since the experience of many large-scale, foreign investors shows that regardless of legal instability and a turbulent political situation in Russia, it is still possible to carry out long-term and highly efficient investment and commercial operations.

Investment activities, such as buying shares and making portfolio investments, generally require no special permission, except when:

- An individual or a group of individuals want to buy more than 15 percent of shares in an enterprise, they must notify the Russian Ministry of Finance five days in advance; or
- A legal entity or a group of legal entities want to buy 35 percent or more of shares, they can only do so with the consent of the State Committee for Antimonopoly Policy and Support of New Economic Structures.

The above requirements do not apply to founders of private or public limited companies or foreign-owned businesses. Besides commercial investments, your activities as a foreign investor in Russia can be carried out in three ways.

- Open an office or an agency that represents you as an individual, foreign businessperson in Russia. This business structure is easiest to set up and can help you make contacts that allow a later joint venture. You are not required to register this form of business since the actual transactions and services supplied — activities such as consulting, locating suppliers, or finding customers — either take place outside Russia or require no monetary transactions through Russian banks, or both.

- Establish in Russia an affiliation or a branch of your business that already exists in another country. Registration of this form of business in Russia is similar to registering an alien corporation elsewhere.

- Incorporate or form your Russian business as one that fully or partially belongs to you as a foreign investor in accordance with the laws of the Russian Federation.

This third way to start a business applies to both joint ventures — businesses that involve a Russian partner and a foreigner — and to businesses that are owned wholly by foreign businesspersons. When you register this type of business with the state and form it under Russian law, your business is given the status of being a 'legal person,' also known as a 'juridical person.' This is similar to the legal entity status granted to businesses in the United States. In the United States, a legal entity has the legal standing to enter into a contract, such as a corporation is considered a legal entity since it is a person in the eyes of the law.

Russian laws regulating businesses

If you would like to do further research, the basic legislative deeds regulating these activities are the *Law on Foreign Investments* (dated July 4, 1991) and also the *Law on Property* (dated December 24, 1990), the *Law on Enterprises and Business Activities* (dated December 25, 1990); and the new Civil code in force as of January 1, 1995.

Besides those, there are a number of presidential decrees and government orders to supplement or amend these deeds. Questions dealing with how to issue securities and their turnover, are covered by *Government Decision No. 78* (dated December 28, 1991).

Keep in mind that the Russian legal system is evolving constantly and changing quickly. Always seek qualified legal advice before you start a business or project.

Choosing a legal form

The new Russian civil code provides for the following legal forms of organization for profit-oriented enterprises with foreign investments:

- General partnerships;
- Kommandite partnerships — similar to limited partnerships;
- Private limited companies — like limited liability companies;
- Closed-type joint stock companies — similar to close corporations; and
- Public limited companies — the same as public corporations.

State-owned enterprises may be operated in the form of what are called unitary enterprises — federal or municipal — or in any of the other legal models described above. Additionally, cooperatives and individual enterprise forms of organization are legal forms of organization reserved for Russian participants. A cooperative has no Western equivalent, but is an enterprise form that evolved under the former command economy.

Advantages and disadvantages of legal entities

In practice, general partnerships are infrequently used by foreign investors, since among other reasons, as an individual or partner in such an entity, you bear unlimited liability for the business' debts and obligations. Because they provide limited liability, to date, mostly private limited and public limited companies have been used by foreign investors. Liability is limited to the investments of the participants or the package of shares belonging to them. The essential differences from a Western perspective between the legal forms used by foreign investors are:

- Public limited companies can issue public shares, whereas private limited companies cannot. Public limited companies are managed by a board of directors elected by shareholders.
- Private limited companies and closed-type joint stock companies are similar to closely held corporations, in which stock is held by a small group of people and not publicly traded. A private limited company may have as few members as only one shareholder.
- A private limited company is organized more like a partnership, since the shareholders are expected to assume active roles in the management of the business.

- Kommandite partnerships resemble limited partnerships. For kommandite partnerships — liability is limited with respect to the money of the contributing members. Full members of kommandite partnerships and all members of general partnerships bear unlimited, sole liability on the obligations of their businesses. The participants of an enterprise having unlimited liability bear the liability on the obligations of his or her company within the limits determined in accordance with its charter.

At present, legislation defining enterprise forms more clearly and specifically has been introduced only with respect to private and public limited companies. The legislation dealing with such companies contains detailed provisions for the establishment and operation of public limited companies and creates a detailed legal framework for such companies. As a result, a relatively solid track record exists in relation to public limited companies.

The *Enterprise Law,* however, contains very few provisions relating to private limited companies. This lack of legal basis for private limited companies has both advantages and disadvantages. On one hand, it allows the founders of a private limited company to organize the company as they desire. On the other hand, it puts the company and its founders at risk. This lack of a strong legal basis gives government officials and other parties, with which the private limited company must deal, room to create their own interpretations and requirements.

The question of which form you should adopt is chiefly a question of which of the below considerations are most important to you. If certainty about laws regulating your business is your priority consideration, then you want to organize as a public limited company, so long as you are willing to accept the increased operational burdens entailed by this form of investment and to have two or more owners of the company. The public limited company also can generate financing by issuing shares and has the ability to incorporate a number of minor equity partners without permitting a significant role in its management.

If you want only one shareholder, then a private limited company is the better choice. If flexibility and simplicity are more important, then a private limited company is probably the better choice, as well, so long as you are willing to accept some amount of uncertainty.

In practice, the private limited company is by far the more prevalent form for subsidiaries. In general, when choosing between public limited companies (corporations) and private limited companies, you should look at the worldwide distinctions between them — a public limited company has continuity when a member departs and can participate in the free transfer of shares, whereas private limited companies lack transferability of shares and may even cease to exist when a member dies or resigns.

Starting your business

In order to start operating a business on the Russian territory, you will need to open an account in one of the Russian banks or in a foreign bank licensed to carry out banking transactions in Russia. However, before such an account can be opened. you must provide either a certificate from the tax office, or a letter of credit from your corresponding bank, or both.

General partnerships are not 'legal persons' (legal entities) by law, but they may open bank accounts in the name of an appointed person as provided for in the business' formation documents.

All businesses and individuals must show that they have registered with the tax service before being able to open a bank account. To get a certificate from the tax office, you must show that you have registered your business with all of the relevant authorities. The general requirements and procedures for registering your business are outlined below. Specific information for each type of business enterprise form are given at the end of this section.

For a small business, you will need to register only with the local authorities. If your business with foreign investments has charter capital of more than 50 million rubles, you will also need to register with the local branch of the State Committee on Antimonopoly Policy. Businesses that have foreign investments of more than 100 million rubles, plan large-scale construction projects, or have an environmental impact must prepare to get through a registration triangle consisting of:

- The Russian Agency for International Cooperation and Development, which will coordinate placing you on the state register of enterprises with foreign investments, registering you with the Ministry of Finance, and obtaining permission from the Russian Cabinet of Ministers — the Cabinet of Ministers must issue permission or give reasons for refusal within two months of when documents are submitted to the Ministry of Finance;

- The local branch of the State Committee on Antimonopoly Policy, which has coordinating functions with the other authorities; and
- The local registration authorities.

When you apply for registration, the Russian Ministry of Finance or other authorized state body must, in no less than 21 days after the application is submitted, register the enterprise with foreign investments or give reasons for any refusal.

Registered enterprises with foreign investments are issued registration certificates. From the moment of registration, enterprises receive the rights of a legal entity. The local body of power will give you a document providing the registration information and it is to be displayed at the enterprise's location. You must publish an announcement of registration in the newspaper and have a seal made, similar to corporate seals in the United States.

As a foreign investor, whether as an individual or as a legal entity, you will need to provide documentation to the registering authorities in order to register your business. Generally, you will need to provide a certificate of solvency from your bank and an excerpt from the commercial register of your country of origin or some sort of equivalent. For a U.S. business with a legal entity status, this documentation could be your listing with the U.S. Securities and Exchange Commission, your certificate of incorporation, or articles of organization. For enterprises organized in Russia with foreign investments, you can use your founding documents, which must define the:

- Subject and aims of the enterprise's activities;
- List of participants;
- Amount and order of creating the charter capital;
- Amount of the participants' shares;
- Structure, content, and competence of the management bodies;
- Procedures for making decisions;
- List of decisions that need unanimity; and
- The enterprise's liquidation procedures.

Other issues that do not contradict the current Russian legislation and reflect the specifics of the enterprise's activities can also be included in the founding documents.

For investors who do not have a legal entity status, providing documentation can be even more difficult since you can not produce an incorporation certificate or similar documentation. Overcoming this status hurdle can be both time-consuming and expensive. While a Russian official may possibly be satisfied just looking at your passport — as would be sufficient for a Russian entrepreneur — you are better off having as many documents as feasible, in the likelihood you will need them.

Having adequate documentation at the start will be worthwhile if it allows you to start your business sooner. Examples of documentation you can provide could be papers from your employer, stating your place of work and job title, or papers containing data on your company's annual turnover. Little importance is placed on where your papers are from — your country's embassy in Russia, your employer, or your local police station.

Many Russian officials still demand that foreign documents be legalized by Russian consulates abroad. Officials may disregard any certificate of authenticity issued by your country. Therefore, to avoid misunderstandings and to save time, you can visit a Russian consulate at home to arrange having your documents officially translated into Russian before you take them to the registering officials. This is an acceptable substitute for notary certification of the translation authenticity that would be done by a Russian notary public.

To summarize the process for opening a business in Russia, you will need to gather the documentation required for your status; register your business with state and local authorities as needed, depending on the size of your investment; register with the tax office; and finally, open your bank account.

Specific registration requirements

Now that you have an idea of the basic procedures and requirements for registering your business, the specific requirements for each type of enterprise with foreign investments are given below.

Joint ventures

A joint venture in Russia refers to a business or partnership that involves both a Russian entity or individual and a foreign entity or individual. The documents you will need to register a joint venture are:

- A written application of the founders asking to register the created enterprise;
- Two notarized copies of founding documents;

- The conclusions of the respective examinations in cases provided by law — for example, a conclusion on the ecological safety of an enterprise to be established;
- For Russian legal entities — a notarized copy of the property owner's decision to create the enterprise or a copy of the decision of the body authorized by him or her as well, as notarized copies of the founding documents of every Russian legal entity participating in the creation of the joint venture;
- For foreign investors — documents of each foreign investor's solvency issued by his or her bank or other credit-finance establishment, with a notarized Russian translation; and
- For foreign investors — excerpts from the trade register of the country of the investor's origin or other equivalent proof of his or her legal status in accordance with the legislation of the country of his or her location or citizenship of permanent residence, with a notarized Russian translation.

100 percent foreign-owned enterprises

- A written application for registration from the foreign investor;
- Two sets of notarized copies of the founding documents;
- Documents of the foreign investor's solvency issued by a bank or other credit-finance establishment, with a notarized Russian translation;
- Excerpts from the trade register of the country of the foreign investor's origin, with a notarized Russian translation; and
- Conclusions of the respective examinations in cases provided by legislation — for example, a conclusion on the ecological safety of an enterprise to be established.

Outlets and subsidiaries of foreign-owned enterprises

- An application, signed by the head of the enterprise creating the outlet, asking to register it;
- A notarized copy of excerpts from the resolution of the respective appropriate management body to create an outlet;
- Two notarized copies of the regulations of the outlet;
- A power of attorney in the name of the head of the local office;
- Notarized copies of the founding documents of the enterprise creating the outlet;

- For foreign legal entities — excerpts from the trade register of the investor's country of origin or other equivalent proof of his or her legal status, with notarized Russian translation; and
- Conclusions of the appropriate examinations in cases provided by legislation — for example, a conclusion on the ecological safety of an enterprise to be established.

Accredited offices of foreign businesses and organizations

To open an accredited office, foreign businesses and organizations must submit to the Russian Chamber of Commerce and Industry the following documents:

- A written application, translated into Russian, containing the title of the foreign business, date of its creation and location, the nature of its business, its managing bodies and top executive representing the foreign firm in accordance with its charter, purpose of its accredited office, its activities, information about its business contacts in the Russian Federation, as well as about prospects of such cooperation;
- Charter, articles of incorporation, or its substitution as required by local laws;
- Registration certificate or an excerpt from the commercial register of the business' country of origin;
- Declaration of a bank containing information on the foreign business' solvency; and
- A power of attorney in the name of the local representative conducting negotiations on behalf of the foreign firm.

All documents mentioned immediately above should be notarized by appropriate local authorities and by a Russian consular office abroad and translated into Russian. Opening an accredited office requires special permission stipulated by local laws. A copy of such permission, notarized by local authorities and by a Russian consular office abroad should be attached to the application.

Besides these documents and information, the foreign business, upon request from the Russian Chamber of Commerce and Industry, shall submit other documents relating to its activities, such as the foreign business' joint stock. Foreign businesses, before obtaining permission to open an accredited office or to prolong their function in the Russian Federation, shall pay an established registration fee.

Setting up a business venture in Russia is complex and challenging. However, the rewards can be extremely great. Listed below are some tips that will help you avoid several of the potential pitfalls of doing business in Russia.

Evaluate the need for a new legal entity

From the very beginning, you should evaluate whether it is necessary to create a new legal entity or person. Because of the complexities of organizing a business under Russian law, if you can avoid doing so, you will be better off. Alternatively, if you organize your business under U.S. law, and then register as a foreign business in Russia, you can define relations with your Russian partners in a detailed agreement on joint operations.

You can most likely define your interrelations — such as separation of duties with regard to financing, management, specific economic operations, and division of profits — better in such an agreement than you can in the founding documents of an enterprise. In addition to saving time on registration, you will also save money on overhead and upkeep — money that could be spent on operations.

Include special clauses for liquidation and resignation

Liquidation of enterprises with foreign investments is done in accordance with procedures defined by current Russian legislation for various organizational and legal forms of enterprises. Liquidation can be either state-mandated or voluntary.

After a one-year period, if an enterprise with foreign investments has no documented confirmation that every participant has invested no less than 50 percent of his or her share into the charter capital, as according to the founding documents, the state body that issued the registration certificate considers it void and makes a decision to liquidate. De-registration of liquidated enterprises with foreign investments is carried out by the body that registered it on the basis of the liquidation committee's act and a liquidation balance confirmed by an auditing company. Liquidation announcements are published in the newspapers.

Be aware that the wording normally used in the formation documents of legal entities does not protect the interests of minority shareholders in case the company is reorganized, one of its members resigns voluntarily, or the state mandates liquidation.

You will want to introduce corresponding amendments to the constituent documents or insist on including special clauses to protect investors in case conflicting situations arise or if and when a member resigns.

Carefully word the liability limits of company members

In most formation documents, the following wording is normally used: "The members bear liability to company obligations within the limits of their share (package of shares belonging to them)." Based on this wording, any creditor has the right to sue any of the company's members even without a claim to the company itself, to receive payment.

Besides that, since the price of shares is not a constant quantity and depends not only on the financial status of the company, but also on variations of the stock market, the investor is incapable to even approximately foresee the limits of those financial claims that may be suddenly brought up by creditors of the company.

In order to avoid such consequences, you should agree beforehand that responsibility of investors may arise only in the case of an incomplete payment for the shares belonging to them, within the limits of the sum unpaid, and only within the limits of the exact time period set beforehand.

In the case when the shares or stocks have been fully paid for by the investor, the investor should have a total absence of liability — clearly and unambiguously — on all company debts and commitments, both in the course of its functioning and in case of its liquidation. To make sure that these provisions are formulated correctly, enlist the services of a lawyer qualified and experienced in this sphere.

Clearly state the rights and duties of directors

Existing legislation in Russia provides fairly weak protection to shareholders against possible tyranny of the executive body and the company board. Many cases have been recorded where pressure has been exerted on shareholders — even to the point of pushing them out of the company — such as preventing shareholders from participating in various forms of control, infringing upon shareholder's interests, and concealing profits from shareholders to avoid distribution.

To avoid such situations, pay particular attention to how these questions are regulated in your formation documents. Provide for well-developed and detailed documents concerning elections, nominations, and company control of the executive body, and adopt these provisions on the highest possible level.

You want to state point-blank that company directors are allowed to execute their functions only on the basis of the contracts signed with them, which must determine comprehensively their rights and duties to the company. Making such contracts is an extremely responsible work and should be done by experienced lawyers. Based on the experiences of others, you are recommended, in the beginning, to sign contracts with company directors for terms no longer than one year. At the same time, provide for guarantees — both legal and financial — to protect against the unmotivated removal of good directors or nonextension of contracts with them.

Regulate questions of company financing

Pay attention to the authorizations delegated to company directors to draw credits and issue long-term obligations on behalf of the company. You want to set exact limits for each loan, in both absolute sums and in length of term, which would be applicable both to the administration as a whole and to the individual directors. For large credit sums or issues of promissory notes, make sure that consent or a decision must be obtained from a higher authority. Include a corresponding provision in the contracts signed with the directors to ensure that they have full financial liability for unmotivated debt growth, as well as for exceeding the fixed limits permitted for them.

Define the value of your contribution into the charter capital

Charter capital can be formed both in Russian rubles and by foreign currency. Contributions in kind toward the charter capital should be agreed upon by all of the participants in the joint venture. If you make your contribution in rubles, you will have to prove that they were legally procured — for instance, an individual can present a document certifying that the currency was exchanged in a bank, while legal entities can provide documents showing that the rubles were earned in a legal manner. Keep in mind that customs duties are not levied on in-kind property contributions of foreign investors towards the charter capital.

If you make your contribution to the charter capital in foreign currency, the created entity is considered an enterprise with foreign capital. If payment to the charter capital is made in rubles, the enterprise is still considered to be with foreign capital if you have more than a 50 percent share in it.

In-kind contributions into the initial capital of an enterprise with foreign investments can be determined according to an agreement between its participants on the basis of world market prices. In the absence of such prices, define the value of the contributions according to an agreement between you and the other participants. The value can be determined in both Russian currency and in foreign currency, with the conversion of each new value into rubles at the rate fixed by the Central Bank of Russia for foreign investment transactions.

Other provisions of Russian laws

While you may never have to deal with issues of bankruptcy or judgments, you should have a basic understanding of the Russian laws governing these aspects of business.

Bankruptcy

Effective as of March 1, 1993, the *Russian Law on Insolvency (Bankruptcy) of Enterprises* — the *Bankruptcy Law* — provides for the voluntary and involuntary liquidation of enterprises, as well as methods for the reorganization of enterprises in an attempt to restore their solvency.

An enterprise may be declared insolvent if it is unable to meet its creditors' claims within three months of the date the claims are due. The debtor, its creditors, or in certain situations, the public prosecutor, can petition the debtor into bankruptcy through the court of arbitration or one of the other designated courts.

If a request for the reorganization of the debtor through outside management or rehabilitation has been included with the petition, the court can decide to suspend the judgment on the insolvency of the debtor and allow the reorganization to proceed. The court will only permit this procedure if there is a realistic possibility that the solvency of the debtor will be restored. The outside limit on the completion of the reorganization process is 180 days. If the reorganization procedure is not successful, bankruptcy proceedings will begin.

Once the estate of the bankrupt enterprise has been distributed to the creditors, the receiver prepares a report of the activities and submits the same to the court. On the endorsement of this report by the court, the bankruptcy proceedings are concluded and the debtor enterprise is struck off the state register.

In addition to the provisions of the *Bankruptcy Law* that allow for the involuntary liquidation of an enterprise, the 1990 *Enterprise Law* provides that an enterprise may be liquidated voluntarily if the owner of the enterprise or the authorized state body so decides, and the personnel of the enterprise have consented.

An enterprise can be voluntarily liquidated through a defined liquidation process, instructions for which are described in the *Enterprise Law*. Through the liquidation process, a liquidation commission is required to establish a list of all outstanding claims of the enterprise and is obliged to collect such claims. Creditors who have contractual relations with the enterprise are required to receive written notice of the liquidation. The liquidation commission values the assets, settles accounts with the creditors, draws up a liquidation balance sheet, and makes a final report.

Jurisdiction

Generally, no provision in Russian law requires the exclusive jurisdiction of Russian courts in disputes between parties to contracts. The new *Civil Code* provides that disputes must be dealt with by the courts of the Russian Federation. Disputes that are in Russia's jurisdiction, for example, are:

- Cases regarding immovable property situated in the Russian Federation; and
- Claims against a carrier that has its registered office in the Russian Federation.

Arbitration

The Russian Federation, as the legal successor of the former USSR, is a member of the New York Convention of the Recognition of Enforcement of Foreign Arbitral Awards (1958), which provides for the recognition and enforcement of foreign arbitral awards.

In addition, the *Code of Civil Procedure* and the 1988 *Decree on the Recognition and Foreign Judgments Enforcement in the USSR of Decisions of Foreign Courts and Arbitration Tribunals* provide for the recognition and enforcement of foreign judgments. The general rule is that foreign court decisions are recognized and enforced if it is so provided in accordance with international agreements concluded between the former USSR and the jurisdiction where the judgment was rendered. There are also conditional agreements for the reciprocal enforcement in the Russian Federation of judgments rendered in all of the former socialist countries, as well as in Finland, Italy, Greece, and Cyprus.

Enforcement of foreign judgments rendered in other treaty states will be refused in Russia on the following grounds:

- Under the legislation of the jurisdiction where the judgment was rendered, the judgment did not come into effect;
- The party against whom the judgment was entered did not receive due procedure;
- Hearing of the case is subject to the exclusive jurisdiction of a Russian court or body;
- A Russian court decision already exists that was legally binding on the same parties and on the same subject, or a procedure was commenced before a Russian court between the same parties and on the same subject;
- A period of three years had elapsed after the filing date of the claim; and
- The enforcement of the judgment would contradict the sovereignty of Russia or threaten the security of the Russian Federation, or contradict the basic principles of the laws of the Russian Federation.

Settlement of accounts

The *Civil Code* provides that debts must be expressed and paid in rubles. The *Civil Code*, however, provides that subject to other legislation, debts may be paid in foreign currency if the judgment is rendered in that currency.

Summary and recommendations

All basic enterprise forms known to Western practice, with the exception of trusts, are accepted in Russia. The draft legislation on trusts and trust transactions recently has been prepared and currently is being debated in the DUMA (parliament).

Registration of enterprises in all their forms is of no special difficulty now — except for banks and insurance companies where a specific licensing procedure has been prescribed — and the government has declared its intention to simplify and liberalize this process even more.

At the same time, the lack of effective laws on companies and securities demands that you pay special attention to:

- How formation documents are drawn up;
- How the business functions; and
- How securities are issued.

When you start a business venture in Russia, keep in mind that deadlock situations have a high probability of occurring if any of the following situations arise:

- Conflicts between the founders or partners;
- Conflicts between the business' management and shareholders; and
- Turnover and redemption of shares if securities have been issued.

Foreigners coming to Russia to do business face many problems, mostly due to incomplete legislation regulating activities of foreign investors, including not only registration but also taxation, currency, and customs control.

Be aware that you cannot rely much on presidential decrees or government decisions regulating certain matters. Presently, the decrees and government decisions are subject to confirmation by corresponding Parliamentary approvals. For more information on currency and taxes, refer to chapters 5 and 7.

Five keys to success

You can avoid a number of problems by following the advice in this chapter and keeping yourself informed of the rapidly evolving legal and economic reform environment. Concluding this chapter are five key principles to help eliminate potential problems.

- At all stages of legalizing a foreign company in Russia, consult experienced local lawyers and consulting firms. For your undertaking in Russia to be successful, you will need reliable information and qualified advice on the complicated and sensitive legal and economic aspects of Russia.
- When choosing your legal form of business and overall plans, take into account your initial and future goals. Also consider the character of possible relations with your local partners. Your financial capabilities and the size of your intended investment are also important parameters.

- The conditions by which you participate in a Russian business must be scrupulously reflected in the organizational documents and in the rules by which the executive body is formed. Trying to save effort and time in these matters, as experience shows, will inevitably result in lengthy and expensive conflicts, which are sometimes impossible to be solved even in court.

- From the very beginning, you will want to work on the establishment of a Russian enterprise in close cooperation with the bank that will keep its accounts. This will save you a great amount of paperwork and provide you with valuable support by the bank legal offices, which later will work with the documents of the business, solving its financial problems and supporting its investment projects.

- In the earliest stages of establishing a Russian enterprise, you should be, first of all, oriented toward the extent of its financial activities. If, in the future, your enterprise will actively draw bank credits or attract means in the Russian financial market, you will need to consult with the bank, reliable brokers, and lawyers familiar with these matters. Consultations with all of these professionals are necessary at all stages, from when the company is set up throughout the development of its activities.

The next chapter describes how the banking system in Russia works and what you will need to know before choosing the bank with which you will do business.

Chapter 5

Banks and Banking
Банки

Banks in Russia

What is a Russian bank? A Russian bank, such as Sanct-Petersburg Bank, is capable of paying annual dividends of 1,000 percent in rubles, which is a solid 250 percent in dollars. A Russian bank is a bank that only five years ago was huddled in two rooms, and now grants dozens of millions of dollars in credit — now the well-known Incombank. A number of young, growing banks can now offer up to 300 percent per year for ruble deposits and up to 35 percent for dollars, and they are indeed paying such high interest each quarter of the year and even per month.

According to 1994 data, half of the 20 largest banks in Russia made more than 200 percent on invested capital, and some of them as much as 500 percent and more. A Russian bank is an institution that knows how to make money in Russia. Therefore, you will find this institution useful to deal with because it possesses the experience and knowledge that foreign investors in Russia usually are missing.

The basic mass of national capital in Russia is controlled by banks — other financial institutions, such as insurance companies, credit associations, and investment firms have not yet developed properly, and their role in the financial market is not significant.

Choosing the right bank

Before choosing a bank, you should ask yourself several obvious questions:

- What banks should you consider for cooperation?
- How do you choose an appropriate bank?
- How do you establish contacts?
- What form of cooperation should you choose?

These questions, of course, can only be answered if you have decided upon:

- The sphere of your activities in Russia;
- The approximate forms in which they are to be carried out;
- The circle of your potential partners; and
- Your final goal — whether it is getting profit from a single transaction, creating a network of permanent clients, or arranging a prospective venture.

Based on those decisions, in one case, you may need support from a large bank with regional affiliations; in another, the important consideration might be a specific connection the bank has in a certain field or region of the country; and in yet another, you might need a bank that can be a full and equal partner in your investment project, bearing a considerable share of the risk.

Currently, two banking sectors co-exist in Russia — the Central Bank sector and the commercial bank sector. The Central Bank sector includes Central Bank's divisions and agencies throughout the country and Central Bank's holdings in some of the largest banks. The second sector is comprised of all other commercial banks, including those that are under partial or total control of foreign capital — foreign also meaning former Soviet Republics.

The Central Bank sector

The Central Bank occupies a similar position in Russia as the Federal Reserve occupies in the United States, with responsibility as the main overseer of the banking system and monetary policy.

The Central Bank maintains the leading role in Russia's credit market. Because of its right to mobilize up to 20 percent of the credit resources of any commercial bank, and because of its exclusive right to emit money, it provides up to 60 percent of all credit resources in the country in addition to the credits of international organizations distributed through its system.

The Central Bank provides resources either in the form of an interbank credit or as a contribution to the capital of commercial banks. Part of the interbank credits are provided by the Central Bank as priority-oriented financing to support certain sectors of the national economy or specific investment projects. These resources may be available to foreign investors under certain conditions. You may want to consider the possibility of getting support from the Central Bank well before the start of a project, but naturally this makes sense only when your projects are of national importance.

Another path to Central Bank support can be directed through investments in sectors of the economy that are shown favor and given preferential credit because fit within plans envisaged by the government programs. Projects that involve conversion of defense industries, aid to farmers, or housing construction fall into this category. In these cases, you have to approach the banks through which these programs are usually financed by the Central Bank.

Commercial bank sector

By November 1994, there were 2,474 commercial banks and 5,328 affiliations in Russia — many of the latter are foreign and former Soviet Union affiliations. Of the total number, 974 banks and 1,359 affiliations were in Moscow.

Commercial banks in Russia can be divided into three groups:

- Banks established on the basis of former state banks or those originated on their authority;
- Banks established by former government ministries or regional and local administrations; and
- Banks established by independent investors — enterprises and private persons.

Former state banks, and banks created on their basis, still play the leading role in this 'second' bank sector of Russia. Eight of the ten largest Russian banks are former state banks, and one is an international bank established with several former state banks' participation; of 100 top Russian banks, the share of those leading eight banks is no less than one-quarter.

Still, with all their impressive power, the former state banks have common weaknesses. They maintain the old, bulky Soviet structure that is not always efficient under new conditions, and they are excessively dependent on centralized credit resources. Perhaps only Vneshtorgbank — the Bank for Foreign Trade — has managed to eliminate these weaknesses in the course of its reorganization, now almost completed. However, Mosbiznesbank has also significantly strengthened its position through aggressive credit policies and client selection. Other banks in this group are clinging to their positions, sometimes even being forced out by younger and more aggressively developing banks.

The largest Russian banks

Some of the larger and specialized banks in Russia are profiled below. The capital assets of these banks are very important to you, since they indicate the degree of reliability for the safety of your funds. Banks in Russia do fail, and bank deposits are still not federally insured as in the United States. You also want a bank that has the capability of providing you with financing.

Many of the banks in Russia specialize in specific industries, which can make obtaining financing and doing business in general easier for you. For example, if your project will involve construction, you may want to contact Promstroibank, which specializes in construction and also has connections to the State Property Management Committee.

Vneshtorgbank

Vneshtorgbank, the institution known as the Bank of Foreign Trade of Russia, currently is the country's largest bank with 750 billion rubles in assigned capital — 95 percent of it being paid in hard currency — and 13.6 trillion rubles in total assets as of June 1, 1994. Sixty-five percent of the bank's stock capital belongs to the Central Bank of Russia — previously 90 percent. Among other shareholders are Norilsk Nickel Concern, Olbi Trading Company, Naftan Joint Stock Company, and Gazprom Joint Stock Company, also called the Gas Industry Holding Company.

Gazprom is rapidly transforming itself from a gas monopoly into a large financial and industrial group, whose interests extend to all spheres of economic activity. In an attempt to dominate gas distribution in Western Europe, Gazprom began constructing its own pipeline in Germany and has already bought DM 1.7 billion (1.7 billion deutsche marks, equal to approximately $1.24 billion) worth of real property there. The latest development shows that Gazprom is expressly interested in the banking business.

Vneshtorgbank is certainly a good goal for Gazprom. The bank now handles 30 percent of Russia's foreign trade transactions. In the first five months of 1994, Vneshtorgbank earned a profit of R 162 billion (162 billion rubles, equal to approximately $45 million as of January 1995).

Gazprom's acquisition of a significant part of Vneshtorgbank does not mean that Gazprom will take the bank under its control. On the contrary, this may help to loosen the grip of the government, which, through Russia's Central Bank, once owned more than 90 percent of Vneshtorgbank's equity and influenced many of its decisions. It is noteworthy that Gazprom was invited to participate, with the evident purpose to eliminate the government's majority ownership.

Vneshtorgbank's total receipts in 1993 was 428 billion rubles. With expenditures of 249 billion rubles, it produced a balance profit of 179 billion rubles — 9.4 times its 1992 profit. At that time, the exchange rate was approximately 2,000 rubles to the dollar. On the results of 1993, 250 percent dividends were paid for common shares.

Vneshtorgbank supports more than 6,000 business clients — the bank prefers not to deal with individual customers. More than $4 billion of its assets, as well as its entire gold stock, is deposited in leading foreign banks.

Agroprombank

Agroprombank, known as the Agrarian Industrial Bank of Russia, is the leader in total sum of assets — 8.6 trillion rubles at the beginning of 1994. In balance profit figures, Agroprombank is second only to Sberbank. It maintains a leading position in financing agriculture and the crop processing industry, with the Central Bank dominating among its shareholders.

Sberbank – The Savings Bank of Russia

Sberbank is Russia's leader in the volume of attracted deposits and loans — respectively 4.7 trillion rubles and 4.2 trillion rubles at the beginning of 1994. Its balance profit value of about 400 billion rubles in 1993 ranked tops in the country. Sberbank has the largest number of branches and divisions, and a record number of customers — more than 80 million. The Central Bank owns more than 50 percent of its joint stock — about 350 billion rubles at the beginning of 1994. It leads all other banks in balance profit figures — 850 billion rubles in 1993.

For all its success, Sberbank maintains its position on the rather fragile basis of guarantees declared by the government to its depositors — but never proven — which allows the bank to attract deposits from the public at relatively low interest rates.

Should the expected compulsory insurance of deposits be introduced at all banks, this advantage of Sberbank will end. If the Parliament requires Sberbank to index deposits against inflation made in 1991 and earlier that were placed in the bank as 'full-weight' rubles, Sberbank will have to apply for large budget subsidies.

Promstroibank

Promstroibank, as mentioned previously, is known as the Industrial Construction Bank of Russia. This bank is still in the top ten banks in spite of the fact that its former divisions in Moscow and other regions of Russia broke away and became top banks themselves, maintaining their place on the list of 100, and even 50, top banks of Russia.

Promstroibank is still a major investor in leading branches of industry. Indeed, it acts as a government agent since the state renders credit support to most important enterprises. The government possesses a considerable share in the bank's capital through the State Property Management Committee and through some state-owned enterprises.

However, the new law on banks adopted by the Parliament on January 20, 1995 intends to prohibit the penetration and participation of the Central Bank in the affairs of commercial banks. According to this law, the Central Bank is to be barred from being a shareholder in Vneshtorgbank and Sberbank within the next six months. It is undecided yet whether its shares will be sold from second auctions or become the property of other government agencies

Sectoral and regional industrial banks

In the sector of nongovernmental commercial banking — banks founded by state-owned enterprises within one certain industry or in a certain geographic region — those connected with leading export sectors, such as Imperial Bank, Neftechimbank, Bashprombank, Yugorsky (oil extracting and processing), Avtobank and Avtovazbank (automobile industry) are natural leaders.

A major player among these banks is Gazprom, which not only bought 30 percent of shares of Vneshtorgbank, but also placed its chairman in the seat of chairman of the board of directors at another major bank, Imperial Bank.

The fact that Gazprom's leader, Rem Vyakhirev, became Imperial's chairman was no surprise to analysts, since the bank has always maintained close contacts with Russia's largest gas producer. In the long term, the merger of banking and industrial power may not only strengthen the commercial banking sector, but also help restore industrial production capacities.

Banks originating from less rewarding segments of the Russian economy generally lag behind, and if the situation in their 'basic' sector worsens, they will immediately face trouble.

Private banks

In the regional banking sector, private banks in Russia can be quite aggressive in finding space for themselves in the market. The most successful are those oriented by the founders to expand only in the banking sphere, such as Stolichny, Credobank, Russian Credit, and Incombank.

For these banks, attracting and keeping large-scale, reliable clients is a question of life or death, so they often are leaders in introducing new forms of services and privileges for their clientele.

Foreign banks

Banks that belong to foreign capital are just starting their activities in Russia, and so far they specialize in dealing with nonresidents. But Russian banks consider them a competitive threat, particularly since some of the most successful Russian enterprises actively deposit their free resources abroad where Russian banks, naturally, cannot compete yet.

Moscow's bank ratings

Moscow's most reliable banks are listed in Table 13 below. Another table, at the end of this chapter, shows the ratings of Russia's top 100 banks.

Table 13: Classification of Moscow Bank Reliability

Group AAA – highest reliability group

Agroprombank of Russia – Agroindustrial Bank
Vneshtorgbank of Russia – Foreign Trade Bank
Mosbiznesbank – Moscow Business Bank
Mosindbank – Moscow Industrial Bank
Promstroibank of Russia – Bank of Industrial Construction
Sberbank of Russia – The Savings Bank of Russia

Group AA – very high reliability group

Autobank – Car Industry Bank
Vozrozhdenie – Rehabilitation Bank
Imperial – Imperial Bank
Mosmezhbank – Moscow International Bank
Neftikhimbank – Oil and Chemical Bank
Orgbank – Organization Bank
Unicombank – Unified Commercial Bank

Group A – high reliability group

Alpha Bank
Conversbank – Conversion Bank
Mezhkombank – Inter-Commercial Bank
Mostbank – Bridge-Group Bank
Neftegazstroibank – Oil and Gas Construction Bank
Stolichny Bank – Bank of the Capital

Source: Rating Analytical Center, July 3, 1994.

Laws regulating Russian banking

In Russia, bank activities are formally regulated by two laws:

- The *Law on Central Bank*
- The *Law on Banks and Bank Activities*

Both dated December 2, 1990, these laws charge the Central Bank only with control and supervision over banks working in Russia. But in fact, the Central Bank goes far beyond that authority to directly interfere with rules of the game, changing them at its discretion.

In contrast to practices in other countries, the Central Bank is also an active 'player' in the credit sphere, and is able to change rules of the game it is playing — even though it is one of the players. Naturally, the banking system only suffers from this situation.

This practice stems from Russian legislation, which introduces policies that later are 'explained' and 'brought' to the public through various 'instructions' and 'directives.' In addition to parliamentary laws, there are 'explanatory' documents of the Central Bank, decrees by the President, and other decisions by the government. These decrees often counter 'basic' banking laws, which leads either to a change in those laws or amendments to the decrees. It is difficult to predict the winner in such situations, so life is never boring for Russian bankers.

Banks in Russia may be constituted in any legal form of an enterprise envisaged by law. Still, there is no case of a bank established in the form of an unlimited liability company. As a rule, banks take the form of a private limited company or a public limited company. Large banks prefer public limited company forms, since this enables them to increase their capital through public subscription to shares and earn additional profits on the growth of the stock market share quotations.

By mid-1994, there were about 2,200 banks in Russia. In the previous 18 months, 144 banks were liquidated because of emerging financial hardships — some were transformed into branches of larger banks.

"The network of our commercial banks is developing in line with our expectations" said Mr. Gerashchenko, the former chairman of Russia's Central Bank, at the official opening of an international banking conference attended by about 300 foreign and Russian bankers. Most banks are located in Moscow and St. Petersburg, while the banking infrastructure in Russian provinces is underdeveloped. At least 70 percent of all payments are conducted through Moscow banks.

Gerashchenko said the Central Bank would support those banks that invest in production and would take "a more casual approach" to those dealing in trade, while considering possible candidates to go bankrupt. Gerashchenko reiterated he favored broader participation of foreign banks in Russia but said licenses should be given to 'first-class' banks that have traditional links with Russia.

Banking associations

In 1994, Interbank Financial House established a Council of Experts to reorganize the Russian banking system, using the United States' Federal Reserve System as its basis.

Sixteen banks of the Tyumen Region have established a banking union in Khanty-Mansiisk, Western Siberia. The administrations of the Khanty-Mansy autonomous region and the cities of Surgut and Nizhnevartovsk, and the Yugra financial and industrial corporation are also incorporated in the union.

The banking union is planning to create a clearing chamber and organize an information exchange between its members. All investments in the development of the oil industry of the Khanty-Mansy autonomous region will go through the banks, which are members of the banking union. The assets of the union's banks total R 2 trillion. The banking union has a charter capital of R 25 billion.

Crime in banking

A separate problem — discussed further in Chapter 9 — is the penetration of organized crime through gaining control over existing banks and by organizing new banks. Informed sources indicate that about 400 of 2,100 banks in Russia are in some way controlled by crime groups. Usually, these are small or medium-sized banks, although there is evidence that certain large banks cooperate with organized crime groups on a permanent basis.

On occasion, conflicts arise between commercial structures controlled by criminals. In 1992–93, three prominent bank leaders were shot dead by hired killers — Vladimir Rovensky, Technobank president, on December 9, 1992; Ilya Medkov, Pragmabank president, on September 17, 1993; and Nikolai Likhachev, Agroprombank board chairman, on December 2, 1993. Investigations have failed to identify the killers, those behind them, or reasons for the assassinations.

Getting reliable information on such cases is difficult, but personal contacts in investigation agencies and bank unions may be very useful in this respect. At the same time, information may sometimes be found in the open press, in newsletters, and in the Central Bank's materials. Even if you don't hear of such events, you should pay attention to cases when a whole group of shareholders suddenly is replaced, when key figures in a bank's administration are removed, or when top clients shift to other banks.

Politically minded banks

As time goes by, Russian banks have gradually come to the understanding that money is not only money and not just power. Today, politically minded Russian banks are beginning to form alliances in order to influence the coming elections. Banks are beginning to finance political campaigns and form power groups. Your Russian partner will consider the political affiliations of a bank when choosing which one to do business with. Here is how some analysts have recently classified Russia's largest banks.

Menatep

This bank is on good terms with everybody, and does this so adroitly that to say which political side it is on is impossible. Only once did the bank take a particular stand on an issue by taking an uncompromising attitude against having foreign banks operate in Russia.

By no means can Menatep be considered as the government's opponent. A well-known fact, though, is that when the Supreme Soviet was in power, Menatep attempted to carry the needed decisions through factions opposed to the government.

A Menatep representative in the State DUMA is a member of the Agrarian Party, which often disagrees with the government. Menatep is an authorized bank of the Moscow Administration in charge of city budget accounts.

Bank Stolichny

This bank's political position is self-evident — Stolichny supports the Russian President. During the December 1993 elections, Stolichny sponsored the pro-governmental political party, Choice of Russia. The Russian presidential office has accounts in this bank.

Most-Bank

This bank is a staunch supporter of the Russian President and the Moscow City Administration, which can be exemplified by the position of the *Segodnya* daily newspaper and Independent Television (NTV) channel sponsored by Most-Bank. This does not mean, though, that Most-Bank is poised to side with any force that supports the President. Most-Bank had a conflict with the Choice of Russia. Despite its pro-presidential position, Most-Bank is known for its flexibility.

Natsionalny Credit (National Credit)

Although young, this bank does not conceal its strong political ambitions staked on young reformers from the political party, Choice of Russia. The bank financed the remodeling of the Choice of Russia headquarters.

Incombank

This bank first entered the political scene when it supported the Entrepreneurs' Initiative political movement headed by Konstantin Zatulin. During the election campaign, the bank supported Sergei Shakhrai, who was on the PRES political party list and was elected to the State DUMA.

Incombank has also been known for its support of Grigory Yavlinsky, a candidate for presidency and past deputy prime minister with the reform movement. Although the bank prefers to keep its contacts with presidential and other political structures quiet, those contacts are rather intense.

Rossiisky Credit

Although the bank tries to keep silent about its political position, this does not mean that it has no political preferences. Previously, Rossiisky Credit was managed by people who were close to the former Supreme Soviet speaker. Most likely, the bank will take a centrist position and abstain from participating in political life.

Imperial Bank

This bank was set up by Gazprom and Russia's fuel and energy complex. Since Prime Minister Viktor Chernomyrdin is a major lobbyist for Gazprom, he strongly supports the bank.

Kredo Bank

This bank blazed the trail for commercial banking in Russia. There were rumors that the bank was established with Communist Party-Soviet Union money. However, no facts confirming this speculation were ever found.

Nonetheless, there is indirect proof of this allegation. When an open conflict occurred between the President and Supreme Soviet, Kredo-Bank sided with the people's deputies in opposition to the Supreme Soviet. Its leader, Yuri Agapov, was the only banker who visited the Supreme Soviet.

Promstroibank, Mosbiznesbank, and Narodny Bank

These are former state-run banks, which do not participate in political life. Their priority is keeping up good relations with the Central Bank and the government since their successful operation primarily depends on centrally allotted credits.

These banks basically employ older personnel whose mentality is closer to the Communists and Agrarian Party members.

Alpha Bank

The political orientation of this young, commercial bank became clear when Petr Aven, the former minister of the Foreign Economic Relations Ministry, joined the bank's board. Petr Aven supports Yegor Gaidar, ex-prime minister of Russia, which determines Aven's political credo. Table 14 below represents the current political and economic connections of the top Russian banks.

Table 14: Top Banks and New Business Pressure Groups

Top structures and first persons formation	Structures and persons promoting the group
Alpha-Group: Alpha Bank	Gaidar team, P. Aven (ex-minister of foreign economic relations)
Bioprocess Joint Stock Company (JSC) – NIPEK Corporation (K. Benukidze)	O. Davydov (Minister of foreign economic relations)
Volkhov JSC – Russian Gold JSC (M. Masarsky)	The former USSR State Committee on Building, administration of Novgorod region
Hermes Concern (V. Neverov, G. Danilov)	Unknown
Imperial Bank (S. Rodionov)	Gazprom Concern, V. Chernomyrdin
Incombank (V. Groshev, V. Vinogradov)	Plekhanov Institute for National Economy
Interagro – Vnesheconom Cooperation Foreign Economy Association	The USSR Cooperative Union – The League of Russian Cooperators and Businessmen, V. Shumeiko
Interprivatization Foundation (V. Stcherbakov)	Connections of V. Stcherbakov as former Vice Prime-Minister of the USSR
Credobank (Yu. Agapov)	BUTEC Concern, M. Bocharov

Top structures and first persons formation	Structures and persons promoting the group
LogoVAZ JSC (B. Berezovsky)	AvtoVAZ JSC, Gaidar team, P. Aven
Menatep (M. Khodorkovsky, S. Monakhov)	The former USSR State Committee on Science and Technology, I. Silaev, former USSR Prime Minister
Mikrodin Trade Company (A. Efanov)	D. Zelenin
Most Group (V. Gusinsky)	Administration of the capital, Yu. Luzhkov
Mosexpo JSC (O. Kiselev)	See Alpha-Group
Neftekhimbank (G. Zhuk)	Divisions of oil chemistry and oil refinery
OLBI Concern – National Credit Bank (O. Boiko)	Vzlyot Scientific Production Association, emigrant circles
ONEXIMbank (M. Prokhorov)	The bank of the Council for Mutual Economic Aid
Stolichny Bank (A. Smolensky)	Unknown
TOKObank (V. Yakunin)	Former USSR and Russian Federation State Committee on Supplies

Banking problems in Russia

A number of factors related to banking are having a profound effect on Russia's economy and the prospects for economic recovery. Regulations about foreign banks in Russia are incomplete and conflictive, creating an atmosphere of uncertainty and risk, which does little to attract foreign investment capital. While negotiations are continuing between Russia and the world banking community, Russian banks are experiencing difficulties opening branches abroad because of the ill-feelings caused by Russia's regulations of foreign banks. Meanwhile, the export of capital, especially the illegal outflow — and this is one area that Russia, through regulation, has a dire need to control — has had an impact on Russia's foreign debt, inherited from the former Soviet Union.

Beginning a new economic system in a country is a complex process that cannot be resolved overnight. However, businesspeople who understand the nature of the problems can still conduct a profitable business and at the same time become part of the solution to some of the long-term economic problems.

A brief history of foreign banks

The history of the advent of foreign banks in Russia resembles a soap opera, where the protagonists lose, then win, or simply leave the scene for a while. The new episode hinges on two documents signed by President Yeltsin, one which determined the admission procedure of foreign banks into the Russian market, and the other, an agreement with the European Community concluded on the Ionian island of Corfu. Writing for the English-language paper, *Moscow News*, Mrs. Irina Yasina, a well-known commentator on bank affairs, describes the situation.

> *Several dozen foreign banks have had offices in Moscow for a while. The first banking license by a branch of the Credit Lyonnais was received back at the end of 1991. The Central Bank began to issue licenses quite actively after more than a year's interruption.*
>
> *Russian commercial banks then decided that their own domestic market could "escape." Since our banks naturally did not have enough strength to compete with international giants, they used more customary methods and talked to the authorities. Thus, the struggle for the Russian market between "us" and "them" ended at that moment with a victory by "us": a presidential decree was signed in November 1993, at the height of the election struggle, which prohibited foreign banks from serving Russian residents for two years. Of the 12 foreign banks which had received Central Bank licenses by that time, only two avoided an actual transfer to an off-shore regime: Credit Lyonnais (Russia) and the BNP–Dresdner Bank, since they already had resident clients. Despite rented premises and hired personnel, the rest had to be content with little, i.e., with non-residents.*
>
> *The sides which came out "for" and "against" the presence of foreign banks are known. In this case, the supporters of the two positions are not divided by any "national" principle. Russian banks, which are liberal in other areas of economic life, came out in a concerted manner against foreign competition. But there were also a few dissenters: several commercial banks, including the Moscow International Bank and the TOKO-Bank, think that foreign banks are necessary in our financial market. Former special banks were also not threatened by a possible invasion of foreign banks.*
>
> *The country's President changed his position with the flow of the political struggle.*
>
> *The Central Bank of Russia supported the limited presence of foreign bank capital, for which it introduced a decision that the total authorized*

capital of foreign banks in Russia should not exceed 12% of the authorized capital of Russian banks.

After last year's presidential decree, foreign banks, who had already spent money on equipment and personnel, felt that their interests were threatened. They hastened to announce that they would retaliate by not allowing Russian banks to open branches abroad. It should be noted, though, that foreign branches of our banks existed only in offshore zones, so it was somewhat premature to speak about retaliatory measures.

The confrontation seemed to have ended with the agreement on partnership and cooperation with the European Community, signed by President Yeltsin on Corfu. Dmitry Tulin, Vice-Chairman of the Russian Central Bank, recently spoke of what this document will mean for foreign banks in Russia.

The agreement with the European Community envisages two transitional periods during which Russia has the right to impose restrictions on foreign capital banking operations on its territory. During the first period (until January 1, 1996), all European Community banks, except banks which have received a Central Bank license and had begun to serve Russian residents before November 15, 1993, will not be able to conduct operations with Russian residents.

During the second period (before the end of June 1999), Russia can impose a ban on the transactions of foreign banks with shares in Russian companies and can also establish the minimum balance a Russian resident must maintain in a foreign bank, amounting to 55,000 ECUs. Moreover, Russia has the right to limit the number of foreign subsidiaries in Russia. (Today the Central Bank allows foreign banks to open only one branch besides the head office on Russian territory.)

After the transitional period, Russia reserves the unlimited right to determine the amount of foreign capital in the banking system of the Russian Federation. On its part, the European Community has promised not to apply the restrictions existing for their banks to Russian banks working in the Community's countries. The question of the activity of American banks in Russia remains undecided. According to the President's Decree of June 10, 1994, since the United States has not ratified agreements on the mutual protection of investments, American banks which earlier received Central Bank general licenses for their branch offices (City Bank and Chase Manhattan) have actually been deprived of the right to work with Russian residents.

According to the vice-chairman of the Central Bank, an active search for a mutually acceptable solution is now being conducted. American banks have both representative offices, which "are very easy to open" and two branch banks in Russia, even though they still don't have the right to work with residents. But two first-class (by our standards) Russian banks have been unable to open offices in the United States. (According to our information, Incombank and Promstroibank of the Russian Federation have long been trying to open offices in the United States). While speaking of asymmetry, Dialogue-Bank is a Russian resident "by more than 50%, though off-shore Cypriot companies belonging to American capital, have the right to conduct all kinds of banking operations."

According to Russian Central Bank data, there were 17 banks in the Russian Federation as of April 1, 1994 who had more than 50% foreign capital, including capital of the states of the former USSR. The International Moscow Bank and the Dialogue Bank are also included in the 17 "foreign" banks according to the methods used by the Central Bank. Of the 17 banks, only 9 are Russian companies which belong 100% to foreign capital. The capital of the 17 banks amounts to a little more than 7% of Russian banking capital, which means that foreign banks have not yet reached the 12% quota determined by the Central Bank.

Dmitry Tulin noted positively the recent softening of the position of Russian banks, which actively came out against "foreigners" in Russia. This can be explained by the business that has developed since the beginning of the confrontation, which pushes our banks into international markets. Furthermore, many foreign banks operated at a loss for their first year since they incurred major administrative, economic, and investment expenses and carried out few transactions. Our banks became stronger during this time. According to Central Bank estimates, the share of foreign bank assets is at least three times smaller than the share of their capital.

Citibank and the Russian banking law

The English-language paper, *Moscow Times*, on September 20, 1994, told an interesting story of a U S. bank taking advantage of a vague Russian banking law.

Citibank, the United States' largest bank, has taken advantage of contradictions in Russian legislation to gain more access to the country's market than any of its foreign competitors, bank representatives and government officials said Monday . . . .

Citibank and fellow U.S. bank Chase Manhattan appeared to have suffered a setback in June, when President Boris Yeltsin signed a decree lifting most restrictions on foreign banks' activities. The decree reversed a November law banning foreign banks from working with Russian customers until 1996, but specifically left out the U.S. banks because the Russian parliament had not yet ratified a bilateral investment treaty with the United States. Citibank, however, has continued to serve Russian clients, assuming that since the November decree did not apply to banks that had already opened an office in Russia, as Citibank had, none of the subsequent legislation applied either.

"We are not prohibited to do anything here," said Miljenko Horvat, president of Citibank in Moscow. "And everything we are doing is sanctioned by the Central Bank." The transactions Citibank cannot do, he said, are operations with jewelry and precious metals, which require a special license.

"It is impossible to understand the situation," said Alexei Sitnin, spokesman for the Central Bank. "The November decree allows Citibank to deal with Russians, the June decree bans them. But how can you prohibit operations that have been going on for half a year?"

Horvat said that Citibank asks the Central Bank's permission whenever it obtains a new Russian client, and that the Central Bank has so far never objected. Citibank is thus in an advantageous position compared to both Chase Manhattan, which had not opened an office here before the November decree, and to European Union (EU) banks as well.

Under the Russia-EU partnership and cooperation agreement signed earlier this year, EU banks cannot work with Russian accounts of less than 55,000 ECUs [European Community Units — currency] ($66,000). Citibank's minimum account requirement is $1,000, Horvat said. Leonid Anikeyev, an expert with the Russian subsidiary of Credit Suisse, said CS was not worried by the low deposit requirements offered by Citibank, since his bank concentrated on operations with accounts of at least $75,000.

Meanwhile, Chase Manhattan is in talks with the Russian government to gain access to local clients, according to a spokesperson who asked not to be named. Chase expects an agreement "within weeks, or months, not longer than that," the spokesperson said.

Problems with the export of Russian funds

In his interview to the *Frankfurter Allgemeine Zeitung*, Zbigniew Brzezinski, former adviser to U.S. presidents, characterized Russian bankers as "surprising parasites." He said Russian banks exported

$15.5 billion in 1993, and invested only $450 million in the Russian economy. Brzezinski believes Russian banks are the initiators of this process, but that blame must be shared with both the Russian businesspeople who order that export of money and the Russian system that promotes such actions by creating instability.

Western estimates suggest that between $50–100 billion have been exported from Russia since 1990. This offsets Russia's seemingly positive balance of trade, equal to $16 billion in 1993. The government is forced to get deeper in debts it inherited from the former Soviet Union trying to postpone the clearance of debts. Total debt of about $80 billion corresponds approximately to the sum taken out of the country during the past four years.

Garegin Tosunyan, chairman of the Interbank Finance House, vice president of the Association of Russian Banks, and president of Technobank, replied to Mr. Brzezinski:

> *It would be to his benefit that the Russian banking system would collapse and free access to the Russian market was opened to foreign banks. But this situation, if extended, would be like saying bring in foreign police to manage order, the foreign army to protect, and foreign owner structures to rule.*

Sergei Egorov, ARB president, added: "The Russian banks are only now making breakthroughs into the international market that demand enormous effort, only for the purpose of reinvesting later into Russian economics."

Mr. Brzezinski has a definite shortfall in his criticism. There is no reason why foreign banks, after squeezing local banks out of the Russian market, would suddenly feel so altruistic as to start pumping money from the West into Russia's limping economy. Most probably, the reverse will occur, with Western banks protecting the interests of their clients by exporting money out of Russia.

But the problem remains of how to open the access of Russian banks to the world market capital. The price of money in Russia is known to be high today. Few Russian businesspeople will seriously consider projects with a rate of return on their capital investment less than 30 percent per annum in hard currency. Even short-term loans are not sold below 15 percent per annum in hard currency, while the rate of interest in rubles is unpredictably fluctuating under the impact of inflation and the policy of the Central Bank. At the same time, interest rates in the world float between 7–8 percent per annum.

All this means that investment projects, which are quite effective by world standards, cannot be implemented in Russia, since limited capital in the local market can demand only excessively high profits. Insufficient investments make it impossible to stop the production slump and reach stable economic growth. Even with with such alluring profitability, Russian banks cannot attract foreign capital. This is because risk is a parameter no less important than profitability.

Foreign creditors are discouraged not only by the dark Soviet past, but also by the present position of many young Russian banks. The brutal persistence at blocking foreign banks from entering Russia and driving away the few that have already begun work does not improve the foreign view of investing in Russia.

However, Russian banks themselves are already offering a more balanced approach to the presence of foreign banks in the Russian market. In particular, Vladimir Vinogradov, president of Incombank, proposed to regulate the presence of foreign banks in Russia "not quantitatively but qualitatively." That is, he suggested not to allow them simply to open exactly as many branches as our banks can open abroad, but to limit the total capital of the branches of foreign banks to the sum total of their risk in the Russian market. In others words, their capital should be regulated by the volume of credit lines they open for Russian banks at normal or favorite interest rates.

Russian banks abroad

While about ten branches of foreign banks are in Russia and a countless number of offices, the offices of Russian commercial banks abroad can be counted on the fingers of one hand. For example, many Western participants in a symposium were, mildly speaking, embarrassed as they listened to the tale of Alexander Smolensky, president of Stolichny Bank, about the two-year ordeal the bank went through trying to open its branch in Holland. Stolichny, one of the country's largest commercial banks, became the first Russian bank to obtain a license for a subsidiary in the European Union (EU).

Spokesman Serge Meshcheryakov said the Dutch Central Bank awarded Stolichny with a license to serve both Russian and foreign corporations in the Netherlands and to open a subsidiary in Amsterdam. Stolichny did not have the right to serve individuals. Larissa Solodukhina, a spokesperson for the Russian Central Bank, said the license was made possible by a partnership and cooperation agreement signed between Russia and the EU earlier this year.

Under the agreement, Russian banks are allowed to operate in EU countries, while EU banks will face some restrictions on the Russian market for a period of ten years. Meshcheryakov said Stolichny Bank International N.V., Stolichny's fully owned subsidiary in the Netherlands, would have an initial capital of 25 million guilders ($14.7 million).

Meshcheryakov said Stolichny International would concentrate its own foreign trade operations, providing services, such as letters of credit, documentary collections, and payment orders. He said that two out of three directors and the majority of employees at the subsidiary would be Dutch.

Solving Russia's foreign debt problem

Consideration of Russia's foreign debt problem has become particularly realistic of late. The solutions Russia now has to choose between to solve the problem of its foreign debt are

- Converting its debts into financial or material resources;
- Converting these debts into investments; or
- Selling them to developing nations or Russian and foreign legal entities.

According to Anatoly Sokolov, the director of the Center for International Banking Development and Cooperation in Investment and Credit, Russia as the successor to the USSR, has inherited the former Soviet Union's foreign debts, now standing at $83 billion. Of this, debts of Russia proper amount to $8 billion. In 1991, Russia spent $12.5 billion on debt payments. In 1992, Russia should have paid $15.6 billion, and in 1993, before Russian debts were restructured, this amount was $19 billion, of which it paid only $2 billion. This year, Russia's debt payments must total $32.5 billion.

Rescheduling Russia's debts does not solve the problem. The monotonous and rather humiliating debt restructuring procedure, repeated every year, does not help either Russia or the West. Russian producers continue to be discriminated against on world markets. For example, discrimination on the part of the European Community countries costs Russia up to $3 billion a year.

Terms of debt restructuring agreements are becoming more and more unfavorable for Russia. Furthermore, the solution to drastically reduce the amount of Russia's foreign debt is being complicated by the fact that stabilizing Russia's economy requires financial aid from the West in the amount of four to five percent of Russia's gross domestic product, approximately $14 billion per year, in the next two to three years.

Meanwhile, to help solve some of the problem, creditor countries are demanding that Russia take 'revolutionary' measures in order to check the outflow of hard currency funds abroad. Western financial experts propose that the Russian government examine Russian citizens' accounts in foreign banks, so that tax and other agencies can establish whether the origin of deposits in those accounts is legal.

Western creditors also propose that Russia impose legislative limitations on the export of capital from Russia, especially capital earned by Russian legal entities and private individuals who export goods to their businesses abroad at reduced prices, import goods at excessive prices from their businesses abroad, and deposit the profits into their foreign bank accounts.

According to expert Western estimates, funds deposited by Russian residents in Swiss banks in 1994 totaled $54 billion. An inquiry conducted by the Central Bank of Russia and the Customs Agency showed that in the first quarter of this year alone, of $500 million in export contract revenues, about $70 million (14 percent) was not returned to Russia.

The proposed restrictive measures should not apply only to newly concluded foreign trade deals. The state must launch an investigation of the illegal outflow of hard currency from Russia over the past ten years.

Western experts are also closely following the work on the drafting of laws that permit nonresidents into Russia's domestic hard currency market and allow them to use their ruble earnings for investment purposes. An article at the end of this chapter, "Non-Residents in Russia: Possibilities and Limitations," provides more information about how foreign ruble and hard-currency investment accounts work in Russian banks.

The proposal of the U.S. government to set up a fund for privatization and restructuring to the tune of $4 billion is an important step in this direction. Russia should establish a special ruble-dollar exchange rate that would be higher than the market rate. Allowing nonresidents to take part in Russia's privatization reduces risks for foreign investment in the Russian economy and will sharply increase Russia's rating among investors.

The lack of clear-cut laws seriously complicates the conversion of Russian debts. Large-scale transactions, including capitalization, made with promissory notes instead of with cash, presuppose the use of those funds in the economy that could amount to millions of dollars.

Resolving debts owed to Russia

Another part of the debt problem is the money owed to Russia. Developing countries owe Russia, as the successor to the USSR, $160 billion. The majority of these countries will likely never be able to pay off all of their debts, while some of them can pay only an insignificant part of the debt. Debts of individual countries are quoted in secondary financial markets at not more than 10 percent of their value.

According to Alexander Kurkin, the acting deputy head of the Main Export-Import Department at the Russian Ministry for Foreign Economic Relations (MFER), Russia has already concluded agreements on accepting supplies of goods in repayment of Soviet loans with Algeria, India, Indonesia, Vietnam, Turkey, and Pakistan. It also has preliminary agreements with Mongolia and Laos.

The practice of using intermediary organizations for receiving debt payments existed until mid-1993, when the Russian Ministry of Finance denied these organizations any subsidies on imports. After importers calculated how much they would have to pay for the transportation of goods, customs duties and excise, value-added and state taxes, as well as the size of their probable commissions, they understood that they would no longer be able to sell imported goods in Russia. When converted into rubles, the prices of imports become much higher than the existing domestic market prices. Now a special tender committee will be established, which will include, among others, the Russian Bank for Foreign Economic Relations and the Federal Agency for Hard Currency and Export Control. The committee will choose intermediaries' proposals that prove to be more efficient for the state budget.

Another possible solution to the debt problem is that Russia can also try to sell the debts of foreign countries to Russian and foreign private traders at very advantageous terms. Since the end of 1993, such debts have been quoted at 11 to 40 percent of their nominal value. As Russian debtors' solvency increases and the political and economic situation in those countries becomes more stable, quotations of their debts to Russia may increase to 60 or 65 percent.

Russia has already begun to sell developing nation's debts to Russian legal entities. This year, India's debts were sold to Russian companies for approximately $500 million. Russian businesspeople, who have earned a total of $35 to $40 billion over the past few years, are displaying a readiness towards investing their capital deposited abroad into projects in Russia. The size of these would-be investments can be compared to the amount of Russia's foreign debt owed.

Last year, Russia received $1.3 billion from debtor countries in payment of their debts. India accounted for $600 million of this sum. There is a good possibility that Cuba, Vietnam, and Mongolia, which account for more than 60 percent of all debts of developing countries to Russia, will pay their debts.

Assessing the situation

Rigid restrictions and fiscal pressure by the government will produce a sharp differentiation in the development of banks. The 20 largest banks will ascend to monopolistic positions in their regions and economic fields, while other banks will face bankruptcies. Those extending their activities to foreign markets will have the best chances of surviving.

Meanwhile, foreign banks in Russia, for the most part, will work only with foreign trade transactions, so it is useless to rely upon their support in the development of Russian investment projects. In the future, a day may come when these banks will compete for top Russian clients, at which time foreign investors may find their Russian contacts to be helpful.

Meanwhile, five Russian banks — Vneshtorgbank, Russia's Savings Bank, Tokobank, Incombank, and Imperial — were listed among the world's 1,000 top banks in the July issue of the English magazine, *The Banker*. Although their rating is below that of the acknowledged leaders, the very fact the banks were on the list indicates that Russia's banking system has been developing rapidly.

There are 178 American banks among the world's 1,000 leading banks, but only one of them — Citicorp — is included in the first ten. Japan's banks continue to retain top ratings. According to the amount of their authorized capitals, the Russian banks took the 425th, 462nd, 694th, 945th and 996th places — see Table 15. *The Banker* used December 1993 data for the balances of Tokobank and Vneshtorgbank. For the remaining banks, it used the January 1994 figures.

However, evaluating the real standing of the Russian banks is difficult. *The Banker* used the absolute indicators — the amount of authorized capitals, assets and profits — but it was unable to calculate the key indicator, which is the ratio between the capital and the assets, ranked according to the degree of risk. This ratio should not be less than four percent, according to the method used by the Bank of International Settlements.

At the same time, the ratio between profits and assets shows that the Russian banks are among the most profitable in the world. By this ratio, Russia's Savings Bank is the world leader.

The table below compares how various banks in the world have been ranked internationally.

Table 15: International Bank Ratings

Rating	Bank – Country	Capital $ million	Assets $ million	Profits $ million
425	Vneshtorgbank – Russia	523	6,814	108
462	Savings Bank – Russia	477	6,319	747
694	Tokobank – Russia	249	785	23
945	Incombank – Russia	141	1,480	28
996	Imperial – Russia	126	818	15
997	Banco Banorta – Brazil	126	1,187	26
998	Lake Shore Bankcorp – U.S.	125	1,252	18
999	Wesbanco – U.S.	125	1,040	20
1,000	Caja San Fernando – Spain	125	2,018	62

Summary and recommendations

In spite of the unfinished and uncertain state of banking in Russia, the prudent businessperson can still do business. A few precautions and some research are in order.

If you pay attention to the recommendations below, however, you will be well on your way to your objective.

- Any investment project in Russia should begin with choosing a bank that by its participation will help with legal, fiscal and financial aspects of your project.

- When choosing your bank, pay particular attention to its structure; its constitutors and shareholders; their background; the qualifications of its managers; and its contacts in spheres of central and local administrations. The bank you use must have a general or extended license allowing for hard currency transactions.
- Deal with large or medium-sized banks — those with less than 2 billion rubles in capital lack stability. Make sure you have direct access to top bank officials.
- Seek financial participation by the bank in your project, at least in the 5 to 15 percent range, either in the form of a guaranteed credit line or a subscription to securities planned for issue.
- With long-term or wide-scale projects, you are recommended to join the body of the bank's shareholders for at least the smallest share of its capital to strengthen ties.
- Banks also may be used as a profitable object for investments. Many of them pay fairly high dividends — in rubles and in hard currency — and the price of their shares is growing continuously, thus opening the possibility for profitable stock-jobbing with them.

This chapter has provided an overview of banks and banking in Russia. For more information about making day-to-day banking transactions, see Chapter 8.

Table 16: Rating of the Top 100 Russian Banks

Rating	Name of bank	City
1	Sberbank Rossii	Moscow
2	Vneshtorgbank Rossii	Moscow
3	Agroprombank Rossii	Moscow
4	Incombank	Moscow
5	Mosbiznesbank	Moscow
6	Mezhnarbank	Moscow
7	Promstroibank	Moscow
8	Mosindustbank	Moscow
9	Imperial	Moscow
10	Unicombank	Moscow
11	Mezhfinance Compania	Moscow
12	Rossiisky Credit	Moscow
13	Tokobank	Moscow
14	Onexim Bank	Moscow
15	MMKB	Moscow
16	Menatep	Moscow
17	Promstroibank	St. Petersburg
18	Vozrozhdenie	Moscow
19	Neftikhimbank	Moscow
20	Avtobank	Moscow
21	Credo Bank	Moscow
22	Zapsibcombank	Tyumen
23	AvtoVAZbank	Togliatti
24	Yenisei	Krasnoyarsk
25	Stolichny	Moscow
26	Kuzbassprombank	Kemerovo
27	Alpha-Bank	Moscow
28	Credprombank	Yaroslavl
29	National Credit	Moscow
30	Tveruniversalbank	Tver
31	Chelindbank	Chelyabinsk
32	Bashprombank	Ufa
33	Yakutzolotobank	Yakutsk
34	Kubinbank	Krasnodar
35	Sahabank	Yakutsk
36	Yakutagroprombank	Yakutsk

Rating	Name of bank	City
37	Industriaservice	Moscow
38	Cheliabcomzembank	Chelyabinsk
39	Bashkiria	Ufa
40	Electrobank	Moscow
41	Agroprombank	Volgograd
42	Mezhcombank	Moscow
43	Srednevolzhskii Bank	Samara
44	Sanct-Petersburg	St. Petersburg
45	Bashkreditbank	Ufa
46	Permcombank	Perm
47	Orgbank	Moscow
48	Mitischenski Bank	Moscow
49	Promstroibank	N. Novgorod
50	Komibank	Siktivkar
51	Narodny Bank	Moscow
52	Promstroibank	Rostov-on-Don
53	Promstroibank	Yekaterinburg
54	Conversbank	Moscow
55	Yugorskibank	Nizhnevartovsk
56	Promstroibank	Arkhangelsk
57	Most-Bank	Moscow
58	Complexbank	Saratov
59	Vostskibcombank	Irkutsk
60	Agroprombank	Roston-on-Don
61	Eurofinans	Moscow
62	Samaraagrobank	Samara
63	Vostokinvestbank	Vladivostok
64	Zapadural Bank	Perm
65	Promstroibank	Kazan
66	Sibtorgbank	Novosibirsk
67	Dalnevostochni	Vladivostok
68	Mosstroibank	Moscow
69	Mosstroieconombank	Moscow
70	Lefortovski	Moscow
71	Neftigazstroibank	Moscow
72	Promstroibank	Omsk
73	Promstroibank	Khabarovsk

Rating	Name of bank	City
74	Kuzbassotsbank	Kemerovo
75	Eurazia	Izhevsk
76	Promstroibank	Blagovestchensk
77	Promstroibank	Tomsk
78	Ladabank	Togliatti
79	Kubanbank	Krasnodar
80	Promradiotechbank	Moscow
81	RNKB	Moscow
82	Yakimanka	Moscow
83	Altaikreditbank	Barnaul
84	Vostok	Moscow
85	Business Bank	Moscow
86	Sibirski Bank	Novosibirsk
87	Sotsinvestbank	Ufa
88	Montazhspetsbank	Moscow
89	Kolima-Bank	Magadan
90	SKB-Bank	Yekaterinburg
91	Gazprombank	Moscow
92	Promstroibank	Murmansk
93	Aviabank	Moscow
94	Frunzenski	Moscow
95	Gloria-Bank	Moscow
96	Delovaya Rossiya	Moscow
97	Presentcombank	Moscow
98	Petrovski-Bank	St. Petersburg
99	Resurs-Bank	Moscow
100	Gorni-Altai	Gorno-Altaisk

The total number of banks registered by July 1, 1994 was 2,294.

The definitive criteria of the size of the bank is, as usual, the sum of its assets — total balance sum, hard currency balance — which corresponds to international standards.

Non-Residents in Russia: Possibilities and Limitations

by V. Andreyev

Although Russia has an unfavorable investment climate, its rich natural and intellectual resources and the accumulated industrial potential have always been attractive for foreign capital. Several western companies tried to penetrate the Soviet market during socialist years when they viewed the former USSR as a trade partner at most. However, in those days any such agreement was decided by the Soviet government and there were no possibilities for a wide flow of foreign capital into the economy.

In July 1992 the former Russian Supreme Soviet adopted a law "On foreign investments in the RSFSR" which legalized the presence of foreign capital in Russia and fixed the general rules for the activities of foreign investors. The law strictly specified that the legal regime enjoyed by foreign investors cannot be less favorable than that established for Russian companies and citizens. This law along with others granted several privileges to foreign investors compared to their Russian counterparts with respect to exports of their own goods, taxation, transfer of capital from Russia, etc.

However, it is also necessary to be aware of the limitations which Russian legislation has introduced for non-residents, their subsidiaries and joint ventures. In order to make any investment in the Russian economy a foreign businessman has to transfer money to Russia. In this connection it is necessary to be acquainted with the hard currency control rules established for nonresidents in Russia.

The rules were fixed by the law "On hard currency regulation and hard currency control" adopted in October 1992,

as well as by other laws and normative acts. The very notions of "non-resident" and "resident" are determined by the law "On hard currency regulation and hard currency control" which fixes the rights of non-residents concerning operations with hard currency assets (which include foreign currency, securities in foreign currency and precious metals and stones, excluding articles made of them and their scrap). Non-residents can bring to Russia (transfer, mail) unlimited amounts of hard currency valuables and transfer from Russia the valuables which they had brought in. Non-residents can open hard currency and ruble accounts in Russian and foreign banks and freely transfer abroad the profits and incomes earned through their investments in Russia.

The main body regulating hard currency transactions in Russia is the Central Bank. In future some of its regulatory powers in this area are to be transferred to the Federal Russian Service on Hard Currency and Export Control, which was created in 1992. However, it is evident that this transfer is to be delayed and the Central Bank will remain the only hard currency regulator for the time being.

The Central Bank establishes the sphere and the rules for the circulation of hard currency valuables on Russian territory, the rules for buying or selling these valuables for rubles and the rules governing the opening of ruble accounts in Russian banks by non-residents. It also has the power to issue normative acts, the terms of which extend to both residents and non-residents.

As far as hard currency accounts in Russian banks are concerned, the conditions for non-residents do not differ in principle from those existing for Russian enterprises and citizens. Non-residents can transfer money abroad more easily — in contrast to their Russian counterparts they do not have to explain the reasons for the transfer.

If a non-resident decides to do business in rubles, a clearing account has to be opened in an authorized Russian bank (i.e. a bank licensed by the Central Bank for hard currency operations). Before opening the account and placing money in it the non-resident has to determine strictly which operations the account will be used for.

Non-residents can open two types of accounts in a Russian bank: a "T", or current account, and an "I", or investment account. The "T" account can be used for all types of operations connected with trading and maintaining the offices of foreign companies. The "I" accounts can be used only for deals connected with investments, including privatization.

On March 16, 1993 the Central Bank issued an instruction specifying which finances can be placed in and which withdrawn from "T" and "I" accounts respectively. A non-resident in Russia can have only one "I" account and investments through correspondent accounts in non-resident banks are banned. A foreign company can conduct the following operations with its ruble account in Russia:

Only the following funds can be placed in an "I"-type ruble account:

• ruble proceeds from the sale of hard currency,

• receipts for shares, equities and other proceeds received as a result of sharing profits (incomes) with a resident,

• funds returned from the budget, or from the sale by a resident of an object of foreign investment,

• fines received for transactions involving objects of privatization and objects of foreign investment,

• funds remaining after a venture has been liquidated and the claims of all its creditors satisfied,

• compensation for the nationalization of objects of foreign investment and for losses,

• proceeds from the sale of shares and equities of enterprises which are objects of foreign investment on Russian territory,

Owners of "I"-type ruble accounts can use them only for:

• purchases of hard currency on the internal Russian hard currency market,

• transactions involving objects of foreign investment and privatization vouchers,

• payment of a deposit to the seller for transactions involving objects of foreign investment,

• fines anticipated in transactions involving objects of foreign investment,

• payment of a commission to the authorized bank servicing the "I" account,

• transfer to a "T"-type ruble account belonging to the same non-resident.

All other types of settlements, including the granting and repayment of credits (deposits) and the placing and withdrawal of cash, are made only through "T" accounts.

It is necessary to note that money earned by selling hard currency can be placed both in the "I" and in the "T" accounts. All other transactions can be made only with the same type of account. For example, although a non-resident sells hard currency through an authorized bank and can place the rubles either in a "T" or "I" account, they can use only the "I" account to buy hard currency back. As it is forbidden to buy hard currency using "T" accounts (as well as to transfer finances from "T" to "I" accounts), a non-resident cannot use rubles earned through foreign trade operations to pay for imports to Russia.

While a "T"-type ruble account can be opened in a non-resident bank (to act through its correspondent account in Russia), an "I" account can be opened only in an authorized Russian bank.

Although the Central Bank has not yet used to the maximum the possibilities provided by such a split of rubles of non-residents, the aim of introducing such limitations is clear — to make it more difficult to export capital from Russia. The same aim is evident in many other documents adopted by the Central Bank to control hard currency proceeds from exports and the internal hard currency market in general. Most of the present hard currency control regulations only apply to Russian residents, but non-residents should be aware of them especially if they plan to create subsidiaries or joint ventures in Russia.

V. ANDREYEV
Expert of the Agency
Banking Information Agency
Tel. (095) 250-4898

Reprinted from
The Moscow Times

❄

Chapter 6

Real Estate in Russia

Недвижимость

On real estate and democracy

The rise of a Russian real estate market is one clear indicator that a new way of life actually is coming to this country, where for almost 80 years, land and construction — the immovables, as they were called — 'belonged to the people.' In other words, they belonged to the Communist Party and Soviet (municipal) bureaucracy. The legal consequences of this muddled formula are very much felt in Russia's expanding real estate market.

Today, land mostly still belongs to the state, which one way or another leaves it in the hands of various bureaucrats. In principle, according to such foreign experts as the people from the accounting firm, Deloitte & Touche, business methods developed to appraise real estate for Western companies are appropriate for valuation of real estate in Russia. But though this field is becoming a booming sector of the Russian economy — particularly in large cities — investors still must overcome much of the heritage of the Soviet past.

Today, most of the long-term projects that fail, involving foreign investments in Russia, collapse because of the unsettled problems of land ownership. Many Russian decrees mention real estate property, special agencies are commissioned to deal with relations in this field, and even taxes are imposed upon land owners. But one thing missing is the real estate itself.

An article in the 1993 *Constitution of the Russian Federation* states that land in Russia may be private, state-owned, municipal, or in other forms of property ownership. Those aware of Russia's history recognize the inclusion of this clause as a major first step in forming a democratic state — perhaps more important than the popular election of Russia's first president. That is why, in spite of the constitutional clause, a battle is raging around this issue in the Parliament and in Russian society.

The legal situation for real estate

The first time the term 'real estate' appeared in the Russian legal situation was in the decree of the President of Russia *Concerning the Regulation of Relations with Respect to Land and the Development of the Agrarian Reform in Russia No. 1767*, (dated October 27, 1993). In the first clause of the decree, real estate is defined as "a plot of land and all that is solidly connected to it."

The same decree declares that "the state guarantees the sanctity and protection of private ownership of land, as well as the protection of land owners' rights in transactions involving land." True, unlike in that first clause, the state guarantee is given with respect to private ownership of land, not real estate, although it is evident that land is not a legal term, while the concept of real estate also includes plots of land as such. But you must put up with this misunderstanding, at least until the *Basic Legislation on Land in Russia*, promised to be adopted soon by the Parliament, comes into force.

The same decree also states that the legal status of any plot of land is established by the *Certificate of the Right for Ownership of Land*, which is to be documented in a special register. Without this document, any transactions with land are considered invalid.

Foreigners generally are not permitted to own land, but they are entitled to own the building that is situated on the land. However, according to explanations given by the U.S. Foreign Commercial Service in Moscow, pursuant to the presidential decree of June 14, 1992 (*No. 631*, dealing with the sale of land), privatized state and municipal enterprises, including those enterprises that are backed with foreign investments, are permitted to purchase land by means connected to the privatization process.

You can — and may even want to — have a real estate transfer to you documented with the *Certificate of the Right for Ownership of Land* and issued in your name. However, you must realize the absolute necessity for the Russian side that is acting as your partner to have this certificate before you invest in any project.

In relations between Russian participants, doing without this document often is possible because they have other means to clear up controversial situations. But these means are not acceptable for foreign investors, who should consider only projects that involve participation by a Russian partner with a legal *Certificate of the Right for Ownership of Land.* Lack of such certificate by a Russian partner should be a signal of alarm, since according to the decree, state authorities refuse to issue the certificate only for one of three reasons:

- Direct prohibition by Russian laws for granting the right of property for the particular plots of land;
- If ownership of the particular plot of land is debatable at the moment of application for the certificate; or
- If the allotted purpose or use of the plot is to be changed.

The existence of any of these situations places a real estate project in the critical category, and investments are possible only if special guarantees and compensation are provided that secure full reimbursement of your resources in case of any negative developments. Be particularly wary of situations in which only specific purposes are allotted for a particular plot of land, especially in protected historic sites, forest park zones, or preserves.

All of these potential problems require detailed consideration, since practices vary in different regions of the country, legislation is quite chaotic, and even those legislative norms that seem unambiguous are sometimes interpreted in the most arbitrary and fanciful ways by local authorities.

Investments in large cities

For now, this chapter will dwell only upon investment practices in large cities — particularly in Moscow and St. Petersburg, for these are regions of extensive foreign investments into construction and renovation, and land-related expenses are most significant here. In other regions and industrial development areas, expenses for land are a minor part of total project costs. Sometimes, you can even reach agreement with local authorities on mutually acceptable conditions for just the use of land.

The city of Moscow stands out in terms of real estate investments for three reasons:

- Moscow is the capital of the country;
- The city is both a municipality and the seat of government; and
- The government of Moscow rejects the concept of private ownership of land within the bounds of the city.

The Prime Minister of the government is also the Mayor of the city, so local authorities themselves set the conditions for land use — and they can change those conditions when they find it necessary. In most cases, these conditions are declared to the investor as a final statement, not subject to discussion. At least, that is how it looks, although in reality, a discussion always takes place. The results of that discussion may differ from the initial version if the investor is prepared to 'have an open discussion' — that is, to discuss not only the conditions that are to be written down, but also the conditions 'to be understood.'

Land regulations

In Russia today, a huge gap exists between regulations on plots of land and regulations on the buildings upon those plots. In other words, the investor must have separate packets of documents and contracts for the land and for the building.

Since private real estate of citizens and of legal entities is not officially recognized by Moscow local authorities, private persons in Moscow can only get land plots for use on conditions of rent or use for an indefinite term. The right for land tenure in Moscow is legalized either by a contract, such as when renting, or by a unilateral act (decree) of the administration, which in all cases acts as the sole proprietor of all land plots and territories in Moscow. You should note straight away that none of these documents provides full confidence for the investor, but a contract still is better than a unilateral act since the contract allows for the possibility of claiming compensation for infringements if these compensations are included in the contract.

In principle, the most reliable route for you to get access to a land plot is through a joint venture established directly with the Moscow administration. However, a serious drawback to this scheme is the opening it creates for Moscow bureaucrats to interfere in management of your venture. Such interference will not necessarily take place, but you should keep that possibility in mind when formulating the by-laws of your joint venture. In practice, there is great potential for conflict here because final agreements can come into question if and when certain officials are replaced. Thus, in the end, many investors prefer to work under riskier conditions but without the vested attention of the local bureaucrats.

So, you should have a rent contract for the land. The length of the period you can rent for now is up to 49 years, and the draft of the *Agrarian Code* provides a possibility of increasing this period to 99 years. Documents must have double registration.

- The first document shows the decision by local (city) authorities, with the number and date of authorization by the appropriate agency of that local administration.
- The second authorization is part of the land tenure act in the local districts. Without the latter registration, any documents on the use of the land are considered invalid (*Clause 3, Decree No. 1767*).

Be aware that these procedures are applied only for the use of the land. If you want to have a building, you will need to follow additional procedures.

Buildings and structures

The 'second level' of rules in Moscow for handling real estate concern the rights for buildings and structures. Here the situation gets even more complicated, depending on which of two strategies you choose.

First strategy. The simplest strategy is to get the land allocation or rent the land in accordance with the registration procedures described above, and then build a new building on it. In this case, the investor usually is required to make the following commitments:

- To transfer, free of charge, to the Moscow administration a part of the residential flats — up to 50 percent — although this is bargainable and not necessarily required to be in the same building or even in the same district; and
- To include, also free of charge, the municipal government as a shareholder for office buildings, with a right to part of the space or profits; and to pay a rent for the land and often a one-time payment for purchase, at auction, for the 'right to rend' — the right to rent or sell.

The ban on rendering land plots as property in Moscow was established by *Order No. 23-PM* (dated January 17, 1994) of the Mayor of Moscow, and the rules for rendering land for construction and other use were established by *Order No. 51-PBM* (dated January 31, 1992) of the Vice-Mayor and *Order No. 168-PM* (dated February 3, 1993) of the Mayor.

Second strategy. The second strategy for rights to buildings and structures is the reconstruction and renovation of already existing buildings. In this case, investors must sign the so-called 'investment contract' with the Moscow administration, in which the part of the building rendered to the investor for renovation — usually no more than 50 percent — is to become his or her property only after the completion of all work. Besides, the authorities usually demand the investor to provide apartments if the building under renovation has tenants to be moved out. Alternatively, the authorities may require you to cover part of the expenses for general communications, such as new telephone lines, in the area subject to development. All this may be part of negotiations.

In this variant, making sure the legal documents are drawn up appropriately is extremely important. Because such projects are often carried out on the basis of shared participation, you will want to make sure that all the documents are in order and in the name of one of the partners, and that all the others involved in the negotiation, such as the authorities, have definite and clear contracts with that partner concerning their mutual rights and responsibilities.

Here, for instance, is the list of the required documents.

- The *Certificate of the Right for Ownership of Land* certifying the rights of the bearer for the object in question — if the building is state-owned or financed by the state;
- The documents confirming the registration of property rights, such as a certificate from the Moscow Committee on Property or other authorized administration agencies;
- Reference from the Moscow City Bureau of Technical Inventory with a certified floor-by-floor plan of the building and the surrounding territory attached to it;
- If the building is on lease, a certified copy of a lease contract is required; if it is on a sublease, then you have to provide copies of both lease and sublease contracts; and
- Documentation of compliance with the land tenure act already mentioned above.

In accordance with the existing regulations, *Moscow Government Decree No. 868* (dated September 9, 1993), commercial property used as nonresidential quarters in Moscow may be rendered for the following purposes:

- For full commercial management authority, only to commercial enterprises and institutions established by order of the Mayor or by the decree of the Moscow government — in this circumstance, the business is authorized to operate a former state property for profit, with a partial return to the government of the proceeds;
- For operating management, only to organizations financed by the budget — in other words, per this arrangement, the government is still the owner of the property;
- For lease;
- For sublease; or
- For sale to legal persons (entities).

In Russia, the sale of buildings and constructions has to be done by means of price competition or auction to the highest bidder. The sale at auction results in issuance of the *Certificate of Ownership*.

Nonresidential quarters rendered on the basis of operating management, full commercial management, and lease are subject to mandatory registration with the Moscow Committee on Property and the Moscow City Bureau of Technical Inventory. Certificates confirming proper registration are issued by the Moscow Committee on Property on the basis of the following documents:

- A standard application;
- Orders issued by the Mayor or the government of Moscow;
- An excerpt from the reference of the Moscow City Bureau of Technical Inventory, floor-by-floor plan, and explanation;
- A copy of the certificate of registration in the name of the user and his or her founding documents; and
- Indemnity obligations (insurance) for repairs or restoration and other documents concerning the plan of using the quarters.

Since June 1994, Moscow has required registration with the Moscow Committee on Property of all operations with property of private individuals or legal entities. Any transactions — including mortgage operations — involving any private quarters and buildings are subject to registration, except for apartments belonging to citizens.

Ensuring the legal process is followed

If you want no problems in your relations with authorities or with your partners, you should be particularly thorough in following all the regulations for handling real estate in Moscow. At all stages of the process you should rely on services from a qualified lawyer, since these regulations tend to change often and not always in a predictable way. Especially note that you should not rely on those Moscow officials who sympathize with you and provide assistance, because often, even the seemingly most reliable agreements — verbal or written — lose all effect if you fail to follow the required details and provisions of Russian real estate law.

One such example is the claim lodged by Oscar-Film Association against Tagansky Commercial Bank. In October 1991, Oscar-Film acquired from the Tagansky Regional Executive Committee a 0.4-hectare plot of land — almost an acre — for temporary use, with a half-wrecked building on it. The building was restored by the company and sold to the Tagansky Commercial Bank in October 1992 for 5.4 million rubles. Then, Oscar-Film presumably received a better offer and decided to get the building back by going to court.

The Moscow Court of Arbitration accepted the case and, in May 1994, decided in favor of the plaintiff, Oscar Film. The sales deal between the bank and Oscar Film was declared invalid and the bank lost its building because, "At the moment of transaction, the plaintiff (it turned out!) had not yet acquired the right of ownership for the house at issue." In other words, Oscar-Film did not have all the required documents in its hands and so, got the building back.

Keep in mind that Moscow real estate is a matter of permanent conflict between the federal and Moscow administrations. Moscow demands that all transfers of quarters on its territory be coordinated with the city's administration; federal authorities insist on their right to dispose independently of property in Moscow. Endless debates continue over which objects should be considered federal property and which are city property.

One of the most recent examples is the direct appeal of the Moscow administration to the President of Russia that he cancel an order of the State Committee on Property concerning the transfer of approximately 20 buildings in different regions of the city to Exicom Joint Stock Company. The buildings were designed according to the plan to be the state's share in the joint assigned capital of the Exicom Joint

Stock Company. The city appealed to the President on the grounds that real estate in Moscow is the property of the Moscow government, which has sole discretion over what goes up for sale, lease, as investment, and to or with whom.

This battle in Moscow for some sort of autonomy is an invitation to other major cities of Russia to follow suit. The same situation, or nearly the same, is happening in St. Petersburg.

Summary and recommendations

As with many other laws in Russia, real estate regulations are in confusion and disarray, especially when compared to the Western concept of property ownership. Of course, you could not expect the conversion — from 100 percent state-owned properties to private ownership — to happen overnight. In many cases, the various regulations only serve as preliminary steps toward the privatization of state assets and property. Ultimately, the plan is to have property ownership rights that resemble Western practices.

If you contemplate any involvement in real estate as part of your investment plans, consider the following observations:

- The understanding of market value widely accepted in the West can be used in contemporary Russia, with certain reservations.
- One of the key problems in Russia's real estate market is a lack of information. This is a field some Western agency could successfully develop.
- In many Russian towns, you can freely trade residential buildings and offices. For many other forms of real estate, an open market has not yet been formed.
- The Russian real estate market is still in its embryonic state. Both buyers and sellers still have only a confused idea of the workings of the market, based on sporadic and often imprecise data.
- External factors influencing market values in Russia include government prices for construction and plots of land and various types of limitations placed on the trade of real estate.
- The accounting systems of Russian enterprises, even where they exist, usually do not meet international standards, which makes them difficult to use for the purposes of property evaluation.

- The cost approach is the one most commonly used to determine the value of real estate in Russia. The problem with this approach is finding the necessary data on construction prices. The American corporation Marshall and Swift, a world leader in construction cost reference books, has opened offices in Moscow, so hopefully this problem will be partially solved for the benefit of foreign investors.
- Instead of data on deals actually completed, evaluators often are forced to use data on proposed sales.
- The future potential for Russia's real estate market is most promising, according to a recently held international construction conference in Moscow. In terms of volume, the Russian market may be compared to the present U.S. market.

Chapter 7

Taxes and Taxation
Налоговая система

The Russian system of taxation

Foreign investors will find many inconveniences in the Russian system of taxation. You will not be happy with the annoying habit of Russian authorities to permanently introduce new taxes and revise retroactive dates for tax legislation.

You certainly will be annoyed with the necessity to study numerous texts of taxation laws and instructions, written in a language that is hard to understand even for Russians, and which quite often contradict each other. Your spirits will not be improved when you learn that, according to strict academic calculations, taxes due from your commercial enterprises are figured at 110 to 120 percent of profits earned.

You will find many things to learn about the Russian taxation system, and what you learn will not always be a pleasant discovery. For example, in the rules for bank profit calculation:

- The expenses for salary suddenly become part of the profit;
- Commercial insurance falls under the category of blamable leisure — that is, not viewed as a deductible expense — because fiscal authorities refuse to consider insurance expenses as a cost of production; and

- An accidentally expressed desire to achieve profit immediately materializes into a corresponding tax bill — advance taxes on expected profit.

In addition, you will often discover disagreement between:

- A legislator's understanding of tax laws;
- The interpretation by central financial agencies; and
- The application of the laws by local tax officials.

According to Harvard Law School graduate, Leonid Rozhetskin, a native of St. Petersburg now in private practice in Moscow:

At the same time, lawsuits brought and won by taxpayers throughout Russia in the past two years indicate the willingness of the courts to review critically the actions of the State Taxation Service and, where these are not consistent with an objective interpretation of the legislation, to invalidate them.

The objective of this chapter is not to consider in detail the mass of Russian laws and regulations on taxes. Instead, the important and necessary task here is to give an account of basic principles of the taxation system in Russia, to characterize the most important types of taxes, and to give a general idea of the work of taxation agencies. These issues will be considered with respect to their effect on foreign investors, and in cases of joint ventures, on foreign investors and their Russian partners.

Formally speaking, the Russian Parliament is the main and ultimate source of tax laws. But in fact, both the President and the Ministry of Finance directly and actively participate in creating tax laws, as do local authorities within their level of competency. In addition, the effect of tax laws may be altered or supplemented due to international treaties and agreements that Russia has signed with foreign countries.

Three levels of Russian taxes

Taxes are levied on three separate levels in Russia. There are:

- Federal taxes, including federal taxes shared with the regional level;
- Taxes of republics and regions; and
- Local taxes.

The federal level consists of 14 taxes. Six of them — value added tax (VAT), excise tax, customs and duty tax, taxes on bank profits, taxes on insurance company profits, and taxes on operations with securities — are included in the federal budget. Revenue from the other eight types of taxes, the most important being corporate and individual income taxes, the stamp tax, and the inheritance tax, are divided between federal and local budgets in various proportions.

At the regional level are four types of taxes: the corporate property tax, the water utilities tax, the forest tax, and the natural resources tax. At the local level, there are 22 types of taxes of which only three are compulsory: the personal property tax, the land tax, and the sole proprietorship tax. The remaining taxes may be imposed, or not imposed, at the discretion of local authorities.

Before 1992, foreign companies had practically no relations with local tax agencies, but by 1994, nonresidents were obliged to pay quite a number of taxes. Table 17, Taxes for Nonresident Enterprises, located at the end of this chapter, shows the rates of the more commonly applied taxes.

Edict from the State Taxation Service

In answer to many inquiries, the State Taxation Service of the Russian Federation announced the following instruction:

1. In accordance with article 11 of the Law of the Russian Federation, No. 2116-1 (dated 27 December, 1991) on the profit tax of enterprises and organizations, foreign legal entities receiving income from sources on the territory of the Russian Federation shall be subject to tax on the income from the source of payment. Such incomes received from sources in the Russian Federation include in particular:

1.1. Dividends paid out by Russian residents and also income from profit created in Russia at an enterprise with foreign capital and paid out to a foreign participant;

1.2. Income received from shares held by foreign partners in a company;

1.3. Additional remuneration paid to shareholders in monetary or other form;

1.4. Profits distributed by voucher investment funds (funds specializing in privatization investment).

1.5. Interest payments on:

- *promissory notes of any kind, including bonds that give the right to receive the profits of a company and convertible bonds — premiums paid for the redemption of securities previously sold with a discount, an insurance or reinsurance premium — fines and penalties for the violation of contractual and shareholding obligations.*

1.6. *Income derived from copyright: fees for the use of copyrights, including publication rights to literature, art, and scientific publications, the right to use cinematographic works, including feature films and videocassettes for public viewing in cinemas and on the television, and for the right to broadcast records.*

1.7. *Income from the use of inventions, working models, industrial models, trademarks, brand names, service signs and other similar assets, including business reputation (prestige), contacts, clients, and employees of a company.*

1.8. *Income derived from leasing out property on the territory of the Russian Federation.*

1.9. *Income from an increase in the value of property or real estate located on the territory of the Russian Federation — shares and other securities — claims for the payment of debts — the property of a permanent representative or an independent subdivision which a foreign legal entity owns on the territory of the Russian Federation; — ships, boats and aircraft, railway transport and motor transport facilities used in international transportation and moving stock related to such uses.*

1.10. *Other incomes whose receipt is not connected with the activities of a permanent representative, in particular for work and services of any kind, carried out and provided on the territory of the Russian Federation, including for:*

- *the issue of a company license for production or sale of goods or services under the firm name of the given company;*
- *the right to use an IBM program and data base;*
- *the use of technological, organizational, or commercial information (know-how), including secret formulas and processes;*
- *managerial services;*
- *the rendering of assistance needed for efficient use of property or granted rights;*
- *the rendering of assistance needed for installation and operation of equipment, lines, mechanisms, and appliances;*
- *consulting, advice, and services connected with the management of any scientific, industrial or commercial project, plan, process, or joint venture;*
- *services and consulting services rendered by a foreign company to its subsidiaries connected with the conduct of the above business activities*

in Russia, and also for services and consulting provided for the benefit of the representatives of the main office of a foreign legal entity;

- income from services for the issue (including income from an independent issue and its servicing) and distribution of the shares of any entity resident in Russia;
- carriage of cargo (freight);
- sale of goods imported from abroad on an intermediation contract with Russian enterprises on the territory of the Russian Federation. In this case, the income, the source of which is on the territory of the Russian Federation, shall be considered as the difference or part of the difference between the sale price quoted by a foreign legal entity and the more profitable price at which the intermediating enterprise sells imported goods.

In the absence of documents testifying to the importation of goods from abroad by a foreign legal entity for their sale on the territory of the Russian Federation, the income, the source of which is on the territory of the Russian Federation, shall be considered as the gross earnings paid to the foreign legal entity for the sale of goods.

The revenue of a foreign legal entity received from foreign trade operations, which is carried out exclusively on behalf of that foreign legal entity and is connected with the export into the Russian Federation of goods, shall not be subject to tax at source.

2. The revenue of foreign legal entities from sources on the territory of the Russian Federation shall be subject to taxation at source, taking into consideration the provisions of current agreements on the avoidance of double taxation.

A case study of tax problems

In the Russian tax system, departmental 'instructions' — the interpretations by local authorities of the law — often turn out to be stronger in Russian legal practice than the legal decrees of the Parliament, but at least there is hope that a court will confirm the advantage of law over 'instruction.' The worst tax situation is when contradictions arise between law acts. Then, even courts often are powerless. Just such a situation has emerged between the general laws protecting the rights of the public and administrative laws establishing the rights and duties of the tax department. This conflict first affected foreign investors, despite government assurances of its desire to encourage foreign investments.

One example of contradictory tax laws involves a tax department ruling that any taxpayer can appeal a decision of the Higher Tax Board only to arbitration courts. The taxpayer also can appeal to any local tax agency about a decision in a local court, but only after the Higher Tax Board or another tax agency makes the final decision. But since the same law requires a preliminary administrative hearing before you can have an appeal and since the Higher Tax Board almost always acts as the higher authority confirming decisions made by tax agencies, the only way to appeal its decision is to apply to the Higher Court of Arbitration.

However, when the taxpayer appeals to the Higher Court of Arbitration, he or she faces new problems. Indeed, this court can hear any argument if there is voluntary consent by both parties — except cases against government administration. Naturally, in order to prevent conflicts with the administration, the Higher Court of Arbitration simply prefers to avoid any hearing on that type of case.

The scene described above was exactly the situation regarding a claim from a large Finnish firm that was fined $2 million in early 1993 by the local tax agency. Both the local court and the Higher Court of Arbitration declined to hear the firm's claim based on the ruling cited above. The firm was compelled to lodge its claim with the Moscow City Office of Justice, which succeeded in getting a hearing in local court by referring specifically to *Clause 4* of the *Law on Foreign Investments*, which states:

Foreign investors, as well as enterprises with foreign investments, enjoy the right of lodging claims in local court for the protection against illegal actions of state organs and their authorities.

Finally, the local court decided in favor of the Finnish firm. This success, however, is not the rule. In similar cases, getting assistance from the Office of Justice either was impossible, or such intervention was not successful. Either way, the taxpayer falls into a deadlock situation when the local court refuses to accept a claim for having a hearing and the Higher Court of Arbitration, even if ready to do so, due to its nature, cannot guarantee that its decision will be executed by the party that loses the case.

Tax collectors always prefer to interpret the law exclusively in the agency's favor, and it is difficult to make them change their minds. Of course, with a strong argument you may bring the case to court, but it is a long and costly process, during which the tax authorities can cause you a great deal of trouble. They can carry out various arbitrary actions that are not regulated at all by law. They can take measures ranging from confiscating your accounting documents 'for investigation,' which might take a very long time, to freezing your bank account.

Even if you avoid such conflicts at the local level, all your tax-planning efforts can be destroyed in a flash by the actions of the federal administration.

Many examples can be provided of federal actions arbitrarily applying retroactive taxation, such as the well-known instruction by tax authorities that banks should pay advance profit taxes for the first half of 1994 in the sum of five times the tax paid for a similar period of 1993. Since many banks did not increase their profits five-fold during that time, the tax exceeded their ability to pay and they faced bankruptcy.

The situation displays the convoluted logic of the system. Those banks that paid taxes honestly the previous year were penalized, but not those banks that previously used all the tricks known to bankers to reduce reported profits and avoid taxes.

Good news for foreign companies

Don't be discouraged yet about starting your business in Russia. There is goods news for you: nonresident companies have a number of advantages over resident companies under current tax regulations. For example:

- Instead of presenting actual balance sheets every three months, a nonresident company just hands in a tax declaration on profit and expenses only once a year, which includes expenses incurred outside Russia, but in connection with Russian activities. As you may well understand, these figures are harder to verify than actual balance sheet figures.
- Foreign companies are not liable for payment of an excess salary tax.
- Unlike resident companies, foreign companies are not obligated to convert 50 percent of their foreign exchange income.
- Depreciation may be accounted for in accordance with the norms of the country of registration, which reduces Russian tax liability considerably compared to resident companies.

- Foreign legal entities are not required to pay VAT on rented living and office space.

Note, however, that every foreign legal entity operating in the Russian Federation, through its permanent office or representative, must register with the local tax agency whether or not its future activities will be acknowledged by the tax agency as subject to taxation.

Three ways of treating taxes

Your tax liabilities in Russia may be treated in three ways. You can pay them according to the law, not pay them at all, or negotiate different payment arrangements. The advantages and disadvantages of each strategy are described below.

Pay all taxes in full in accordance with the law

While this should be the recommended method, unfortunately no examples worth mentioning exist of its practical implementation in Russia's business life. Indeed, this tax strategy more often than not leads to bankruptcy. If you choose this method, consider these consequences:

- You immediately will have to accept that all your profit belongs to the government; all your business activities will be burdened by such tax risks as changing, sometimes retroactive, tax legislation, and by possible changes in the attitude taken by tax authorities of various levels.
- You will have to maintain substantial tax analysis services to deal exclusively with matters of tax obligations for the business.
- You will have to establish a reserve system — a tax-free money fund to assure an uninterrupted performance of your business — in case your bank account is frozen by an arbitrary decision of a certain tax authority.

Pay no taxes at all

This strategy leads you into direct confrontation with the fiscal administration; yet, it is less risky than the first strategy because it leaves you a chance to stay in business — although permanently balancing on the edge of the law.

The most widespread practice of implementing this strategy is establishing a parallel payment turnover in cash — be it in dollars or rubles. In this scenario, minimum sums go through the main bank ruble accounts or through other bank accounts controlled by tax authorities, while basic payments are made in cash. The business may also play the so-called 'overtake game' or 'catch me if you can,' in which for each big transaction a separate company is created and then left at the disposal of tax authorities as soon as all its money is transferred to the accounts of other firms.

This tax strategy is not necessarily a direct violation of law. For example, parallel payments in cash may well be interpreted as loans of private persons or even as 'presents,' neither one of which openly contradicts the law. And since the bankruptcy of any particular firm is a normal occurrence in Russian market economics, when a certain businessperson suffers several such misfortunes in succession, it has still to be proven that they were caused by his or her orderly plans rather than simply bad luck.

In Moscow, for example, money is collected from the credulous public in such a manner. A financial company with minimum paid-up capital is organized, advertisements are published promising inflated profits, and when a certain substantial sum is collected, all the money is drawn from the accounts leaving the company to be tortured by the fooled depositors and tax collectors.

What is most surprising is that authorities are unwilling to pursue such swindling. For example, the Central Bank says it has no grounds for control of such operations because these operations do not have bank licenses, and the prosecutor's office doesn't want to interfere unless there are complaints from depositors. Such complaints emerge only when the firm stops payments, by which time the money and the swindlers are gone.

But these are extreme cases. In fact, some taxes must be paid unless you are prepared to give up your business and leave with all its cash.

Make arrangements with authorities to reduce or lift taxes

This tax strategy not only can save your venture, but it allows you to broaden the scale of its activities. You can negotiate to have some or all of your tax duties reduced or lifted. Of course, you will need an experienced team with established, broad connections, which means not everyone can do it. However, this is the most reliable strategy in providing the highest degree of protection against arbitrary actions of fiscal agencies, since it is based on a direct agreement with higher authorities.

Certain estimates suggest that up to one-half of all foreign trade turnover is done on 'favorable terms,' without confiscatory taxation and without compulsory exchange of export profits from investment activities. These agreements are strictly established and are valid only for the particular venture and activities indicated in the corresponding documents. The Russian government never questions these agreements and quite openly offers them to potential investors.

Such an agreement, involving the discharge of taxes, was made between the Russian branch of Coca-Cola — Coca-Cola St. Petersburg Bottlers — and St. Petersburg's mayor, Anatoly Sobchak. According to that decision, the company, which is constructing a new factory for production of patent beverages in the Pulkovo area, is exempt, effective in 1994 from taxes on profit (22 percent), property (2 percent), home upkeep, and advertising. In addition, for the period of construction, this business is also exempt from payments for renting the land plot (43 hectares). This is the first such 'package' tax exemption deal made because the magistrate did not want to lose a potential investment of $35 million and more than 2,000 new jobs. Before that, Proctor & Gamble had walked away from its planned investment of $300 million when the company failed to find a 'common language' and reach a similar tax exemption with St. Petersburg authorities.

Special tax agreements becoming more common

In other regions, such practices already have become widespread, and authorities consider preferential taxation agreements as a suitable alternative to budget subsidies as an instrument to win the competition for investors — a competition in which many of the Russian provinces are involved.

Chuvashia and Kalmykia already have announced provisions for new investors that provide either long-term 'tax holidays' or reduced taxation, similar to practices in off-shore financial centers. These examples give hope to investors for similar treatment in other regions of Russia, or at least that authorities will provide for some kind of protection against taxation bankruptcy. The following story appeared in a Moscow English-language paper.

The Autonomous Republic of Tatarstan has introduced a three-year tax holiday for foreign-owned companies and joint ventures, joining a handful of Russian regions that are pioneering the use of local tax breaks to attract foreign investment.

On January 1, Tatarstan will suspend local property and profits taxes for three years for all manufacturing and service companies registered in the republic with at least 30 percent foreign ownership and assets worth at least $1 million, a Tatar official said Thursday.

"We want to attract foreign investors," said the official, who asked not to be named. "The main thing is for them to come here and start working."

Companies will still be subject to a 13-percent federal profit tax, but will reap "significant" savings by avoiding Tatarstan's local profits tax of 22 percent and property tax of at least 2 percent, the official said. Most regions impose a 25 percent profits tax, the maximum allowed by law.

"It marks one of the first occasions when a region of Russia is specifically going out to make itself attractive to outside investors by using the tax system, the way countries do all over the world," said Steve Hasson, senior tax partner with the U.S. consultants Price Waterhouse to a Moscow Times *correspondent. "If it spreads that might be a good thing."*

Foreign consultants said the tax holiday in oil-rich Tatarstan, a region the size of Portugal about 800 kilometers east of Moscow, was the first they had heard of that offered across-the-board tax breaks to a broad category of companies and was aimed at stimulating regional development rather than creating a tax shelter, as the southern republic of Ingushetia has attempted to do.

Both newcomers and some 160 foreign-owned enterprises in Tatarstan will enjoy the tax breaks introduced in a decree entitled "On the Attraction of Foreign Investment" and signed October 31 by Tatarstan President Mintimer Shaimiyev.

Hasson said the tax breaks would probably not lure large consumer-oriented companies away from major commercial centers, but could encourage more investors to start joint ventures with Tatarstan's giant KaMaZ Truck Factory or in the oil industry.

John Braden, tax partner at Ernst & Young, said several foreign companies had decided to register in the Moscow and St. Petersburg regions rather than in the cities themselves because taxes were slightly lower in the suburbs.

"It's not a significant difference, but it's enough to influence the decision," he said.

Sometimes, the local administration will consider giving a rebate on tax and rent payments as payment for a share in a joint venture with a foreign investor — such agreements already have been made in Moscow. At the federal level, it is known that Mars, a U.S. concern, was offered a big rebate on taxes if assignments were made to Russian investment projects. Thus, both central and local authorities in Russia are willing to provide exclusive tax allowances when they are interested in projects offered by investors.

In the near future, considering relations established between the legislative and executive powers and the assurances by President Boris Yeltsin not to allow measures that worsen the situation for foreign investors, few will dispute the legality of such deals. On September 27, 1993, the President of Russia signed a decree that gave businesses with a share of foreign capital a three-year immunity from acts of Russian authorities that might be to their material detriment.

Russia has a specific internal government policy to hand out special and exclusive privileges to 'priority' enterprises and sectors of the economy. In the past, broad and exclusive privileges were rendered to miners, oil companies, car makers, the largest enterprises in other sectors, and to certain specifically patronized foundations and concerns. Early in 1994, extensive tax privileges were rendered by presidential decrees and government instructions to the National Sports Foundation and to the National Sport Center under its patronage, including reduced custom duties for the export of commodities such as cement, black oil, and metals. By *Decision No. 521* (dated May 5, 1994), similar privileges were rendered to a sports lottery.

More and more, officials at the federal level understand the need for a general reduction of the fiscal burden and the necessity to stimulate investments. In May 1994, the President issued a special decree *Concerning Certain Aspects of Fiscal Policy.* This decree provided for an overall reduction by 10 to 20 percent for the tax rate on profits and added value; the introduction of rapid depreciation in high-tech fields; and a two-year income tax exemption for ventures with a foreign capital share of no less than 30 percent, involving at least $10 million. An order by the State Customs Committee (SCC) dated June 1994, lifts the VAT and other special taxes on certain imports. This order is designed to encourage investments, including foreign investments. The text of *Order 297* by the SCC is reprinted at the end of this chapter.

Looking forward to 1995, Mr. Alexander Pochinov, Vice-Chairman of the Parliamentary Committee for the Budget, Taxes, Banks, and Finances, made this statement:

Many have been looking forward to fundamental changes and a drastic reduction in taxation pressure. The alternative variants of the budget offered by different groups are based precisely on this. However, serious reforms should be prepared without undue haste.

Today, minor changes have been introduced into laws, which are now in effect. Another six legal acts proposed by the government will be adopted until the end of the year, and by the end of 1995, the Taxation Code, which will finally reform Russia's taxation system, will be introduced. The Duma's Committee for the Budget, Taxes, Banks, and Finances has considered several drafts of this document.

On the whole, due to the complexity of life, today's taxation system cannot be simple. A system which is primitive and accessible to all is not possible, either is it possible to cut all taxes in half. The state's expenditures have already been lowered in the draft budget for next year, which is a basis for the subsequent reduction in taxes.

There is arguably no greater obstacle to foreign investment in Russia than the tax system.

The climate for all forms of investment in every sector of the economy is affected by such mainstays of the Russian fiscal system as galloping tax rates, the ever-shifting contours of taxable income and transactions, and the vagaries of interpretation by local officials.

Summary and recommendations

Based on the present situation in Russia, you can expect a reduction of the tax rate level with respect to investment activities in general, and specific privileges for investments from abroad. Further, you should expect special tax rebates for particular projects and ventures of priority interest to the development of Russia's economy.

Listed below are several recommendations to help you survive — and even prosper — in spite of the present Russian taxation system.

- For short-term investments, you should provide your business with a 15 to 20 percent reserve money fund to protect against the unexpected introduction of new taxes or an increase of customs duties.

- For long-term investments, especially with major businesses, make agreements with authorities beforehand to provide for tax rebates of 20 to 40 percent. Make such rebates one of your main conditions for carrying out the economic project.

- Have a permanent consultant on taxation who maintains business contacts with the appropriate fiscal agencies and helps formulate your tax strategies — such as written protests, appeals to a higher authority, or appeals to court — whenever the rights of your company are threatened by tax laws.

- Address taxation issues at the very first stages of planning your investments in Russia. In many cases, the tax situation will determine not only the sum of investments and their time schedule, but the type of investment you will make, such as whether to make direct investments, provide credit or credit combined with portfolio investments, provide financial leasing services, or deliver supplies with payment by installment.

- Pay special attention to producing a complete and documented declaration of venture expenses outside Russia. If your expenses conform with the character of the main activity of the venture, you can often use them to reduce your overall tax bill in Russia.

- Use the assistance of qualified consultants to keep abreast of general changes in the tax policy of Russia. Also, keep active relations with local tax agencies. Have preliminary talks with them on taxation issues with regard to new capital investments, operating ventures, and financing of new projects. In these talks, you should ask for the official answers or other explanations by the tax officers.

Although you have been introduced to most of the legal aspects of doing business in Russia — forms of business organization, banking, real estate, and taxes — you are probably uncertain as to how all of this translates into actually conducting business operations. The next chapter covers some of the more intangible differences — those not covered by law — of carrying out daily business operations.

Table 17: Taxes for Nonresident Enterprises

Type of tax	Tax (%)	Application of tax
Value added tax (VAT)	20.0	Sale turnover on Russian territory (food: 10 %)
Special tax	3.0	Tax for development of Russia's key industries
Transport tax	1.0	The total sum that is to be paid to employees in the form of salary
Dividend withholding tax rate	15.0	of the amount to be paid as a dividend
State pension tax	31.6	of the sum paid to employees in the form of salary
State fund of population employment tax	1.0	of the sum paid to employees in the form of salary
State fund of social interest tax	5.4	of the sum to be paid to each employee in the form of salary
Assets tax	2.0	(for enterprise) of balance sheet value of all assets of an enterprise
Advertisement tax	5.0	of the cost of an ad
Tax on car acquisition	20.0	of the price of a car
Profit tax	38.0	paid by an enterprise on its net profits from most of its business activities, including: federal profit tax (13%) and local profit tax (25 %)

Taxes when Importing Certain Goods onto the Territory of the Russian Federation

Order 297 of the SCC (State Customs Committee), 20 June 1994

For the realization of Decree 1199, dated June 10, 1994, "On certain measures for the encouragement of investment, including investment using foreign credit."

1. Equipment, machines and mechanisms imported onto the customs territory of the Russian Federation and intended for the capital development of enterprises, organizations and institutions in accordance with contracts signed prior to January 1, 1993 and which were registered in accordance with SCC (State Customs Committee) Order, dated February 4, 1993, No. 124, and SCC Instructions No. 1-12/464, dated April 26, 1993, shall be freed without exception of VAT and special taxes (except excise duty) levied for the support of important industries.

VAT and special tax paid prior to June 16, 1994 (the date when the President's Decree No. 1199 of October 6, 1994 came into force) shall not be returned by the customs bodies directly but shall be compensated by the procedure established in Article 16, of the President's Decree No. 2270 of December 22, 1993, they shall be compensated by the tax authorities to the full amount when putting the capital assets into operation.

This article shall apply to both direct import of specified goods by enterprises, institutions and organizations for their own capital development and when importing such goods on contract for the same goals.

Use of the above-mentioned goods for purposes other than that or which the exemptions from VAT and special taxes was granted, shall be allowed upon obtaining permission from the customs authorities and payment of VAT and special taxes.

2. VAT and special taxes (except excise duty) shall not be collected when importing goods onto the territory of the Russian Federation within the framework of the use of credits granted to the Russian Federation by foreign governments and international financial organizations, and on goods imported in payment of loans granted to foreign states by the former USSR and the Russian Federation.

Exemption from payment of VAT and special tax (except excise duty) when contracts as envisaged shall be granted under the existing directives of the Russian SCC.

3. The provisions of Article 1 of this Decree shall be extended to the goods mentioned in it which are imported onto the customs territory of the Russian Federation after January 1, 1994 and registered with customs before December 31, 1994.

Article 1 of this Order shall come into force from June 16, 1994 (the publication date of the President's Decree 1199, dated October 6, 1994).

4. When registering goods with customs as specified in Article 1 of this Order, the code for exemption from payment of VAT and special taxes in form 36 for customs freight declarations until June 30 should be 41 and after July 1, 1994 should be a Russian L.

When registering goods with customs as specified in Article 2 of this Order, the code for exemption from payment of VAT and special taxes in form 36 for customs freight declarations until June 30 should be 41 and after July 1, 1994 should be M.

5. To supplement Article 4 with its Classification of preferences, privileges and other exceptions in paying customs duties, as approved by the Order 162 of the Russian SCC April 25, 1994 (in Appendix 11 to the Instruction on the procedure for the filling out of a customs freight declaration) with the following:

L – equipment, machines and mechanisms imported onto the customs territory of the Russian Federation in 1994, intended for the capital development of enterprises, organizations and institutions in accordance with contracts signed prior to January 1, 1994 and which has been registered in compliance with SCC Order 124, dated April 2, 1993 and SCC Instructions 01-12/464, dated April 26, 1993.

M – goods (with the exception of excise duty) imported onto the customs territory of the Russian Federation within the framework of credits granted to the Russian Federation by foreign governments and international financial organizations and also goods (with the exception of excise duty) imported to pay off state loans granted to foreign states by the former USSR and the Russian Federation.

6. The heads of customs authorities shall bring the subject-matter of this Order to the notice of staff members and those submitting customs declarations.

First Deputy, SCC
V. Kruglikov

Chapter 8

Everyday Operations
Дела повседневные

Change since 1990

At a law and economic conference held at the Kremlin Palace in September 1990, a professor of history at a leading Ivy League college told an incredulous audience of 600 American lawyers, "If anybody here tells you that they know what's going on, that person is either a fool or a liar." That statement was probably true in 1990.

People, events, and institutions just weren't what they seemed or were represented to be. Since 1990, many revolutionary changes have occurred in Russia, political and economic. Information that foreign businesspeople must rely upon to assess the viability of potential markets in Russia continues to be suspect, but credibility is improving.

Current periodicals indicate that Russia does not have a stable business environment because production is falling at a rate of 25 to 30 percent a year. However, the statistical information indicating the fall in production pertains to the monolithic, macroeconomic enterprises organized under the former Soviet state's command economy. The decline and disintegration of these giant industrial 'elephants' — which have always been and are now ill-suited to supply products to a market economy — has obviously had a negative impact on the country's budget and output.

What you should note is that published economic data relating to production is only tied to these giant, dependent, elephantine enterprises, which in the past produced for the pleasure of the Kremlin 'ringmasters' in the 'circus of the Red Star.' The data does not measure the production of the new entrepreneurial sector of the private economy, which can be collectively and metaphorically distinguished from the elephant sector as the 'honey bee' sector. The honey bee sector is energized and tirelessly seeking to bring fruit to the Russian economy through its microeconomic efforts, while requiring little or no subsidization or support from the state.

Very little data is available to accurately measure the productivity of the newly created, honey bee, private-sector industry. The Russian government is in the process of establishing a committee to evaluate statistics for the emerging, private entrepreneurial sector and, at the same time, is presiding over and defending the conversion and dismantling of the antiquated institutional giants.

Understanding the dichotomy presented by the eclipse of the command economy and the emergence of the 'mindless' market economy is the core issue for Russian economists at this time, according to Abel Aganbegyan, Rector of the National Academy of the Economy, an economic think tank for the Russian Federation and the Commonwealth of Independent States. To compound the woes of the economic analysts of the Russian government, estimates show that a substantial portion of the economy may not be taxed at this time and, therefore, the gross domestic production for Russia may be substantially under-recorded. Indeed, for the traveler going to Moscow and other parts of Russia, the signs of economic revival are everywhere to be seen, notwithstanding pessimistic press accounts.

From Marx to the market

What makes the Russian businessperson tick? The fundamentalist Marxist claim to socialism's economic rationality has been thoroughly challenged and refuted through the actual experience of the former Soviet Union. However, vestiges of Communist ideology continue to linger at all levels in Russia. Many Communists seek to reconcile Marx with the market and establish an economic system that will accommodate socialism.

Understanding this aspect of Russian reality is very important for any Western businessperson seeking to do business in Russia. Before the Soviet Union was dismantled, not a single educational institution in the country trained businesspeople and managers. The subjects of business and how to make a profit were simply not taught in Russia. The current Russian businessperson was reared under the Soviet system, which branded on his or her psyche the unquestionable superiority of the socialist 'blueprint.' The premise of this belief is that central planning will assure a stable movement of the economy, and that output and input will be balanced, thereby allowing appropriate use of resources and labor.

The theoretical linchpin of the Communist system is that socialist ownership of the means of production will afford every member of the society equal access to decisions regarding:

- How the means of production are to be applied; and
- How the distribution of the means of production are in fact to be distributed.

The concept of public ownership with the state as the 'owner' is derived from this idea.

Marx believed, and many Russian managers still believe, that human beings have the capacity to organize every aspect of the economy rationally under the 'right conditions' and that socialism will create those 'right conditions.' The essence of this belief is found in *Capitalism, Socialism and Democracy* (Fifth ed. Allen and Unwin, London: 1976) by Joseph A. Schumpeter, who wrote as follows:

> *There are cases in which capitalist industries are so circumstanced that prices and output become theoretically indeterminate .... In a socialist economy, everything — limiting cases without practical importance alone excepted — is uniquely determined. But even when there exists a theoretically determined state, it is much more difficult and expensive to reach in the capitalist economy than it would be in the socialist economy. In the former, endless moves and countermoves are necessary and decisions have to be taken in an atmosphere of uncertainty that blunts the edge of action, whereas that strategy and that uncertainty will be absent from the latter .... This means more than it seems at first sight. Those determinate solutions of the problem of production are rational or optimal from the standpoint of given data, and anything that shortens, smoothens, or safeguards the road that leads to them is bound to save human energy and material resources, and to reduce the costs at which a given result is attained. Unless the resources thus saved are completely wasted, efficiency in our sense [under a Socialist economy] must necessarily increase.*

Sounds reasonable, but events have proven Mr. Schumpeter and Karl Marx, to be flat wrong. Russian businesspeople now freely admit that command economies, for all their perceived efficiency, are not the most efficient economic systems. The forces of the market make businesses lean and efficient, and thereby, better ensure the most efficient use of a nation's available resources.

The fact that a thriving entrepreneurial class is emerging from the wreckage of the former Communist state is a testament to this realization and to the pragmatism, resourcefulness, and flexibility of the Russian business mind. Among this class of entrepreneurs, who have no time to grieve over the lost opportunities of Russia during the 70-year debacle of Communism, is Victor Penenkov, the founder of the Russian business, Likchel Company, a medium-sized firm and an example of the type of successful new business that is the mainstay of Russia's emerging private market economy. The company name, Likchel, means "business with a human face" in Russian. During an interview for an article that appeared in the Russian magazine *Russian Life* (Vol. XXXVII, No. 2, Spring 1994), Mr. Penenkov was asked the following question:

> Question: *Many entrepreneurs nowadays justly complain of the unpredictability of the political and economic situation in Russia and the contradictory nature of governmental decisions concerning the activities of private companies and enterprises. Would operating in the West be easier for you?*

> Answer: *I am not altogether sure. There are other difficulties there, like cutthroat competition and saturated markets. These barriers would be extremely hard for fledgling Russian businesspeople to surmount. If and when political stability comes to Russia, market conditions for companies like Likchel will turn out to be highly favorable. Judge for yourself: colossal mineral resources, a limitless market volume, and the all but total absence of the service sector — it would be a crime not to make use of all these things.*

Planning for profit

Profitability is a function of three components volume, price, and cost. The dynamic relationship and correlation of these factors is the core of business planning anywhere in the world, including Russia. Descriptions of each of these components as they relate to the Russian mind set and market are highlighted in this section.

Volume – the vast markets of Russia

Potential markets in Russia are currently enormous for virtually all of the goods and services already established and sold in Western markets. The command economists of the Soviet Union had no appreciation of the market and no need to develop and implement production to serve the marketplace. The military-industrial complex in Russia was just that — a military and industrial complex. It produced simultaneously, and often at the same plants, both military and general consumer goods. Unlike the United States, where private defense contractors contract with the government, no such distinction existed in the Soviet Union and everything was contracted for by the government — everything was the government.

In the Soviet structure, every means and aspect of production was controlled by the state — from goods for the armed services to household products and other civilian goods. In some cases, machine guns were manufactured at plants that also produced washing machines. Central planners of Soviet Russia believed that in this way technology could be centralized and economies of scale could be enjoyed. The Soviet military also sought to veil the production of military goods behind a facade of the production of civilian consumer goods — so reliable production data is not available in many cases.

This mind set is still prevalent with Russian managers and companies, which like Likchel, initially diversified by producing many different products at their plants, ranging from children's toys to industrial pumps. Likchel, according to Mr. Penenkov, has since learned to focus on the most profitable lines, and the first key to profitability is whether people want your product.

Pricing – can you get hard currency?

Profitability depends upon whether your customers have the means to afford your products and are willing to pay high enough prices for these products to allow for an operating profit. Pools of hard currency are available in Russia — currently estimated at $18–20 billion in U.S. dollars and growing — and consumers are ready and willing to pay prices that exceed the cost of production, thereby ensuring a profit.

The availability of hard currency is an important factor for the foreign businessperson since rubles are only traded within Russia and are not convertible on the world market, yet. As soon as you get off the plane, you will see that Russians are anxious to get consumer goods of all types and will pay a fair price — rubles or dollars — for them.

Controlling costs – practical considerations

The key factor for profitably doing business in Russia is cost control and effectiveness. You will need to make sure that your Russian partners and employees understand that costs — direct and indirect — affect profitability. To be successful in any business anywhere in the world over a sustained period of time, the business must:

- Generate revenues
- Control costs
- Achieve operating profits
- Manage assets
- Maintain productivity
- Satisfy customers

These criteria, by which businesses attain success in the United States, are equally relevant in Russia. You must educate your Russian partner about the importance of each of these criteria to success. Remember, all of these aspects of doing business are alien concepts to the Russian workforce since state-run enterprises did not have concerns over profit. If your partner does not have a Western business education or background, consider investing in a course of study in Western business practices for him or her.

Currently, several American universities and educational enterprises have established programs of business education in Russia. For example, the American Institute of Business and Economics, located in Moscow, states its designated mission as "the preparation of young Russian men and women for leadership roles in their country's market economy."

Courses are taught by faculty from the United States and other English-speaking countries, using standard American course materials to teach students aspects of American culture, including participatory democracy, initiative, honesty, fairness, and the ethical conduct of business.

The Russians have not adopted all features of the American model for doing business, and it is unlikely that they ever will. But, they are trying to understand it.

Junior Achievement – Russian style

Junior Achievement, an educational program for schoolchildren originating in the United States, was introduced in Russia in 1991. The Junior Achievement economics textbook, *Project Business*, is currently used by more than 42,000 schoolchildren throughout Russia. At the 1993 International Junior Achievement Conference, a group of Russians became the first non-American team to win the international entrepreneurial contest award!

When the Junior Achievement Program was imported from the United States, the program's creation and direction reflected a perestroika-era approach of emulating U.S. society. Evidence of Russian reluctance to accept the American model for doing business comes from the current Russian leadership of the Junior Achievement Program, which has asked that the organization reframe its American-based ideas for a Russian context.

According to Sergei Micksin, a former director of a communist youth organization who now works as executive director for Russia's Junior Achievement Program, "If Junior Achievement attempts to alter its own program to adapt to Russian society, then it risks losing the integrity of its ideas. The current Russian economic business structure may be uniquely Russian or just uniquely collapsed." Micksin has solicited professors at Moscow State University to adapt examples and theories in a new translation of the Junior Achievement textbook. "We must reform, but we cannot believe that all was bad [in the former Soviet Union]. After the Cold War, we need a cold analysis."

Micksin's comments may reflect the attitude of a former Communist bureaucrat and the desire of a socialist to combine socialism with the market economy.

Inquiries about Russia's Junior Achievement Program can be directed to the organization's Moscow office.

Junior Achievement Program – Russia
095-930-37-11
FAX: 095-930-05-42

Another example of resistance to the American model are the comments of Sophia Astakova of the Russian Academy of Sciences, Institute of World Economy and International Relations, reported in her article on mortgage lending in Russia, which appeared in the *Business World Weekly* (December, No. 12/105).

The performance of the credit system is an indicative criterium for determining the country's maturity in terms of economic relations. The most developed credit system in the world exists in the United States of America. But Russia's experience shows that the American model, however effective, should not be thoughtlessly adopted but studied and adapted to fit our specific conditions.

Ms. Astakova goes on to report that:

Although a number of mortgage banks are officially registered in Russia, no actual crediting is yet in progress. This is mainly due to the absence of a legal mechanism for registering mortgages and collateral claims. So neither the creditor nor the mortgagee have any legal protection ....

Easily, you can realize that until the legal mechanisms catch up, implementing an American model for doing business — including mortgages — is not entirely feasible.

You need a business plan

The problems experienced in day-to-day operations in Russia will be magnified by the absence of an effective business plan because of the ever-changing and unpredictable legal and economic environment in Russia. A flexible business plan is a must first step. Your Russian business plan will differ from a regular plan because you must work out sufficient details and be flexible enough to accommodate a number of obstacles. Your plan should include:

- A reliable analysis of the available market;
- An estimate of proprietary position;
- An assessment of barriers to entry of the market;
- Plans for obtaining funds to purchase materials and machines;
- Sources and methods for providing a reliable and uninterrupted supply of materials and machinery necessary for production;
- Methods for obtaining a reliable labor force;
- Designation of management authority and rights;
- Provisions for establishment of a reliable and modern means of communication;
- Specifics of accounting methods for recording expenses and revenue and tracking sales dynamics;
- Procedures for collections; and

- An analysis of claims on revenue relating to both direct and indirect operating costs.

As you can see, a plan for doing business in Russia requires that you think through many details that are taken for granted with a business in the United States. For example, determining direct and indirect costs in the United States is a relatively simple operation compared to the Russian system.

In Russia, in addition to the usual overhead costs, many of your indirect costs are 'hidden' costs, such as payments or negotiated expenditures towards organized crime or 'community development.' Your business' success or failure depends on understanding the Russian system of getting through the red tape.

The following sections of this chapter offer information, advice, and solutions for solving other problems — such as accounting methods and bank payment options, communications, transport, and obtaining a reliable workforce — that are outside the usual experience of U.S. business plans.

Accounting and payment options

The success of any business depends upon truth and trust. Trust is built on a foundation of truth. Too often, your Russian counterpart will want to impress you with a rosy picture of the current and future situation. This is natural since your expectations and those of your partner regarding economic performance may differ.

Accounting. Insist upon the accuracy of information supplied and reported to you. Agreements should spell out in detail material representations of fact and the consequences of fraud. Explain to your Russian partner that only with truth will each of you be able to ascertain where your business has been.

If you know where your business has been as a starting point, then you will be able to determine where your business currently is. Given those two points of reference, you will be able to project with some accuracy where your business is going.

Simply stated in an accountant's jargon, quickly educate your Russian partner on the importance of:

- A financial statement — where you have been;
- A balance sheet — where you currently are; and
- A cash flow projection — where you are going.

As banks develop and investment capital becomes more plentiful, the availability of accurate financial data concerning your business will be vital in providing the analysis of the three Cs of creditworthiness — character, capacity, and collateral — that lending institutions look for before making loans. So don't forget to highlight this potential benefit of using realistic accounting practices with your partner.

Familiarity with Western accounting principles varies substantially among Russian businessmen and women — from a few Harvard MBAs to the bottom of the bell curve. The foremost reason for this fundamental lack is due to the short history of free enterprise in the country. Under the Soviet command economy, making a profit was not a relevant consideration — the task was simply to produce the needed commodities, using the available workforce. Without this orientation towards profit, the Russian enterprise system naturally is ill-equipped to deal with the pertinent aspects of profit. This also explains why the banking and taxation systems are not well enough developed to easily fit in with the Western style of doing business.

Payment options. Russia's banking system is just barely six years old, and has expanded substantially in the past few years, becoming the fastest developing sector in Russia. Refer to Chapter 5 for more information about the banking sector.

At one time, regular business transactions between Russian companies sometimes took months to execute, whereas now, most transactions are completed in days. Improvements in the system have made it possible for foreign companies to perform a number of traditional banking transactions that were not previously possible, including transferring money to and from foreign and domestic banks.

If you are planning to do business in Russia, you should be aware of the various methods available for Russian and foreign companies to settle payments. One method not available is payment by check, since there is no such thing as a checking account in Russia. Russia's payment system, developed for a centrally planned economy, does not have a well-developed infrastructure for payments, since payments traditionally were secondary to both production and locating supply sources.

Most consumers in Russia only use cash for retail transactions; however, debit and credit cards are becoming popular. Most foreign businesspeople find that the easiest payment method to use is a hard currency credit card. Russian credit cards are structured differently since most Russians have no credit history. Cards are issued based on payment of sufficient funds in advance.

Debit cards are becoming commonplace as employers distribute these to pay employees' wages and salaries. Debit cards reduce the paperwork and accounting involved in distributing pay.

Enterprises and government agencies make transactions using payment orders and purchase orders. Electronic debit and credit transfers are made based upon the manual paperwork that must be processed, which until recently took a couple of months to settle. Many commercial banks are now members of the Society for Worldwide Interbank Financial Telecommunications (SWIFT), which greatly improves the speed of cash settlements. International cash transfers can now be settled in fewer than three days and domestic cash transfers within Russia take four to five days. SWIFT also makes it easier to finance trade with letters of credit.

To use letters of credit, your bank in the United States will need to have a correspondent relationship with your trading partner's bank in Russia. Establishing a corresponding relationship between the bank of the foreign investor and a reliable Russian bank at the outset of business operations may pay dividends when future financing of an investment project is necessary.

Communications

Communications in any Russian business are currently inferior and substandard at best. Russia's telecommunications system is severely outdated, however, the present obsolete infrastructure is impossible to replace wholesale due to hard currency shortages. Russian fax lines are unreliable and the quality of faxed messages is often poor. E-mail is a more reliable tool of communication in comparison to fax machines.

While Russian communities are seeking investments by foreign phone companies, for now, you will have to tolerate static, cut lines, and misrouted calls. In some areas, you can use cellular phones, solving some of the local problems. For international calls and faxes, you will want to subscribe to one of the new satellite services.

The mail service is also antiquated, unpredictable, and unreliable. However, many larger cities now have courier services you can use. Keep in mind how many sales you may lose because of poor communications, and solve these problems beforehand in your business plan.

Transport

One of the largest problems you may have is providing for reliable and uninterrupted shipments of supplies, materials, and equipment. Likewise, you will also need to consider how to ensure dependable distribution of your products and goods.

Several factors in Russia contribute to the present inadequacies of the transportation sector. The first factor has to do with attitude. The transport network in Russia is based on the previous command economy, which means the focus is on production — not service, reliability, timeliness, efficiency, or in the case of passengers, comfort.

The second factor affecting the transport system is the rising cost of fuel. The rising prices have eaten up revenues, with the net result being the lack of funds to upgrade or even maintain facilities in some cases, and the bankruptcy of other transport firms.

The third factor hurting the industry is the lack of modern technology and equipment needed to stay abreast of the changes in the types of freight being shipped. Instead of heavy industrial goods and machinery, much of what is shipped today consists of lighter consumer goods.

Each segment of the transport industry — railroads, trucking, airports, and shipping port facilities — suffer universally from these factors, plus have unique problems within each segment, as well.

Added to the weaknesses of the existing system are the sheer size of the land itself and the increased demands brought about by the new market economy. As trade levels continue to increase, so will the need for better equipment, improved facilities, and better airports, road networks, and railroads.

Although improvements are on the horizon with planning, funding, and bidding in the works, you will need to work out immediate solutions as part of your business plan. To succeed requires patience and innovation — the desired result is a steady supply of quality products and a high level of service.

Some U.S. businesses have solved the problem by creating their own distribution networks. For example, Certified Industries International, Inc., with offices in Los Angeles and Moscow, distributes more than 100,000 products to hotels, supermarkets, restaurants, and embassies throughout Russia. The business determined, first of all, through market research that virtually guaranteed delivery would be a key element for success. To accomplish this goal meant arranging all the details for ordering goods and providing freight, transportation, customs, warehousing, security, and eventual delivery to the customer. Certified Industries had to become a very service-intensive operation.

A complex part of this service is getting goods through customs. If you plan to set up your own distribution, take the time to learn all the intricacies of your local customs authorities. Customs procedures in Russia are like most other law functions — bureaucratic, confusing, and subject to frequent changes without notice.

Some U.S. businesses are able to use the existing distribution network. These businesses establish joint ventures with those local entrepreneurs who are well-connected and know how to do things the old way.

If you are going to ship to the Russian Far East, you have some further considerations. The biggest mistake you can make here is to try to ship from the European Continent. The system of roads is extremely poor, a number of natural obstacles are located on the route, few gas stations are found along the way, and the 6,000 miles between Moscow and Vladivostok create considerable wear and tear on your cargo.

Although the vast trans-Siberian railroad could be an option, entire train cars and containers have disappeared from this route. Your best solutions are either shipping by air or ocean transport. An international airport is located in Khabarovsk, two hours from Vladivostok.

If you plan to ship by ocean transport, the Maritime Administration of the U.S. Department of Transportation has initiated an award program for those shippers who use substantial services from U.S. flagged vessels. The agency also has a helpline to provide guidance on shipping waterborne goods. For further information, contact:

Maritime Administration – Office of Market Promotion
U.S. Department of Transportation
(202) 366-5517
(202) 366-5508 (Helpline)

If you would like a list of transport companies operating in Russia, contact the Business Information Service for the Newly Independent States (BISNIS), which is described in Chapter 13.

Labor force problems

As you become acquainted with the qualities and idiosyncrasies of the Russian workforce, you will at first be convinced that the incompetent and substandard workers of the world are seeking to unite. But, don't be fooled by appearances. In actuality Russia's labor force is very literate and highly skilled. However, after 70 years of socialism, old habits are difficult to break. Jobs used to be life-long and unemployment was nonexistent. The prevailing attitude about money-making being a dirty game still lingers.

For example, Russian employees, if not trained to accommodate Western standards, will not give appropriate attention to phone, fax, or E-mail messages. A phone will be left ringing, while a roomful of employees look on without even considering picking it up. Your workers will hold back on taking responsibility since motivation was previously frowned upon and even penalized. Accordingly, letters and messages you send should be addressed to the individual intended to receive the message, thereby increasing the chance that the message will be received. Addressing anything with, "to whom it may concern," simply will not work. Traditional Russian business is a slow process — often phone calls are not returned for three or four days, if ever.

In the past, Russian businesses have only circulated information along a vertical hierarchy basis. Russian employees should be encouraged to develop horizontal links of communication among departments and people of the same level to encourage and stimulate productivity. Form horizontal task groups to introduce the concept of personnel informing each other about solutions to problems. Keep in mind how much noninvolved and disinterested employees will cost.

Deal directly with cultural differences — such as everyday behaviors, like those described above, and business ethics — existing between Russian and foreign employees, and develop plans and take action to overcome these differences. The interaction of both Russian and foreign personnel together is beneficial towards this goal. Interaction serves to educate foreigners to the realities of Russia's current business environment and imperatives, and increases your Russian employees' familiarity with foreign technological management and behavior patterns.

Housing. In providing living accommodations for foreign personnel living in Russia, keep in mind that the availability of Western-style apartments and office space is limited and the prices are extremely high — prices rival those charged in Tokyo, Japan. Foreign personnel assigned to Russia should anticipate substandard apartment quality if you cannot locate Western-style housing for them.

Conditions in Russian apartments are described as tolerable only to the very young or the very hearty. Problems encountered with landlords include the landlord not adhering to the agreed lease period, renting out apartments for which he or she has no right, and leaving his or her personal belongings in the apartment for the tenant to live around. In Moscow heating is centrally controlled for large parts of the city. Of course, the heat goes off in the spring, even though it is still needed and does not come on again until later in the fall, even though it was needed much sooner.

Hot water in Moscow undergoes a similar procedure each summer for several weeks as portions of the system are shut down for cleaning — apparently according to an unpredictable schedule of rotation. Space heaters and a small hot water heater can solve these inconveniences. Realize that substandard living conditions have been one of the leading causes of foreign personnel leaving Russia.

Strict and hidden labor laws. Labor in Russia is extremely regulated and Russia's labor code is massive. Pay particular attention and carefully analyze existing Russian labor laws and the forms of contracts entered into with employees before entering into employment relationships. For example, in a recent case reported in *The Wall Street Journal*, two female employees who were fired from the Moscow Radisson Hotel successfully sued the hotel and were awarded damages by a Russian court, interpreting a little-known Russian labor law. The women were also allowed to keep their jobs, notwithstanding that their work was substandard and their one-year contracts of employment had run out!

The old Russian labor code, which is still in effect, all but guarantees employees their jobs after they have completed a three-month probation period. While foreign businesses can hire Russians freely, firing them is another matter. You must compile a record of absences or other transgressions — except for extreme employee misconduct — in order to fire a worker at all.

Under Russian law, contracts with time limits are viewed as binding in the case of executive employees, but such clauses as to term of employment are not applicable for workers. Russian employees also have the right to take very long maternity leaves and other leaves with pay. You also must allow the organization of trade unions, with which you then must enter into collective compensation agreements. Avoid direct employment by an American company if the choice of law in the contract is Russian.

You should also be aware of a political perception that Russians should not be slaves of Western businesspeople. Look out for substantial indirect costs in this area!

Loyalty. An additional problem that has presented itself in Russia is that well-qualified workers, aware of the marketplace and lacking in loyalty, tend to jump ship. They will leave you, as their employer, without notice in order to join other businesses, which will pay them more, even though they have signed contracts of employment for two or three years and may even have been sent to school and trained by you. Offer bonuses to your employees to keep them loyal.

The patriots. The current generation of Russian businesspeople have been trained in an obsolete economic system and have watched the collapse of their nation as a superpower. This has caused some to become personally selfish and, on occasion, untrustworthy. As has been indicated in Chapter 2, the most essential ingredient for success at doing business in Russia is the selection of an appropriate partner.

A class of Russian society, known as 'patriots' by their countrymen, are characterized by high intelligence, patience, integrity, dedication, resourcefulness, and courage. These are the best people of Russia, and they may be found at all levels of society, and in all religions. These are the people you will want to employ or to have as your partners. Their loyalty is to their families and children and to Mother Russia (RODINA). If you doubt this, remember these 'patriots' smashed Nazi Germany 50 years ago for love of country — not for Karl Marx and not because of the fear of "So So" DJUGESHVILI (Joseph Stalin). The United States has no common experience, yet it is something every American businessperson should respect about the potential capabilities and the determination of Russians.

Summary and recommendations

The business environment in Russia can be likened to a labyrinth, created by an imperfect government with imperfect legislation, designed imperfectly with convoluted paths leading to the contradictory regulation of activities of foreign investors, including registration, taxation, currency, and customs control.

Additionally, the presence of organized crime cannot be underestimated — the next chapter discusses this topic. For these reasons, to be successful in Russia, reliable information — the truth — must be sought and obtained from qualified personnel, including lawyers and consulting firms, as well as governmental institutions.

The cost of consultants is a direct cost. Legal entanglements are the quintessential examples of indirect costs. Below are the key points to consider during the day-to-day operations of your business.

- Understand the mind set of your Russian partner and the mind set of Russian workers. Be aware that there is a resistance to abandon the cultural heritage of Russia entirely and, in some cases, the experiences of 70 years of socialism. Naturally, most Russians seek to minimize the humiliation of having been held back for the most productive 70 years in human history, as well as having been forced to invest a good portion of their lives under the control of a bankrupt and thoroughly refuted ideology. But, do remember the triumphs of Sputnik, Oksana Bayul, and Stalingrad.

- Understand the importance of educating your Russian partner in the elements of profitability, the importance of productivity, the elements of creditworthiness, and the requirements of successful, sustained business operations.

- Before entering into any employment contracts, seek out appropriate consultation and legal advice concerning the requirements of Russian labor law, including the applicability of length of employment clauses and noncompete provisions. Be aware that mandatory injunctions prohibiting defecting employees from leaving your company and taking a better job do not exist. Encourage loyalty through perks.

- Remember that Russia has undergone enormous change in the past 100 years and that the people have demonstrated a patience and resiliency unequalled in the modern world. Russia contains a highly literate and skilled labor force, and the transition to the market economy has actually been occurring at an exponential pace, considering the state of the country in 1990 and notwithstanding pessimistic press accounts written by the 'chicken littles' of this world.

- Be aware of the particular environment in which your foreign employees will find themselves in Russia, and be aware of and mitigate the hardships that they will encounter while there.

- Insist upon truthful communications and representations at the outset in all dealings. Insist on truth as a condition for trust.

- Be skeptical of official economic data relating to productivity released by the Russian government since very little data is available on the emerging privatized businesses and industry, which currently comprise approximately 50 percent of the Russian economy.

- Be aware of the existence of organized crime and all other forms of indirect costs, which may develop into claims on revenue for your operation.

Above all, breathe some of the exhilarating spirit of a new capitalism, which is spreading through Russia like a wildfire. It will open your mind and reinforce your faith in the importance of the market economy. You may be privileged over the next decade to watch the transition from embryo to super economic power. ZA RODINU (a toast meaning, "To the motherland!").

Chapter 9

Organized Crime in Russia
Преступность

Crime in the news

Mass media of the Western democracies has brought the art of reporting bad news to absolute perfection. Sometimes, watching U.S. television newscasts and programs, a Russian wonders how on earth people can live in such a violent country as America. And yet, foreigners who come to the United States see many rural people not locking their homes. Furthermore, suburban homes have more windows than walls, and the thickness of those walls is very often such that a criminal does not need to have a black belt to break into the house through them. Of course, big city crime is another subject, but people — particularly foreigners to the United States — tend to forget that New York City is no more the whole of America than Moscow of Russia.

Post-Soviet media, at one time specializing in reporting good news of events at home, has quickly and brilliantly mastered the art of sensationalism and the macabre. Now, this sensationalized news is picked up by foreign news correspondents in Russia and reported to their home bureaus. And why not? This is what the Soviet media did in the old days as propaganda. Beyond any doubt, the new methods of news coverage being used by the Russian media have become one of the many reasons for the decrease of trust in Russia's present-day administration.

In a random poll among Russia's urban populations, 1,600 people were asked by the Russian Center for Public Opinion and Market Research: "Is corruption among today's Russian authorities encountered on fewer occasions than among Soviet leaders of Brezhnev's times?" The results were not encouraging — only 4 percent believe that today's authorities are less corrupt, 34 percent believe things are the same as before, and 47 percent think today's politicians are more corrupt. Other results revealed in the survey show that in big cities, 18 percent had been subjected to paying bribes — 23 percent in Moscow — but in small towns, the figure was less. Furthermore, only 9 percent still believe in Boris Yeltsin's honesty. As Yuri Levada, the director of Public Opinion Center, put it, "Power corrupts, anarchy corrupts even more so." (*Moscow News*, October 14, 1994)

Mr. Sergei Khrushchev who is the son of Nikita Khrushchev, the late shoe-banging General Secretary of the Soviet Communist Party, is indeed repeating the truth in his article published in the *Washington Post* that, "Racketeering, hostage-taking, bank bombings, constant shoot-outs on the streets and in the restaurants, even the use of heavy weapons in disputes between criminals — all these things worry today's Russians more than the increasing problem of unemployment." Since young Khrushchev now lives in the United States — which seems to be typical for children of ex-leaders of the Communist Party — he naturally repeats what he has read in the Russian papers and on Russian news programs that are transmitted to the United States.

What worries Russians

Russians are indeed less worried by the growing rates of unemployment, but for wholly psychological reasons. In Russia no unemployment occurred, in the Western sense of the word, for almost 60 years. A constant demand for work hands was the norm because of the lack of modern technology. So, the people cannot believe that this is now a current threat.

For almost the same reason, the Russian people are panicky today about crime. For 60 years, it was absolutely safe to walk in the streets of any town, including Moscow, at night or in the small hours of the morning. Now Russians do have to worry about crime, not only because they hear about it more due to the sensationalized news media, but because of an actual increase.

Extortion

Many of the worst crimes in Russia can be attributed to organized crime. As a Russian government official said at a business security conference sponsored by the U.S. Chamber of Commerce in Moscow:

Sooner or later, one expects to meet up with racketeers. But paying up is a big mistake. Contacts with Russia's underworld often end up in violence. Nine businessmen have been killed and 293 — both Russian and American — kidnapped, a 10 percent increase from 1993.

According to the *Moscow Times*, the majority of incidents involving foreigners took place in St. Petersburg, and extortion was the most popular crime against foreigners. Russian anticrime experts note that this type of crime usually starts with security demands, then is followed by a request to put their people on your staff in a minor position. Soon the racketeers are running your business. The recommendations of anticrime experts are:

- Stall for time
- Contact your embassy
- Contact the antiorganized crime police

So far, the antiorganized crime police report 100 percent effectiveness against the Mafia when a foreigner reports the trouble quickly.

Steven Zaiesner of the *Moscow Times* relates a U.S. government official as saying:

The more noise a person makes, the safer he or she will be. The Mafia will move on to easier targets. If you coordinate with your embassy and the police, it becomes too much of a hassle for the Mafia to bother with you. There are plenty of easy targets here.

In a recent survey by the U.S. Chamber of Commerce of 199 businesses operating in Russia, only 19 have been approached for protection. While only four decided to pay, the rest had no repercussions.

Economic crimes

A major problem faced by the Russian government is that of financial crimes. With a fledgling economy and underdeveloped monetary laws, these crimes pose a major threat to Russia's economic well-being.

The infiltration of organized crime into the banking industry is a significant contributing factor. According to Tass Agency Reports (Spring 1994):

As a rule, the means for processing illegal activities, including theft of government property, bribes, and cheating, lie in their transferral to foreign bank accounts. In achieving this, tax evasion and the breaking of the customs and bank laws of foreign countries are common occurrences.

Joint ventures, exchanges, organizations implementing government programs, barter agreements and bank operations connected with ruble conversion and the use of credit cards are all being used for money laundering purposes. Crimes connected with import/export operations of large state enterprises, are the main source of "dirty" money, utilizing commercial firms and middlemen.

Posing with foreign partners as owning supplies and products, they cause the existing detriment to manufacturing enterprises. They quote false prices, either very low import prices or very high export prices, embezzling the payment under a fictitious import contract and delaying the transferral of the hard currency proceeds upon receiving the full proceeds for deposit, and then illegally transferring the hard currency proceeds from the legal entity to the private individual.

Another, much more wide-spread form of crime is happening in the credit-bank sphere. The goal appears to be embezzling huge sums of money from its last conversion to foreign hard currencies through exchanges and commercial banks. According to the calculations of experts at the Ministry of the Interior, close to 2.68 billion dollars passed through the Moscow Interbank Currency Exchange (MICEX) in 1992. No less than one-third was acquired through false letters of advice. Falsified bank documents are used even more often, in particular as liabilities guarantees which are given out by various government structures, agreements on the fulfillment of work and services, and also documents which certify individuals of foreign partners.

A very typical source of crime can be found in the financial-bank establishments which have been reduced to the following:

- *Reporting false information about members' transactions, presenting falsified documents which identify individuals as employers or owners of firms and their competence for concluding business transactions and conducting negotiations;*
- *Using distorted information for the registration of enterprises;*

- *Using distorted information, falsified documents for the completion of transactions, such as fictitious licenses and agreements for receiving pre-payments;*

- *Breaching confidences by undoubtedly distorting transactions' meanings, substituting the participation of the contractor and implementing hidden mediation which is usually in the form of a secret middleman posing as the owner of a firm participating in the deal. He then obtains the prepayment, changes the meaning of the transaction and brings in a third party that changes the quantity of production, form of payment, and sets up the possibility for the embezzlement of the available credits provided for in the agreement;*

- *Full or partial falsification of bank documents, including false information about individuals issuing checks, the size of the sum, which is transferred to the receiver of the check. They then use a fake receiver when the available sum is issued; and*

- *Violating the obligations of the agreement and notoriously misleading the creditors, and misappropriating the credit resources from the deal through the bank employees.*

As is shown by the analysis done by the Scientific Research Institute of Russia's Ministry of Internal Affairs, it is nearly impossible to detect the crimes after the "dirty" money has passed from bank account to bank account in various foreign banks.

The seminar's participants assessed Russia's existing bank, customs, tax, and hard currency legislation for their inadequacy in the new economic process. They also discussed with Russian entrepreneurs the insufficiency in other areas of government control with regards to international economic regulations.

In addition, they announced the need for working off the operating mechanisms of the existing economic, administrative, and criminal sanctions in relation to the offenses of legal [entities] and natural [individual] persons. For example, the procedures for confiscating property, particularly the concentrated amount abroad, for causal detriment compensation were discussed.

Tass Agency sources also report that for the past two years, it is estimated that more than R 500 billion — roughly $140 million — worth of crime has been prevented. The entire task of exposing crime is subdivided into several main areas of economic crime. Table 18 below shows some of the results reported by Russia's Ministry of Internal Affairs for 1993.

Table 18: Economic Crimes in Russia by Type

Type of crime	Quantity	Percent (%)
All registered economic crimes	110,408	100
Serious economic crimes	23,313	21
Embezzlement (not including minor)	60,292	55
Of these 60,292, the number that are very serious	10,699	
Embezzlement including appropriation, squandering, and abuse of official power	37,306	34
Of these 37,306, the number which are very serious	7,537	
Embezzlement through cheating	5,787	5
Of these 5,787, the number which are very serious	1,749	
Bribery	4,497	4
Violations of hard currency operations laws	5,881	5
Manufacturing or marketing counterfeit money or securities	7,061	6
Illegal trading activities	4,525	4

The table reveals more than 110,000 economic crimes. Preliminary results show that 23,313 of them, or roughly one out of every five, are considered to be serious crimes.

As before, the priorities for the Department of Economic Crimes at Russia's Ministry of Internal Affairs remain to be the more severe crimes, which include embezzlement, bribery, offenses regarding hard-currency laws, and counterfeiting money. Nearly 80,000 of the total number of economic crimes fall into this category.

Table 19: Business Economic Crimes by Region

Region	Number of crimes
Moscow	1,580
Rostovski	1,317
Tatarstan	1,245
Novosibirsk	1,139
Krasnodar	1,089

The workers of the Ministry of Internal Affairs are alarmed that most of the crimes connected with embezzlement, misappropriation of funds, squandering funds, or abuse of official power are being committed by registered entities. During 1993, the number of these types of crimes committed by businesses in specific cities and regions are listed above in Table 19.

Table 20 below shows the geographic spread and the proportions and total number of occurrences for all of the types of severe economic crimes. The crimes listed in previous Table 18 are shown by geographic regions in which the crimes occurred.

Table 20: Economic Crimes in Russia by Region

Region	All economic crimes		Embezzlement crimes	
	Total	Serious	Total	Serious
All Regions	110,408	23,313	37,306	7,537
Northern	3,701	718	1,135	275
North-Western	5,353	1,079	889	191
Central	20,341	4,920	6,387	1,282
Volgo-Vyatski	5,350	1,041	2,101	391
Central Chernozemni	5,984	1,269	2,334	431
Povolzhski	13,255	2,383	5,061	925
North Caucasus	12,366	3,560	4,297	1,002
Urals	12,770	2,299	3,854	889
Western Siberia	9,656	2,027	3,700	875
Eastern Siberia	5,960	1,216	2,562	478
Far East	6,145	1,333	1,840	434

* Embezzlement by means of appropriation, squandering funds, and abuses of power.

In a country that has a quickly deteriorating situation in the sphere of money circulation, the urgent need to protect itself — by stabilizing the growth rate of these dangerous manifestations, such as counterfeit money and securities — is apparent.

However, during the last two months of 1994, the number of counterfeiting types of crimes that were exposed rose by more than 30 percent. While the total for 1993 was only 7,061, the number over the past year has increased by 2,120.4 percent. So, efforts to deter these crimes have certainly not been extremely successful.

Solving the problems

In June 1994, President Yeltsin signed a decree granting police sweeping powers, including the right to detain a suspect for up to a month without making formal charges, and examine the financial affairs of anyone suspected of organized crime. The police now have the right to search offices and dwellings without a court order. For the first time in post-Communist times, police have access to bank accounts and other commercial information of organizations suspected of criminal activity.

Police have reason to believe that at least 35,000 Russian businesses are controlled by crime gangs. The decree caused an outcry of protest from Russian liberals and Communists in the Parliament. The eternal dream of liberals to have their cake and eat it too seems to be universal.

However, those who think that Russia's Mafia works only in Russia are deeply mistaken. Today, banks and industries of a number of Western countries are very well propped-up by Russian 'dirty' dollars. Russian Mafia leaders feel themselves much safer abroad, and whereas the U.S. consulate in Moscow is particularly meticulous in issuing visas to unmarried women — the concern is over mail-order brides — some top Russian Mafioso figures are comfortably residing in the United States. For some reason, Russian publications on this subject are never translated for the benefit of American readers.

A new spirit of cooperation, with exchanges of information across international lines, has been inaugurated by the U.S. and Russian security agencies. That is why the working meeting between Louis J. Freeh, director of the FBI, and Victor F. Yerin, Russia's Minister of Interior was of particular significance. The agreed minutes of that meeting are reprinted at the end of this chapter.

Summary and recommendations

In early 1994, Russia's police reported that a substantial number of state-owned enterprises and a high percentage of the private sector are influenced by organized crime in some capacity.

As you are aware, the total damages are extremely high, reaching trillions of rubles in 1993. Experts estimate that if businesses did not have to pay organized crime, prices would go down by 20 to 30 percent.

If you are in business and decide to remain in Russia for some time, you will eventually have to deal with organized crime. If you are approached by soft-spoken, well-dressed men, here are some tips from the U.S. Department of Commerce for how to deal with them.

- Tell them that you are a foreigner who does not interfere in internal matters.
- Tell them you will have to consult your superiors abroad and inform your embassy.
- Ask for time to think.
- Be invariably polite, but resolute and firm.
- Indicate that by harming you they will not get anywhere.
- Use the head of your security department for further negotiations.
- Meanwhile, lose no time — approach your police contacts and the Department for Fighting Organized Crime.

Remember, organized crime elements usually approach medium-sized and larger businesses. The Mafia's preferred method of extortion is to blackmail businesspeople — who supposedly possess hefty sums of cash — over problematic tax-paying records.

While organized crime is one of the major problems in Russian society, you will need to protect yourself from other crimes as well. The next chapter deals with everyday security matters and how to protect yourself and your family.

**Agreed Minutes of a Working Meeting
between
The Director of the Federal Bureau of Investigation (FBI),
United States Department of Justice, and
The Minister of the Interior (MVD) of
The Russian Federation**

July 2–5, 1994, the FBI Director Louis J. Freeh visited Moscow at the invitation of the Interior Minister of the Russian Federation Viktor F. Yerin.

During the course of the discussions the Minister and the Director noted the importance of the meetings between the representatives of the MVD and the FBI held in 1993–1994, in Washington, D.C. and Moscow, which facilitated establishing the necessary understanding and foundation for a long-term cooperative relationship between the FBI and the MVD.

The sides expressed their deep concern about the fact that international organized crime constitutes a major threat to both of their countries. International organized crime groups are committing criminal acts which include murder, theft, extortion, fraud, robbery, kidnapping, drug trafficking, financial crimes such as money laundering, and other serious crimes in both the United States and Russia. They carry out illegal activities on their own, but also establish close contracts with other organized crime and drug trafficking groups.

In the course of the discussions, the sides stressed the need to enhance the exchange of information concerning the activities of organized criminal groups, specific criminals and their associates. Furthermore, the sides concluded that joint and coordinated actions between their respective agencies as well as other law enforcement agencies of the United States within the Department of Justice and the Department of the Treasury are necessary to identify, investigate and prosecute these international criminal organizations effectively. In addition, both sides expressed the desire to develop technical cooperation between the MVD and U.S. law enforcement agencies.

The Russian side welcomed the establishment of a Legal Attache Office of the FBI in the Embassy of the United States of America in Moscow and noted that it would be an important step in enhancing coordinated efforts to combat crime.

Desiring to counteract aggressively international organized crime and to promote cooperation between our countries in the prevention, investigation and prosecution of criminal matters, the Minister of the Interior of the Russian Federation and the Director of the FBI stated the following:

1. Respect for Sovereignty. Both the FBI and the MVD pledge to respect and observe the sovereignty of the United States and Russia, and to comply with the laws and regulations of each nation as well as applicable domestic or international agreements, treaties, or other memoranda of understanding.

2. *Exchange of Information.* Both agencies intend to exchange information, as deemed appropriate, to assist in the identification, investigation, apprehension, and prosecution of suspects in organized crime and other criminal matters of mutual concern to both countries, subject to the existing laws and regulations of each nation as well as applicable domestic or international agreements, treaties, or other memoranda of understanding.

3. *Availability of Personnel Through Embassies.* It is the intent of both agencies to make liaison officers and other employees available, as deemed appropriate, to assist in the identification, investigation, and prosecution of suspects in organized crime and other criminal matters of mutual concern to both countries, subject to the existing laws and regulations of each nation as well as applicable domestic or international agreements, treaties, or other memoranda of understanding.

To further this objective, the FBI will open a Legal Attache Office in the Embassy of the United States of America in Moscow staffed with FBI agents whose job will be to work in partnership with Russian law enforcement officials on criminal and other law enforcement matters of joint concern as discussed above. Likewise, the Russian side expressed the intent to open a Legal Attache Office of the MVD in the Embassy of the Russian Federation in Washington, D.C.

4. *Requests for Assistance.* Any requests for criminal information or investigation of organized crime and other criminal matters of mutual concern to both countries should include a sufficient factual basis to establish that a reasonable belief exists that a person or persons have committed, are committing, or may commit criminal violation(s) recognized by the country providing the investigative assistance.

5. *Channels for Exchanging Information.* Routine communications and requests should be routed through the appropriate FBI or MVD legal attache's offices, when they are opened, located in the respective embassies, while emergency requests may be made directly to the FBI or MVD, with copies to the legal attaches.

6. *Points of Contact.* To ensure that assistance is rendered and information is exchanged in a timely fashion, both agencies will designate additional points of contact. To that end, and to ensure that timely and effective contact is maintained between the agencies, all contact with the FBI should be through the Criminal Investigative Division. All contact with the MVD should be coordinated with the Office of Foreign Relations and the appropriate unit of the Main Department on Organized Crime.

Done at Moscow, this 5th day of July, 1994, in duplicate in the English and Russian languages.

For the United States
Department of Justice:

For the Ministry of the Interior
of the Russian Federation:

_____

_____

Louis J. Freeh

Viktor F. Yerin

Director
Federal Bureau of Investigation

Minister of the Interior
Russian Federation

Chapter 10

Crime and Security

Меры предосторожности

Protecting yourself from crime

Whether you are a diplomat, tourist, foreign businessperson, homemaker, student, or ordinary visitor, your stay in Russia will be enjoyable if you follow the guidelines in this chapter. These guidelines have been put together by the U.S. Department of Commerce. They originally appeared in that organization's publication, *U.S. Firms in Russia: A Handbook for Doing Business in Russia*, and have been excerpted and paraphrased with permission for inclusion here.

In every country, the attitude the local people will adopt towards you as a foreigner is determined by your ability to conform to or act in accordance with their laws — and even their customs and traditions — as well as by your level of knowledge regarding the internal situation. To a large extent, your personal safety and the security of your property depend on this.

Crime is increasing in many countries and Russia is no exception. Therefore, you cannot ignore the problem of security and safety in this country. If you know how to behave in specific circumstances and follow advice and recommendations about personal safety and security of property, you can help reduce the risk of becoming a crime victim.

Currently, Russia is facing hard times. With the disintegration of the Soviet Union, Russian society has experienced some negative phenomena, such as a sharp increase in crime in recent years. The way of life in Russia has considerably changed due to political instability, social and economic shocks, and ethnic unrest in some regions of the area once called the USSR. Many negative elements of society have surfaced like dirty foam on water, making crime a serious social problem. Unfortunately, Russia's law enforcement agencies are not fully prepared and sufficiently equipped to cope with such an abrupt rise in crime.

In addition to traditional crimes committed against individuals and property, new crimes — such as extortion, kidnapping, robbery of banks and financial institutions, and attacks against entrepreneurs — are being reported. These crimes caused by today's economic and political instability, pose a serious danger not only to Russia's citizens, but to all foreigners, including you and your family. Therefore, you must learn and adhere to these elementary security guidelines.

However, the crime rate in Russia — and the Commonwealth of Independent States (CIS) as a whole — is not higher than what is reported in some Western countries. In the United States, during the 1980s for example, as many as 13 million criminal offenses were registered annually with the Federal Bureau of Investigation. Meanwhile, Russia's 1992 crime figure was roughly 3 million. But, you cannot assume because of this that your personal security and the safety of your property are not threatened in Russia. For instance, the 'criminal world' in cities such as Moscow, St. Petersburg, Vladivostok, and Kaliningrad has become very active in recent years. Indeed, the number of crimes against foreign citizens in Russia has nearly doubled. Table 21 below gives some of the crime statistics reported for 1993.

Table 21: Types of Crimes Committed

Type of crime	By foreigners	Against foreigners
Heinous crimes including:	3,971	3,863
Homicide and attempted murder	243	169
Intentional bodily harm	261	234
Rape and attempted rape	173	32
Property theft	5,380	5,970
Violent robbery	750	1,049
Nonviolent robbery	1,167	2,073

Type of crime	By foreigners	Against foreigners
Fraud	653	223
Hooliganism	708	421
Drugs	2,462	79
Other	2,201	302
Total	17,297	13,980

Source: Interior Ministry of the Russian Federation.

Unfortunately, the same tendencies are prevailing in 1994 as you can see in Table 22, which shows the statistics for January and February 1994 by major region.

Table 22: Crimes Committed by Region

Region	By foreigners	Against foreigners
Moscow	1,474	793
Moscow region	256	29
St. Petersburg	1,054	277
Leningrad region	74	33
Russian Far East	407	362
Total	9,041	3,670

Source: Interior Ministry of the Russian Federation.

According to Russia's Interior Ministry, about 75,000 Americans — including tourists — visited Russia in 1993. Police reported 180 crimes committed against U.S. citizens — 103 in St. Petersburg during 1993. The most common crimes committed against Americans were theft (60 percent), robbery (17 percent), and auto theft (11 percent). The same source said that Americans committed six crimes, including one rape, a traffic violation, and petty thefts. In addition, the Russian authorities instituted administrative proceedings against 320 Americans charging them with registration and travel rule violations and residing in Russia with expired documents.

The crime rate is rising astronomically — in the first quarter of 1994, police registered 52 crimes against American citizens, with 34 crimes committed in Moscow and 18 in St. Petersburg.

In 1992 and 1993, Russian police arrested several criminal groups that had targeted foreigners. One of these groups had been attacking foreigners along the Minsk Highway. That group, arrested in December 1993, confessed to eight assaults against foreigners. The criminals' strategy included driving Mercedes-Benz automobiles to search for vehicles with foreign drivers. The group, which was armed with weapons, would stop these cars under various pretenses and rob the passengers.

In recent months, police have arrested several gangs for robbing foreign visitors traveling between international airports in Moscow. Foreign trucks transporting cargo from European counties are another favorite target.

When foreigners visited the former USSR, the KGB's 'guardianship' guaranteed personal security. Now the present situation in Russia differs greatly, and these same foreigners, used to that degree of safety, could be easy targets for criminals.

Personal security and property safety

Statistical data on crimes against foreigners show that almost 30 percent of these crimes occur in the streets and other public places and 50 percent in hotels and apartments. In many cases, the victims were careless. The practical tips listed below should help you avoid many dangerous situations. Many of these recommendations are common sense and are similar to those you would give to visitors in your home country.

If you are threatened by criminal assault or you become the victim of a crime, immediately call for police assistance. You may use one of your prepared Russian text cards — located at the end of this book — to help you communicate your need for assistance. The police emergency number in Moscow and most large cities in Russia is "02." The medical emergency number in most cities is "03."

Remember that swindlers are active in finance — as discussed in Chapter 9. Before doing business with a bank or other financial institution, attempt to verify its solvency, assets, and liabilities. This task can be quite difficult even for the state tax inspectors. Furthermore, do not change money with private individuals. This practice is illegal and many people who offer this service are hustlers or may use counterfeit bank notes.

Often, foreigners fall victim to crime in airports, train stations, sea and river ports, or around shops and hotels, markets and other public places. Criminals sometimes offer assistance in carrying luggage, providing car services, or helping to locate a hotel, among other things. If you need assistance, ask for help from authorized persons — such as porters, airport and train station officials, hotel clerks, and hotel porters.

Practical tips for prevention

Using common sense precautions can increase your safety considerably. The following basic general rules are essential.

- Have a Russian friend or guide help you most of the time.
- Keep a low profile. Do not attract attention to yourself by flaunting cash or expensive jewelry.
- Learn basic Russian words and expressions and write them on paper to show police. Also, prepare and keep handy a card with emergency numbers and the address of your embassy, friends, colleagues, and partners. Two of the emergency cards at the back of the book are prepared for you to fill out your embassy's address and your local address.
- Avoid traveling alone on the streets and in unfamiliar locations at night.
- Avoid trouble — such as brawls, scandals, and arguments.
- Avoid suspicious-looking contacts and never exchange money in the street.

Safety at home

Choosing your living quarters and setting up your Russian home should be done with care. In order to rent an adequate, safe apartment, use an agency's services or recommendations from people you know. Try to find an apartment in areas with large foreign populations.

Establish contacts with the police. Once you have rented an apartment, arrange to go with your landlord or landlady to the local police station to meet the station inspector responsible for your area and building. You will want to establish a good relationship with this person. Talk to the inspector about potential dangers, ask for advice, and get a direct office number and the number of your police station. While dealing with the inspector, use good public relations, the customary small gifts, and a smile. The official will then register your stay for his or her record. You have no reason to be afraid, since the official has no right to infringe upon your constitutional or human rights — or to ask the amount of your rent.

You should also consult the inspector about your hotel or apartment staff and unsafe areas and times in your neighborhood. Invite your local police officer (UCHASTKOVY) for 10-minute tea or brandy and offer a symbolic gift. Time spent this way may be rewarded tenfold later.

Entryway security tips. Preferably, your entrance should have an intraphone or an intercom, a code lock, or both — or even better — a 24-hour concierge behind a telephone-equipped desk. Do not enter elevators with strangers.

Your landing should be brightly lit and, if your neighbor's apartments are in the same corridor, ask whether you can install an additional door to this corridor; share the costs and keys. Introduce yourself to your neighbors, establish friendly relations, and know them by their faces. Exchange useful information, such as phone numbers, and inform them about your guests or relatives, if possible. Discuss with them potential alarm codes, such as knocking on the wall to mean, "Call the police. Danger."

Your own door should be steel, reinforced with side bolts — or at least two wooden doors with one opening inside — and equipped with a peephole and chain. Locks must be foreign-made, but remember the Russian saying, "Locks are for honest folks." Never leave keys under doormats or in mail boxes. Your apartment should be equipped with an alarm system covering the balcony windows and the front door. If you live on the ground floor, by all means install window grids. Alarm systems are recommended for all windows.

Do not open your door to strangers even if they claim to be maintenance workers, electricians, or similar. Also check even if you are expecting a visitor. Beware of strangers calling themselves the police (MILITIA). Ask for their name, precinct number, mission, and whether they know your contact from the local police station.

Helpful telephone tips. Use a telephone with Automatic Number Identification (AON in Russian), which displays the caller's number. Such phones have an easily recognizable tone and scare away obscene or unwanted callers. It also stores the numbers of your callers in operational memory. If you do not have AON and the call seems strange or openly threatening, do not hang up the receiver. Instead, go to your neighbors and call your telephone exchange to have them identify the caller's phone number. Then, in Moscow you can call 943-50-01 or 943-50-05 to learn the address for that phone number. If you want to have your number blocked from those who could be too curious, go to No. 2 Novy Arbat Street and the phone company can accomplish this. Take your passport and about 8,000 rubles to have it done.

Store the local police phone numbers in your phone memory and place them so they are easy for children to locate. Avoid placing classified ads with your home telephone number to sell expensive items. Use your office number or a neutral place for the ads, since crooks have been known to trace people this way. Keep a radio-phone or walkie-talkie at home in case the communication lines are turned off. In case of an emergency, you can call PETROVKA (police) on a Citizens Band (CB) radio.

Preventing burglaries. Today, burglaries in Russia are either solved within hours or never. Thieves typically take only easy-to-carry, expensive items and get rid of them as soon as possible. Burglaries are random and often performed by 'guest teams' — gangs visiting Moscow specifically to perform this task. Because of this, you must take care to properly protect your home when you are away. Remember that long weekends, summer holidays, or weekdays between 9 A.M. and 2 P.M. are ideal times for robbers. Usually, they spend only 15 to 20 minutes inside an apartment.

The most vulnerable places are those with doors that are easily broken through. So, steel doors with bolts and a strong frame can present a major obstacle. Take these elementary precautions before and when you are away:

- Do not flaunt your well-being — be discreet with flashy, foreign or expensive-looking purchases and personal items.
- Lock your door properly.
- Leave your radio and lights on.
- Do not close the window curtains.
- Never leave keys outside your flat.
- Do not talk about your work schedule, holidays, or vacation plans.
- Do not hide valuables in one place. Keep important papers put away.
- Have the numbers of your bonds, banknotes, certificates, and credit cards written down.

Remember: The first places burglars search are wardrobes, cabinets, and cupboards.

Safety in your office

You will be much safer if you have an office within a previously established office space — a factory, government or municipal agency, or business center with its own security personnel. Make friends with the security supervisor in your office building and discuss security issues with that person. Do not forget the public relations — small gifts and a smile.

Visit the local police station or have the head of your security do so. Select your own loyal security personnel — preferably military officers on active duty or retired officers who will work part-time. Install a desk for your security officers inside the building and equip it with an intercom and direct line to the local police. Have a closed circuit video system installed at the entrance.

Have emergency drills for your security staff and require them to record the names of all visitors. Visitors should be accompanied by one of your security officers, while another remains at the front desk.

Nevertheless, neither the local militia nor your own security personnel should know too much about your financial situation and business operations. Also, make sure to have plastic identity cards made for your security personnel so they feel an integral part of your company.

Safety in public places

Always have someone — such as a Russian partner, friend, or colleague — accompany you around. Carry a phrase-book or a list of basic Russian expressions for emergencies. Having small gifts ready in your pocket and a smile can help you through many potential problems.

Do not accept offers or services from unauthorized persons. Exchange money only in hotels or special exchange offices, which are abundant. Beware of counterfeit Russian bills, especially 50,000-ruble notes. Have your Russian partner show you how to check for counterfeits.

Avoid or frighten groups of street children or teenagers who may try to approach you. Shout at them or use your briefcase as a weapon. Be aggressive, even tell them you are a diplomat.

When you flag a car, do not accept the services if more than one person is inside. Select places frequented by foreigners where you will be safe.

Avoid the locations associated with the underworld — such as second-rate cafes or restaurants. You can visit nightclubs and casinos, but have your driver wait for you, or call somebody to pick you up if you will be be there late at night.

If you are in trouble, approach the militia or run to the nearest international hotel or hard currency shop. Do not hesitate to shout for help! Keep a supply of telephone tokens and 1-ruble coins to call a friend or partner from the nearest telephone booth. You may reach the police station free of charge from public phones by dialing "02" in nearly all larger cities.

At night, use the metro, but take a taxi to go straight home from the train, even if you live only one kilometer away from the metro station.

Hotel safety

International hotels are usually safe, but do not forget to observe the usual rules.

- Lock your door.
- Try to receive visitors in public places.
- Do not leave money or credit cards lying around the room.
- Inform the desk about your guests.

Travel safety

Crime on aircraft is unusual. Nevertheless, try to travel with companions. In trains, avoid traveling alone. If you must, purchase the entire compartment for yourself to avoid unwanted contacts: first class (SV) compartments have two berths; second class (coupe) have four berths. The Moscow to St. Petersburg overnight trains are considered to be particularly dangerous.

On the train, lock your compartment and tie the handles inside with a belt or a piece of strong wire. Do not open your compartment door — especially at night — until you arrive at your station. Put your valuables in the box under your bed and never accept invitations to play cards or have a drink from fellow travelers. If you agree to have a drink, do not drink anything offered in a glass, you may be drugged.

Car safety

Common sense rules are absolutely essential if you are going to keep a car or drive in Russia. Here are some of the main points to remember.

- Change your number plates to Russian ones.
- Use Russian-made cars.
- Never leave briefcases, radio equipment, or valuables inside.
- Have a security alarm system installed.
- Use a guarded parking lot near your home or office; hire a chauffeur, rent a garage, or buy a mini-garage — RAKUSHKA, or stall.
- Do not give a lift to people.
- If the car is stolen, report it immediately to the local police. A gift will encourage the search, but your friendly contact will be of invaluable help.

Remember: The police act on a territorial basis, so the cases are investigated where they happen.

Safety for your children

Traditionally, in Russia, children are surrounded with warmth and overprotection. Unfortunately, increases have occurred recently in sexual abuse cases and kidnappings. Sometimes small children become victims for violent teenagers, who extort their pocket money, beat and intimidate, or even organize mock kidnappings to coerce money from their parents. Sex-related crimes against children are also increasing.

Children are quite safe in schools and kindergartens, but they must be openly warned about potential dangers. Children should know their address and telephone number and what numbers to call during an emergency. Warn children about the dangerous places in your city and neighborhood. Get to know your children's friends and their parents. Tell children to avoid public demonstrations and political gatherings because these may turn violent. Advise them not to accept invitations from strangers and people they do not know well.

Dealing with dangerous situations

Despite taking extensive measures for prevention, you may still become a victim or encounter the following situations. Knowing how to properly respond can save your property — and perhaps your life. Once again, common sense rules apply.

Hostage-taking or kidnapping

In 1993, approximately 69 Russian businesspersons were subject to hostage-taking, including 6 children — in 1992, 63 businesspeople and 4 children. All hostage situations or kidnappings so far have ended with the hostages' release and the ransom money returned. If you are taken hostage:

- Do not panic, and show your moral strength.
- Try to remember the people, license number plates, places, and any other identifying information.
- Devise a special coded message to alert your friends and family, and call a phone that has an Automatic Number Identification System.
- Do not irritate your kidnappers.
- Have the police and your embassy alerted by all means.
- Agree to all conditions.

If your family member or a friend is kidnapped, alert your embassy, the police, and the Federal Counterintelligence Service (FSK). Remember: This situation is dealt with by Special Police and Security Forces, or the Organized Crime Unit (OMON). Apply in person to the FSK, and alert friends and business partners. Immediately start recording all of your telephone conversations and messages. Remember, in most cases, kidnappers count on victims' reluctance to call the police. So beat them at that.

Armed break-in or robbery

Sticking to general common sense rules will help minimize dangers if someone wants to rob you.

- Your best protection is a concierge or doorman at your hotel or apartment.
- Beware, criminals sometimes provoke you to open the door and come out of your flat by turning off your electric meter if your fuses are located outside your flat. If your lights suddenly go off, call your neighbor to check.
- If bandits burst into your apartment, do not argue, but try to remember their appearances and call the police after they leave.

- Criminals may try to trick you by posing as police or repairpersons. Look through your peephole or put the chain on your door before your open it. These precautions will save you several valuable seconds, allowing you to give a signal to your neighbors, call the police, and bang on the walls and floor.
- Try to remember visitors you had recently or strange calls since, in 90 percent of these cases, someone has 'led' the attackers to your apartment.

Burglary

If you find your apartment ransacked, do not enter it. Call the police from your a neighbor's apartment, because you might destroy valuable evidence and make a police investigation more difficult.

If you bump into burglars in your flat, do not provoke them since they rarely use violence unprovoked. Try to reason with them, bargain with them, and let them go, showing that you are not aggressive but have no fear. If you find the door of your flat broken, do not enter. Call the police.

Combatting pickpockets

While pickpockets are not the most dangerous characters you may encounter, you can avoid many inconveniences by following a few simple hints.

- Avoid crowds and rush-hour traffic.
- Do not keep your valuables in plastic bags because they are easily sliced open by a razor.
- Keep money in your waist bag or fanny pack.
- If you are a woman, do not keep money or valuables in your handbag.

Dealing with hooligans, drunks, or street gangs

If you are accosted or bothered by hooligans, drunks, or street gangs, don't panic and apply more common sense advice.

- If possible, just go away.
- Try to calm them down.
- Do not provoke them.
- Attempt to disarm them with a smile and say, "NE PONIMAYU," which means, "I do not understand."

- The drunks are the easiest to reason with — just let them talk for a couple of minutes. Listen sympathetically and the situation will usually diffuse.

Defending yourself

You may find yourself in a situation when your life, health, or property are in danger, but you have the opportunity to defend yourself and your belongings by force.

What are the legal regulations of such cases? Russian law allows for defending yourself by force — including harming an attacker. You may use all possible means within the limits of necessary self-defense. According to Russia's criminal code, the limits of necessary self-defense are defined as the equality between a harm caused to an attacker and the threat of an attacker to a person defending himself or herself. The legitimacy of necessary self-defense is based on three conditions:

- A threat or an attack is against a person who defends himself or herself or other people and property;
- A threat or an attack is real, not imaginary; and
- A defense does not exceed the necessary limits — that is, harm to the attacker should not exceed the scope of his or her threat.

Under a necessary self-defense situation, a person defending himself or herself can attack a criminal, too, in order to repulse him. It depends on you, whether to defend yourself with the risk of being harmed, or to yield to force but saving life and health. You are to decide!

Communication for emergencies

To make your communication with Russian officials and Russian people easier in emergencies, you can prepare in advance several cards with requests written in Russian on one side with an English equivalent on the other side. To help you with this project, several cards have been preprinted and are located at the back of this book. The preprinted cards, which you can cut out and carry in your pocket, include the following messages:

- I have not been met. Please help me meet an official in the airport/train station who speaks English.
- Please, where is a telephone booth?

- Help!
- Save me!
- Show me please, where is a militia post?
- Call the police, please. I am a foreigner. I have been robbed.
- I am sick/wounded. Call an ambulance, please.
- Please, where is the nearest toilet?
- Please, help me hail a taxi.
- Please, show me the metro station entrance.
- Help me get home please — showing the card with your address in Russian.
- Please help me contact the U.S. Embassy — showing the address in Russian.

Useful addresses and telephone numbers

The Ministry of Security — formerly the KGB — has been replaced by the Federal Counterintelligence Service. The name may sound intimidating, but this agency mostly deals with organized crime. In Moscow, this agency has a 24-hour special reception bureau on Kuznetsky Most Street, behind the gray-black, new building — Metro 'Lubyanka.' You may approach them in person or by calling:

Federal Counterintelligence Service
921-07-62

More useful phone numbers for Moscow and other large cities appear at the end of this chapter. Do not hesitate to call or go see these officers. Also, you should hire part-time security consultants from among former KGB specialists. They were the best in their field.

Obeying Russian laws

While in Russia, you risk not only falling victim to crime but also pulling illegal actions — especially if you are not aware of principal regulations applicable to foreigners in this country. These regulations are similar to those in other countries.

Legal status of foreigners

The legal status of foreigners in Russia is determined by the Constitution of the Russian Federation and Russia's other legal acts, which regulate the activities and legal status of various categories of foreign citizens. The basic principle of the Russian Constitution is the legal equality of all citizens. Their rights and freedoms are guaranteed by the State, regardless of race, nationality, language, social or income status, place of living, religion, or any other criteria.

In Russia, foreigners enjoy the same equal rights and freedoms as Russia's citizens. They also have equal duties, outside of those exceptions specified by the Russian Constitution, current legislation, and international agreements. Foreigners' rights can be limited by law, if this type of action is necessary to protect the constitutional and legal rights and interests of other people, health of other people, and public morality.

Citizens of other states and persons without citizenship should observe Russian legislation while in Russia. Foreigners' transgressions in Russia are punished by Russian laws with the exception of those persons who enjoy diplomatic immunity.

Foreigners' rights and interests, including their personal security and the safety of their property in Russia are protected by the agencies of the Interior Ministry, with the militia being the main agency among them. The militia is also responsible for the supervision of foreigners' observance of Russian legislation.

In accordance with these responsibilities, the militia registers foreigners coming to Russia, issues them documents for living and traveling through the country, and tries to ensure their personal security and the safety of their property. According to statistics, the most popular administrative punishment applied to foreigners in Russia is fines. Foreigners are seldom arrested.

Registration and passports for foreigners

Foreigners in Russia should have a passport or an equivalent document registered according to the regulations. Passports are to be presented to Russian authorities when requested. If you lose your passport you must report the loss to a host organization and the militia immediately in order to get a temporary certificate.

Foreigners coming into and leaving Russia must pass the posts of the state border control, which are opened for international migration for all foreign citizens bearing passports and persons without citizenship having certificates from the countries of their permanent residence. Entry, entry-exit, exit, or exit-entry visas are required unless a nonvisa regime has been established by a special agreement with the corresponding country. Exit and exit-entry visas are granted in Russia by Interior Ministry agencies.

For foreign citizens whose passports are registered in the Ministry of Foreign Affairs or its representations, visas are granted by these organizations. In specific cases, these visas can be issued by Interior Ministry agencies.

If you are invited to Russia either by invitation of a Russian organization or a permanent foreign representation, you will need to bring the written request of the appropriate organization or representation. For foreign citizens who come to Russia for private business or for permanent residence, and for permanent foreign residents in Russia, for their travel abroad for private business or for permanent living, permission from the Interior Ministry agencies is necessary. Permissions are granted from citizens' written requests.

If you are visiting Russia or living there permanently and you lose your visa, inform the Interior Ministry immediately. Foreign citizens in Russia should have international passports, which should be presented for registration on arrival at your place of residence within three days — excluding holidays. Host organizations register international passports of foreigners for a term not longer than three months. Foreign citizens coming to Russia for a short period of time may stay at a hotel or a private apartment, but must inform their host organizations, foreign permanent representations, or private hosts about their place of residence.

Foreigners who stay in hotels are registered there irrespective of the goal and length of their visit to Russia. Passports of foreigners coming to Russia for private business are registered at the Interior Ministry, according to their visas if there are no other bilateral international agreements. Prolongation of registration is done by the Interior Ministry agencies and in hotels. Host organizations may prolong a registration for no longer than three months. A prolongation of registration is executed after the Interior Ministry has extended an exit visa.

Foreigners may travel throughout Russia's regions freely, but travel plans should be reported. Short-term visitors should notify the administration of their host organization.

Permanent foreign residents and those who have come for private business, including guests of permanent foreign representations' employees should notify the Interior Ministry. On arrival to a destination, you are to register in a hotel, at the Interior Ministry, or at a host organization. To travel in territories closed to foreigners, you should appeal to the Interior Ministry.

Summary and recommendations

Living, visiting, working, and traveling in Russia will not be any more dangerous for you than in any other large city in the world — including U.S. cities like Los Angeles, Chicago, and New York. Besides using common sense, the only obstacle you will have is overcoming cultural and language barriers.

To make your visit easier, prepare as much as possible in advance of your trip to Russia. Some suggestions are:

- Cut out the emergency communication cards at the back of this book to carry in your pocket.
- Try to learn a few Russian phrases to get you by — have your Russian partner help you, or take a class at a local college.
- If you are in Moscow, use the list of emergency phone numbers on the next page.
- Study and read as much as you can about Russia — especially the new Russia, which you can read about in Hedrick Smith's book — *The New Russians*.

The next chapter will acquaint you with what life in Russia is like for an American. Russia has drastically changed in the last two years, so prepare yourself for some new expectations.

Emergency Phone Numbers*

Moscow phone number	Agency
02	Emergency/Police
924-50-26	Officer on Duty, Directorate of Internal Affairs
200-89-94	Department for Fighting Organized Crime
921-07-62	Federal Counterintelligence Service
254-97-09	Criminal Radio Information Channel 'KRIK' Radio code: 'PETROVKA'

* The emergency/police phone number for all major cities is "02." All numbers listed above are 24-hour services, but operators speak Russian only.

Chapter 11

An American in Moscow
Американец в Москве

Getting there and establishing yourself

So, in spite of everything you have read in the previous chapters, you may have decided to go to Moscow and see for yourself what things are like there. Well, in that case, keep in mind some of the following recommendations. While many of these recommendations may have been stated elsewhere in this book, they are important enough to restate here.

How to get a visa

When you go to Russia, you will need an entry visa. You can get a visa using one of two simple methods.

- Buy a tour from your travel agent; or
- Get an invitation from someone you know in Russia — a friend or a potential partner.

The invitation is in essence a visa support document, which you hand in or mail to the Embassy of the Russian Federation in Washington, D.C. or, depending on the place where you live, hand carry it to one of Russia's consulates in New York, San Francisco, or Seattle. For details, you can call the Washington, D.C. office of the Russian embassy.

Embassy of the Russian Federation
(202) 939-8918
(202) 939-8907

Your invitation must mention all the cities you intend to visit. In case you plan to visit cities of the other former Soviet Republics, keep in mind that, today, they are independent sovereign states and demand separate visas.

Extending a visa in Russia is done through the Department of Visas and Registration. However, unless your extension is arranged by your Russian counterpart or host, you should build in some extra time in your original visa and thus, avoid the necessity of contacting a fairly crowded Russian bureaucratic organization.

While in Russia, always carry your passport. However, relatively often foreigners lose their passports. Don't panic: just be sure to inform your embassy and your hosts. Remember: at worst, you can obtain your exit visa at the airport — at the expense of a fairly moderate fine. Make sure you keep a xerox copy of both your passport and visa in a separate location.

You can fly in, drive in, or come by ship or train into Russia. However, most travel inside the country is done only aboard planes belonging to the various local airlines. Foreign airline companies do not cater to passengers inside Russia.

Getting through customs

Before traveling, make sure you get a list of recommendations concerning customs procedures from your travel agent. These recommendations may be somewhat overly cautious, but when abroad, it is always better to be on the safe side.

Going through customs in Russia today has become much easier than what it was in the Soviet days, when you had to make up a story explaining why you are carrying two prayer books or several paperbacks. Customs used to make sure that any books had nothing that could be considered offensive toward the Soviet way of life.

While you certainly will go through a screening procedure, customs officers today are after narcotics, guns, and undeclared valuables, such as money, precious stones, and metals. Remember: if you are using medications that have narcotics as part of the ingredients, make sure you have a copy of your doctor's prescription with you.

Russian money

The money unit in Russia is called the ruble (sometimes spelled 'rouble'). Inflation is such that lesser denominations do not exist. The exchange rate by mid-January 1995 was around 3,600 rubles (R3600) to one U.S. dollar ($1.00). Only four years ago, it was R400 to $1.00. Currently, the ruble is not exchanged in international currency markets. Exchange booths are located everywhere in large cities. These booths are licensed by private — or as they are called in Russia 'commercial' — banks and generally give you better rates than state-owned banks. Using these services is quite legal; however, you want to avoid changing money in the streets with private citizens, who are usually jostling around the exchange booths. You may be paid with counterfeit money or not paid at all. You are allowed to use dollars to pay or tip for services rendered.

Generally, you should avoid carrying a large amount of cash in your pockets. You can always pay with or get cash from your credit card.

Transportation tips

If by any unfortunate chance your host fails to meet you at the airport, take a taxi from the taxi booth in the arrival hall. Do not go with moonlighters unless you are accompanied by a Russian friend.

Often, the taxis at the airport and elsewhere may ask you for astronomic sums. Just remember that you can bargain. Innocents abroad are always welcomed with a smile.

According to statistics, Moscow gets 500 more cars every day on its streets, which creates incredible bottlenecks, particularly in the center. Taking the Metro — subway — is cheaper and certainly faster and safer. Do not use a rent-a-car service unless you enjoy confronting kamikaze-style driving and road hazards.

Experts at the European Bank for Reconstruction and Development estimate the total expenditure needed to repair Russian roads may amount to $4.5 billion in world prices. A twelve-month delay in repairs of the 1,350 kilometers of trunk roads may cause damages, in terms of rapid depreciation of vehicles, of up to $250 million.

Finding accommodations

Finding a room in a Moscow hotel is not really a problem anymore. Not so in St. Petersburg and even less so in the provinces.

Many of the hotels in Moscow and St. Petersburg are managed or even owned by Finnish (Savoy), German (Kempinski), and other international chains (Novotel). Americans prefer the Radisson — the hotel where the U.S. State Department and White House dignitaries usually stay. Two excellent hotels are near the Red Square and the Kremlin: the Metropol and the National, which was just recently renovated. All hotels will take credit cards.

In hotels and restaurants, the personnel speak English. Baseball, football, basketball, and hockey scores are available. You can get newspapers — owned by foreign companies — in the English language: the *Moscow Times* and the *Moscow Tribune*. Furthermore, the quality of news reporting that covers the Russian scene can easily compete with any U.S. paper.

Also available are English-language Russian newspapers, such as the weekly *Moscow News, Business World,* and *The Kommersant (Businessman).* The *Moscow Business Telephone Guide* is a paper advertising businesses owned by foreigners and is available free of charge in almost all hotels.

In your hotel room, or if you get a satellite dish for your home, you can get the following broadcast stations:

- BBC
- MTV
- Super Channel
- Eurosport
- TV-5 (French)
- Pro-7 (German)
- RTL (German)
- CNN
- Reuters Reports Russia
- Thru Kosmos TV

The best-known, English-language programs on the radio are *Sherry and Larry* from 6 A.M. to 10 A.M. and the *Vasily Strelnikov* program daily from 6:00 P.M. to 10:00 P.M., located on the dial at FM 73.4 and 104.7, respectively. So, while in Moscow, you won't miss the *Larry King Live* or the *Elsa Klensch* fashion shows.

The newspapers mentioned above can help you find reliable apartments to rent. Costs on apartments certainly depend on how close they happen to be to the city center or to a subway station. A two-bedroom apartment in the center of Moscow can cost you up to $1,000 a month or more.

Prices in Moscow are not very different from expensive Western capitals. In fact, some say they are closer to those in Tokyo. So, if you plan to stay in Russia for a year or more, you should consider buying an apartment. An apartment is a good investment, and you will always be able to get your money back. A renovated two-bedroom apartment in Moscow could cost you between $70,000–$100,000.

The job market

"It has to be noted that the job market for expatriates is still growing as the overall market is growing," said Richard Goode, managing partner for Korn, Ferry, Carre, Orban International. This firm is considered one of the world's top 'headhunting' firms, according to *Moscow Tribune's* Richard Lein. The executive job market for expatriates may be growing by as much as 25 percent annually, thinks Richard Goode.

For example, a recent classified section listed more than 150 job opportunities for expatriates in corporate Russia. Positions advertised were in the fields of:

- Accounting
- Administrative
- Advertising
- Computers
- Engineering
- Finance
- Legal
- Marketing
- Sales
- Secretarial

In addition to well-known U.S. businesses, advertisers included companies from all corners of the globe — from Singapore to Canada to Italy — that are doing business in Russia.

Russian customs and attitudes

When you are in Russia, you will have to get used to some very different customs and attitudes. Some of the more noteworthy differences are highlighted below for you.

Dressing for success

Russians pay close attention to the way people are dressed. Although teenagers and students tend to wear the now universal, youth 'uniform' of jeans, t-shirts, sweaters, and cardigans, men will need to wear a tie for executive visits, at least in the beginning, for protocol's sake. A blazer will serve you well for all purposes whether the occasion is negotiations, restaurants, receptions, or the theater. Women in business should wear dresses. To many Russians, a woman wearing pants may as well be on the promenade — a prostitute. Remember, Russians have a private joke — if you see a badly dressed foreigner, he or she must be an American. This attention towards fashion can be explained by the fact that good stuff was scarce until only recently, with local products being as ugly as you could only imagine.

Dealing with male chauvinism

Russia has always been and, although somewhat less, still remains a male chauvinist's haven. Even the highest political figures would rarely appear with their wives at receptions or on trips abroad even just a decade ago. The first to introduce the First Lady concept was Mikhail Gorbachev, a leader greatly underestimated today in his country.

Russian men feel it almost impossible to allow a woman to pick up or share the tab. He will insist on treating a woman as a weaker partner, and cases of sexual harassment of female colleagues at work are frequent.

However, attitudes and stereotypes are gradually changing. Today many more women are becoming CEOs, owners of private stores and boutiques, members of joint stock companies, parliamentarians, and government officials, in fact, ministers. In certain ways, Russian women have one up on their U.S. sisters — women have formed a political party that has scored far better than many well-established parties. In fact, the Women's Party did better than President Yeltsin's party in the last DUMA elections.

So, if you are a businesswoman, you may face some old-time, European-style courting or some sort of condescension. But, now that you are aware of the possibility, your intuition and wisdom shall certainly guide you to victory.

Ensuring clear communications

In planning for negotiations, remember that most probably you will have to work through a translator working consecutively — that is, not simultaneously — with what you have to say. Remember that the actual length of the meeting time will be approximately three times longer than what you are used to at home because of the time it takes for translation.

Before going to negotiations, find your own translator: the one you have tested, the one you pay, and thus, the one you trust. Have him or her translate from Russian into English for you, as well as keep control of how well their translator carries over your message. Remember, translating from Russian is harder for Russians than vice versa.

Form a vocabulary of terms and make sure your translator knows them. Your translator may be good at discussing politics or books, but terms in a narrow field are another thing. Terms often have an equivalent in Russian, but rarely do they mean the same thing. For example, the words for limited liability companies in Russia, versus in the United States, mean slightly different things.

If you can, bring your proposals in written form, both in English and Russian. And inform the other side you would like to get their proposals the same way. Another approach that can help is to bring visual aids to any negotiations. Visual aids will certainly facilitate the meeting and prevent misunderstandings.

A further recommendation is tape recording the meeting, then transcribing it into proper form for both sides to sign. Preserve the tapes, and as time goes on, you will have a fully documented history of relations that will help you avoid conflicts.

While you can wholeheartedly believe in the warm, welcoming character of your Russian counterparts, you are recommended to withhold from post-meeting, restaurant celebrations until the final document is signed.

As for tokens of attention, you certainly should bring souvenirs for your Russian counterparts. Understand that often their expectations may be significantly higher than what you intend to bring. Yes, your gift may often resemble a bribe. You will have to decide whether your souvenir will be a Montblanc fountain pen, an invitation to spend a week on Waikiki, or a Jeep Cherokee.

Life in Moscow

In years past — and even recently — you have likely heard a number of horror stories about food shortages, hours of waiting in lines, terrible food and service in restaurants, and other primitive conditions. While everything about Russia has not been Westernized, you will be surprised by what you find about everyday life in Moscow.

Shopping and groceries

Moscow features more than a dozen foreign supermarkets. In the past, going to Moscow was like going to the Sahara Desert — you had to take everything with you from facial tissue to your own stationery. Today, all of that and more is available in Moscow. However, prices seem to be on the expensive side, particularly in clothing. Moreover, the main consumers shopping in the boutiques, carrying world-famous brands, are no longer foreigners. They are the 'new Russians.'

In supermarkets, use your credit card — food will be somewhat cheaper that way because the foreign stores like to deal with hard currency accounts. However, for those who plan to settle in Russia for some time, buying food in Russian stores is much cheaper, particularly in the Russian peasant marketplaces. Meat, dairy products, and vegetables in the peasant market have to pass sanitary controls and are actually better than the ones sold in grocery stores.

Restaurants

Eating out can be more expensive than in the United States unless you know where to go. An Italian aperitif like Crodino costs around $5 a glass at the Fantasia Italian Cuisine Venture; crepes with a creamy mushroom and onion filling and a shrimp cocktail cost $12 each; tenderloin in red wine is $13, with a fresh vegetable salad the cost is $5 more. An iced fruit drink is $3. A real nice dessert will cost you around $8 and tea or espresso $3. A lunch is, thus, in the vicinity of $100 in the very center of Moscow. Eating out in a Mexican restaurant, not far from Fantasia, could cost you as much as $50 for two people: a margarita costs $3, a Guinness beer is $2, guacamole is $5 and nachos are $4. La Cantina makes its own tortillas. Chicken chimichangas are $10, and beef fajitas are $13.

To provide another viewpoint about restaurants in Moscow, a specially written article for the English-language paper, *Moscow Times*, by Jo Durden-Smith on June 28, 1994 is reprinted below.

I went to a Moscow restaurant the other day, and so ridiculously, horrifically expensive was it that I was forced to choose what I could remember of economics — instead of tiramisu or cassata siciliana, or whatever other souped-up farrago they were offering — for dessert.

I mean, this place was a turkey, a lulu. It was mutton dressed up as lamb. The waitresses, who were got up as high-class courtesans, had no idea what they were doing; and the food was what you might have to endure on a very bad night out in Peoria, Illinois.

Still, it had pretensions. It had finger bowls and foppery, napery and drapery for days. But the most pretentious thing about it was the check, which arrived for inspection in a little leather-and-velvet bed all its own. My wife almost wept for shame at the sight of it, in front of the courteous British cameraman who was paying. If I had had to pay it myself, I would probably have had to pawn my children.

I think it is because all the foreigners who come here to advise the Russians on the creation of their marketplace, or else have come here to take advantage of its arrival, are simply not subject to the laws of the marketplace themselves. If they are advisors from agencies and governments and international banks, or Moscow-based managers of foreign companies, they are on expenses. They really don't spend their own money at all. They can pay any money they like, live high on the hog, and call it 'local costs' or 'prevailing economic conditions.'

Which leaves us with another of those nice little East-West ironies: the people who come to Moscow to help create its marketplace actually delay its arrival. The West pays these people hundreds of thousands of dollars each — in travel costs, salaries, and expenses — and call the resultant hundreds of millions of dollars 'aid' to Russia, when actually it is an 'obstacle.' For what these advisors and businessmen are doing through their presence here is creating an artificial, closed-shop marketplace in which prices are so high that few tourists and no Russians — except hoods — can actually afford it.

I am not sure what can be done about this by ordinary people, except to remind these happy-go-lucky 'helpers' of Russia that Western ideas, when imported here, tend to get bent out of shape and turn quickly into their opposites.

Medical aid

A number of medical centers are operated by foreigners in larger Russian cities. Either the doctors are foreigners or the clinics are managed by foreign specialists. Over-the-counter foreign drugs are all available in the medical centers and in specialized drugstores. Embassies also have their doctors, and in extreme cases, they could be of help. If you are in Russia for a short stay, avoid drinking tap water. You have to get used to the local water. Bottled water from

France and other countries is cheap and always available in super-markets. For general first aid service, ask your hotel to call "03."

Religion

Moscow has churches of various denominations: Roman Catholic, Protestant, the Church of England, Russian Orthodox, Bulgarian Orthodox, Greek Orthodox Christian Church, the Moscow Choral Synagogue, the Seventh Day Adventists, and the Baptist Church.

Recreation

You don't have to worry about your sports and cultural pastimes in Moscow or St. Petersburg. World-renowned museums, galleries, theaters, and sports facilities that catered to Olympic and Goodwill Games are at your disposal for a fairly moderate price.

Summary

Of course, you have to remember that these are the conditions in Moscow and St. Petersburg. Much is still unavailable in the provinces. However, without an established Russian link, you are not likely to venture anywhere beyond Moscow or St. Petersburg.

However, many foreigners are already in Russia, and are managing just fine with the conditions they find. To get a sense of the scope of activities going on in Russia, the next chapter highlights recent news clippings from the English-language papers.

Chapter 12

You Won't Be Alone

Вы не единственный

A spectrum of foreign activities

You are aware by now that a large amount of investment activity is going on in Russia. So that you do not feel you are about to go to a *terra incognita*, you can familiarize yourself with some recent activities in Russia by reading this chapter's compilation of clippings from various English-language papers that are published in Moscow. These excerpts demonstrate the spectrum of foreign activities in Russia.

GM and Daewoo competing in the Russian car market

Russia's largest car producer, the Autovaz concern, built in the '60s by Fiat, has to make up its mind whether to work with GM in accordance with the memorandum signed some time ago or give preference to Daewoo. GM offered to put up an assembly line that would produce 20,000 GM cars annually that would be sold in Russia.

"Are 20,000 cars worth opening the Russian market to foreigners and what are 20,000 cars for a giant like Autovaz? The U.S. car producers are not interested in helping us develop VAZ 1116, our new model," said one of the Russian board members of the concern. "In this sense, Daewoo is more daring. It built whole new plants in Pakistan and Lebanon. With or without GM we shall implement our project." Though where will the money come from in a crisis-torn country?

Bayer against Russian headaches

Bayer has begun producing aspirin on Russian territory. In the first year, Russia shall get 20 million pills, but the people at Bayer are optimistic and intend to increase the production in the near future. It is understood that in the beginning, the company will be bringing in everything from raw materials to packaging. Russian Bayer shall be 15 percent cheaper than the original.

St. Petersburg registered almost 1,000 JVs

By January 1994, St. Petersburg registered 985 joint ventures with foreign companies. Of those, 57.9 percent (or $89,475 of the authorized capital) belong to foreigners. Of those really working are 854 joint ventures predominantly in trade and restaurants. U.S. capital is represented by 150 companies; German and Finnish companies share second place.

U.S. West to modernize Russian communications

U.S. West International, an affiliate of U.S. West, Inc., is already most active in Russia and shall take part in a major project laying 50,000 kms of fiber optic cables and putting up 50 digital transit stations that will actually double Russia's existing telephone capabilities. It has already introduced cellular telephone communication systems in the Russian Far East, Bashkiria and the Urals, as well as in Moscow and St. Petersburg. OPIC, the American Private Investment Corporation, has granted U.S. West a $125 million guarantee loan to participate in the development of telecommunications in Russia.

German trucks to be produced in Taganrog

TKZ, a harvester manufacturer in Taganrog, the Rostov Region, plans to produce light trucks in a joint venture with Germany's Multicar Spezialfahrzeuge GmbH.

The joint venture will be set up in September or October. It will produce Multicar-26 trucks equipped with Volkswagen diesel engines. The Multicar-26 truck, which carries 1.5 tons and has a speed of 70 km per hour, will be produced in several versions, including passenger, cargo and snow-cleaning versions and a special version for various farm applications. It will be marketed in former Soviet republics, Bulgaria, the Middle East and Southeast Asia. Its price is expected to be 30 to 40 percent lower than that of the original German truck, currently priced at between DM 36,000 and DM 40,000.

TKZ will produce 500 trucks in the first year and will then increase its annual output to 20,000 trucks.

Sony TV sets to be assembled in Perm

The diversified joint stock company, Stek (Perm), with a turnover of $10 million in 1993, started producing Sony televisions of the KV-M2100K model from Sony-made components, to be sold in Russia, said Alexander Fimin, director of the affiliated firm, Stek — the Sony Service Center.

Stek and Sony signed a contract to this effect on December 15, 1993, with the expiry in August 1994. The sum of the deal is not mentioned. According to Alexander Fimin, Sony will supply components to manufacture 660 televisions monthly. The deliveries may possibly be expanded after the expiration of the initial term. The approximate price will be $600.

Truck giant, U.S. firm set joint venture

KamAZ, Russia's biggest truck maker, plans to set up a joint venture with U.S. venture capital firm, Kohlberg, Kravis, Roberts & Co., to attract $3.5 billion for new equipment. The joint venture had been approved at an urgent shareholders' meeting in Moscow on Wednesday.

Interfax quoted officials as saying the money would be used to finance a five-year plan. Kohlberg, Kravis, Roberts & Co. would obtain 51 percent of the stock in the new joint venture, Interfax said.

GM, YelAZ plan deal

General Motors and the Russian factory, YelAZ, plan to sign a general agreement to finance a $1.5 billion project to produce off-road vehicles in November, a YelAZ official said Monday.

Yuri Martinov, aide to YelAZ's general director, said the two companies planned to set up a joint venture to make up to 500,000 four-wheel-drive vehicles at the YelAZ factory in Yelabuga, Tatarstan.

At the first stage, to begin in the fourth quarter of 1996, GM would supply the joint venture with parts for assembly. The parts would later be produced by military plants in Yelabuga, Martynov said.

Russian-British venture to mine gold in Siberia

A new Russian-British venture, Svetloye, was recently established in Russia to develop the Svetloye gold deposit near the town of Plast in the Chelyabinsk Region, on a production-sharing basis.

Svetloye, established with a capital of R100 million, is owned by Yuzhuralzoloto (45 percent), a Chelyabinsk-based gold-mining company, and by RTZ (55 percent), a British mining company.

Svetloye plans to begin development of the deposit in two years. It will be producing five tons of gold annually. RTZ will supply British mining technology and will invest an additional $100 to $200 million in the project during the first stage of its implementation. The Svetloye deposit is estimated to contain 70 tons of gold.

A duty-free shop in the middle of nowhere

It's as unlikely a spot as you could imagine — it's more or less a hut built on a bog in the middle of dense woodland near the Finnish border. But it's also one of the success stories of Aer Rianta International, the Irish company, which runs the duty-free shops in Moscow, St. Petersburg, and Kiev international airports. The company also has two duty-free shops on the Russian-Finnish border, with a combined turnover of nearly $6.5 million.

The bigger of the two shops, at Torfyanovka, will be four years old in July, while the smaller enterprise in Brusnichnaya was only opened in October 1993 — and it had paid for itself in two months.

Coca-Cola to invest $100 million

The Coca-Cola Company and its bottling partners announced plans Monday to invest $100 million in the development of a Russian bottling and distribution network stretching from the Baltic Sea to the Pacific Ocean. The company said that the new investment should make Coca-Cola products available to around 80 percent of the Russian population. The U.S. beverage manufacturer has already invested $140 million in the Russian market and Monday's announcement comes just five months after the opening of Coca-Cola's Moscow factory, which employs some 300 people.

EBRD signs first Russian shipping loan

The European Bank for Reconstruction and Development (EBRD) has authorized a $75 million loan for Russian shipping.

Loan recipient, Prisco Maritime Limited, is a subsidiary of the Primorsk Shipping Company A/O, the largest tanker shipping company in the Russian Far East. The loan will be used to purchase four new product tankers from the Kherson shipyard in Ukraine.

The transaction does not involve any export credit finance or guarantees from the state. "The commercial banks which have participated with us have demonstrated that financing the Russian shipping sector is commercially viable without state guarantees," EBRD Vice-President Guy de Selliers said in a statement.

According to the EBRD statement, the financing will allow the Russian shipping companies to begin a fleet renewal program.

OPIC to launch new investment fund

The U.S. Overseas Private Investment Corporation (OPIC) is set to launch another investment fund in Russia, according to the organization's president, Ruth Harkin.

"During the Gore-Chernomyrdin Commission, we will be signing an agreement with our fund managers and make an announcement of a $300 million fund for capital investments in Russia," Harkin told reporters in Moscow.

OPIC is a U.S. government agency that provides direct loans, loan guarantees and investment insurance against a broad range of political risks.

Lehman Brothers has been selected to manage the private equity fund, which is intended to make larger size investments in industrial-sector projects. Money for the fund is to be raised privately and OPIC will provide guarantees.

Irish public limited company (plc) explores oil in Siberia

A deal between Ireland's Dana Exploration Plc and three Russian partners last year to develop an oil field in Western Siberia has brought the struggling Irish company back to life, Dana chairman Kevin Burke told shareholders. "Today the company has got another chance to live," Burke said.

The South Vat-Yoganskoye oil field, discovered in 1990, has proven oil reserves estimated at 31.4 million barrels. This could earn Dana millions of dollars, with the amount depending on the price of crude oil and whether proposed tax reforms are brought in by Prime Minister Viktor Chernomyrdin.

At current prices of $17–18, the proven oil is worth $21 million in net present value. If reforms of export taxes and excise duties are introduced, that will double to $43 million. Shareholders approved an 11-for-five rights issue at five pence a share to raise 2.17 million pence ($3.31 million) to help fund the venture.

Financial turnover

RIA reports that a deal between Moscow stock bank Vozrozhdeniye and British aluminum and oil trading company Middlesex Holdings for the purchase of 2.5 percent of Middlesex stock for $1M has been finalized. Pretax profit of the company for the first six months of 1994 was 1.565 million pounds with a turnover of 12M.

According to company representatives, the success of the company in the first two quarters was promoted by successful performance in the CIS mining industry. The company finances the deliveries of raw materials for the aluminum industry of these countries. Payments are made in ready-made aluminum.

The February 22, 1993 issue of the *Daily Telegraph* published an appointment announcement for the company. Alexander Vladislavlev, chairman of the board of AMO ZIL car-making company, joined the board of directors of Middlesex Holdings. This appointment signifies that the business is balancing out in new directions. The price of Middlesex Holdings stock rose continually in the first half of 1994.

U.S. to invest more in Russian economy

The United States' Overseas Private Investment Corporation (OPIC) has signed three protocols supporting U.S. companies operating in Russia. According to this protocol, U.S. West International will be allocated approximately $80 million for its new holding company in Russia with a charter capital of $150 million. This company will work on telecommunications projects involving Western state-of-the-art technologies.

OPIC also plans to allocate $140 million for funding and insuring a project that will be implemented by the Snyder Company jointly with the Russian state-owned oil company, Permneft. The two companies have set up a 50-50 joint venture, Permtex, to resume oil extraction from mothballed oil wells and to develop major oil fields in the Perm region. According to Snyder estimates, the joint venture will extract an average of 1.1 million tons of oil per year.

In addition, OPIC will allocate $100 million to Dresser/Petro-Hunt for funding and insuring an oil extraction project. Dresser/Petro-Hunt plans to sell this oil abroad for hard currency.

New Radisson Hotel opens in Sochi

A Russian/Turkish joint venture, the $50 million hotel overlooking the Black Sea is owned equally by the Sochi Municipal Authority, the Russian joint stock company, Gazprom, and the Turkish firms Gama (a petroleum concern) and Erna (a consumer goods and construction company).

The U.S. Radisson Hotels International holds a 15-year agreement to manage the Lazurnaya in a profit-sharing deal similar to the one it holds at Moscow's Radisson-Slavyanskaya — except that, unlike the latter property, Radisson does not own the Sochi hotel. With its modern amenities, including a casino, two swimming pools, a business conference room and a guest-friendly "Yes I can!" policy for the 600-member staff, the venture makes for an oasis of sorts in Sochi, formerly a major resort for the Soviet elite and the proletariat on state-subsidized leave.

Works in Namibia and Tanzania

Tumanov & Co. has received an offer to conduct geological prospecting in Namibia and Tanzania. The company has set up an international Geological Prospecting Office, whose purpose is to carry out prospecting works abroad. An expedition from the International Geological Prospecting Office worked for six weeks on south Namibia's diamond deposits and succeeded in identifying promising areas. At the moment, a tender from the company is being considered by the Namibian side.

In Tanzania, Tumanov geologists are prospecting for gold. Tumanov & Co. is also expected to be subsequently invited to organize gold and diamond mining in these countries of southern Africa. The International Geological Prospecting Office is prepared to execute other orders from overseas companies interested in conducting prospecting works entailing the mapping and estimating of reserves, and in organizing the experimental mining of minerals.

Another oil pipeline

Russia's Gazprom company has signed a protocol agreement with a consortium of Greek companies to build an oil pipeline through

Bulgaria and Greece. The planned pipeline, estimated to cost $600 million, will carry crude oil transported by tanker from the Russian Black Sea port of Novorossiisk, it said. It will stretch for 350 kilometers from the Bulgarian port of Bourgas to Alexandropoulis on the Greek Mediterranean coast.

The pipeline would be completed in three years and be able to pump 20 to 40 million tons of oil a year. New oil storage tanks, each with a capacity of 1 million tons, would be built at both ends of the pipeline, it said.

Kommersant named the Greek companies involved in the project as the shipping and oil refining company, Latsis, and the construction firm, Kopelouzos. It said a joint venture between Kopelouzos and Gazprom, known as Prometheus, was also involved. The Bulgarian and Greek state oil companies were also expected to take part, it said.

The pipeline would allow Russian exports to bypass the Bosphorus Straits, where Turkey has announced new shipping restrictions to reduce the danger of ecological catastrophe in the narrow waterway.

Russian-German investment fund created

On February 24, a document was signed creating in Russia the first Russian-German investment fund, to be located in St. Petersburg. This financial-commercial agreement united the joint stock bank, Russia and DEG (a financial company with 100 percent state partnership, created with the federal government of Germany). The goal of this fund is to provide assistance to the perestroika structure and to developing industries in St. Petersburg. The German government is setting aside nearly DM5 million for the fund. The founders of the fund have already planned their first project — production of semi-conductor lasers for medical purposes.

GE, Marriot win grants

The U.S. Trade and Development Agency has awarded 19 economic assistance grants worth a total of $6 million to finance feasibility studies for U.S.-Russian projects in areas ranging from real estate development to helicopter building. A press release circulated by the agency Tuesday said that the U.S. government agency has agreed to provide part of the cost of the feasibility studies, while the companies that are going to carry them out will come up with the rest.

Among the 19 projects is a partnership between General Electric and the Kirov factory in St. Petersburg to produce gas turbines. The agency and General Electric are investing $600,000 each in the feasibility study. GE is also considering a partnership with a Russian factory to make helicopters with U.S. engines.

Marriott International is prepared to pay $1.5 million to investigate the feasibility of building a Marriott Hotel in place of the Intourist in Central Moscow. The agency is committing $435,000 to the study. The costly feasibility studies are necessary for the implementation of the projects since financial institutions require these studies to decide whether a project is creditworthy.

A $300,000 grant has been allotted to Lukoil, Russia's biggest independent oil company, which will study plans to build a major oil refinery in Krasnodar with ABB Lummus Crest. The press release said that if the projects are implemented, they may bring U.S. companies about $2 billion in export revenues. According to the press release, the agency has invested $34 million in 80 projects in former Soviet republics since 1992.

Gazprom & Ferrostahl AG plan new port

The Russian concern Gazprom and the German company Ferrostahl AG have registered the joint venture TOO Metaprom. The German side holds 37 percent of the charter capital. This joint venture will design, build and conduct operations at its complex in Arkhangelsk. Its annual production capacity will be 680,000 tons and its port structure will serve to dispatch shipments of methanol. All the methanol will be exported since the domestic demand in Russia for methanol is fully covered, and there is even a surplus.

The German partner is Ferrostahl AG. The methanol complex is planned to begin operations at the end of 1996 or the beginning of 1997. The majority of the equipment will be imported on a turn-key basis. Preliminary financial estimates show that this complex could be paid off in seven or eight years, although profits from its operations would already be seen in the first year.

Study: Russia eats up U.S. food

The U.S. food exporters searching for new markets should look to Russia despite that country's recent economic troubles, the U.S. Agriculture Department suggests.

The Russian market, while still forming, is largely untapped by U.S. exporters and could offer great rewards, according to an article in the current issue of the USDA publication, *AgExporter*. In the first five months of 1994, Russia expanded to become the fifth largest market in the world for U.S. consumer-oriented products, surpassing such countries as South Korea, Taiwan, and Singapore. Also, the market for imported consumer-ready food in Russia is estimated at $2.5 billion and predicted to grow as further economic recovery occurs.

Europe currently dominates the Russian import market, most of which consists of upscale food purchased by the wealthiest 10 to 15 percent of the population. European Union nations alone account for $1.4 billion of the total, mainly because their proximity to Russia allows for quick delivery of specialty orders.

Still, interest in American products is high, and Russian producers provide little competition in the upscale food arena. In 1993, American agricultural exports to Russia rose sharply to $346 million from $126 million the previous year. Exports of snack foods, red meat, and poultry also increased significantly. For the first five months of 1994, U.S. food exports are estimated at $206 million, 280 percent ahead of the same period in 1993.

Though European foods crowd most of the shelves at Western-style supermarkets in Moscow and St. Petersburg, U.S. goods are starting to make inroads, particularly in freezers where American ice cream, pizzas, and processed chicken products are prevalent. Still, Russia's problems cannot be ignored. The food distribution system remains shaky, at best, although improvements are being made. Additionally, the legal and banking mechanisms are not equipped to deal effectively with international trade.

On the other hand, the magazine says that now is the time to enter the market and build up product recognition, since advertising costs are low by American standards and European companies have not spent much in this area. Some high-profile products already known in Russia include Mars, Coca-Cola, Smirnoff Vodka, and fast-food outlets such as McDonald's and Pizza Hut.

Promotional materials are rare in Russia, and owners seem eager to put product displays in their stores. Also, if the Russian processing industry becomes advanced enough to compete in the upscale market, additional export outlets will open up for nonbrand imported ingredients, such as dried fruit, nuts, flavorings, and concentrates for juice drinks.

Tchaikovsky in Japanese

For the first time since the collapse of the Soviet Union, a major international recording company is launching its own program of releases of Russian classical music. Sony, the Japanese company whose classical music division is based in Hamburg, inaugurated its new "St. Petersburg Classics" series in two days of ceremony and music-making in St. Petersburg this week.

Several million dollars have been committed by Sony to preparing the first 100 compact-disc recordings. According to Iris Mazur and Hanspieter Rhein of Mazur Media, Sony's partner in Russia, performances for the first 50 CD releases have already been taped. The first nine CDs will go on sale within days. They include works of Tchaikovsky, Shostakovich, Rachmaninoff, tenor arias from Russian opera, and Russian liturgical music.

The Templeton group considers a Russia fund

The Templeton group, which runs one of the world's top emerging market funds, is considering launching a $300–$400 million fund to invest in Russia. Mark Mobius, who runs the $280 million China World Fund, a recently launched $120 million Vietnam Fund, and $5 billion in emerging markets cash for the Franklin/Templeton group, said in an interview the new closed-end Russian Fund would be listed on the New York Stock Exchange.

"We are looking at around $300–$400 million for Russia," Mobius said. "This is a major emerging market just like China, Brazil, India, and South Africa. Russia is at the same level."

Templeton was also planning to set up a representative office in Moscow soon, Mobius said. It was too early to give a timetable for the fund's launch, which depended on sorting out custodian facilities in Russia, Mobius said. No foreign bank has yet ventured into custodian business in Russia. But Mobius said that, ideally, the fund would like to work with Chase Manhattan Bank, which is planning to develop such facilities in Russia in the near future.

Truck engines for Russia

U.S. firm, Caterpillar Inc., is having talks with the International Finance Corporation and the U.S. Overseas Private Investment Corporation to fund two joint ventures with Russia's ZiL truck maker, officials said.

A senior Caterpillar official said on Thursday that financing was being put together for the U.S. diesel-engine maker's new Novodiesel joint venture with ZiL, agreed June 24, and its Diesel System joint venture signed earlier this year. Novodiesel will produce Caterpillar truck engines in the 150 to 500 horsepower range, starting in 1995. Diesel System will produce Caterpillar fuel systems for ZiL's new line of mid-range diesel engines manufactured near Smolensk.

The Caterpillar official did not give the size of the financing package or likely investments in ZiL ventures. He also declined to say how the ownership would be split. But Russian media reports have said ZiL will own 51 percent of Novodiesel and that Caterpillar plans to invest $100 million in this joint venture.

Novodiesel will also produce Caterpillar truck engines, which will be used by ZiL's new joint venture with U.S. truck manufacturer Paccar Inc., which makes Peterbilt and Kenworth heavy-duty trucks, the Caterpillar official said. "So we can talk of a strategic alliance between Caterpillar, Paccar and ZiL," the Caterpillar official said.

BAT Industries 'helps' Russian smokers

The British-U.S. company BAT Industries, which controls 11 percent of the world's cigarette market, has won a tender for a 75 percent share in a tobacco factory in the Russian city of Saratov. The company now plans to invest $40 million to modernize the factory. The factory's management believes that the investments will pay for themselves within ten to twelve years.

The managing director of BAT industries, Ulrich Hoerter, said his company had been impressed by the factory management's clearcut vision of its objectives and of ways to reach them, which had predetermined the company's choice. The factory plans to increase its annual output capacity to 10 billion cigarettes within three years. Since the factory was privatized in July 1993, labor productivity there has increased 13 percent, although the number of personnel has remained unchanged. The factory now produces 5 billion cigarettes per year. In 1990, it had a capacity of 3.5 billion cigarettes.

BAT industries is now negotiating with another Moscow factory, Yava, which has an output capacity of 14 billion cigarettes per year. The company hopes that Yava and the Saratov factory can jointly produce 30 billion cigarettes annually. Russia's cigarette market is estimated at 250 billion cigarettes.

Japanese credit goes to Lukoil

After two years of negotiations, Russia's largest independent oil company, Lukoil, is set to receive a $700 million credit from the Japanese trading company Mitsui to restore the productivity of oil wells in Western Siberia. Lukoil will use the credit line to purchase equipment and materials from Mitsui for the restoration of the wells. The interest on the credit was low enough to be attractive to the Russian company. Lukoil agreed to put forward a five percent advance payment on the credit. A further ten percent would be paid out after Mitsui supplies the equipment and materials. Lukoil would repay the rest of the credit in ten installments over five years.

$1.5 million export order

According to Viktor Alyakrinsky, director of the Vladimir Technika plant, the plant has received an order for the production of 100 cases for the numerically controlled lathes by Marathon joint venture (Hungary and Germany), which was created on the basis of the Chepel machine-building group of enterprises. Marathon joint venture will supply part of the machine components under the contract. Marathon will also do the final lathe assembly for export to the U.S.A. The order is valued at $1.5 mln to be carried out by October 1995.

American Express launches a fund

The credit-card giant American Express is launching a $750,000 fund to benefit the tourism sector in the CIS and Eastern Europe, company officials announced on Wednesday.

The first major project of the Fund for Central/Eastern Europe is a secondary school in St. Petersburg where some 100 students are enrolled. Under the program, called the Travel and Tourism Program, the students will learn about the tourism industry in coursework lasting two years, American Express officials told a press conference at the Olympic Penta Hotel. American Express officials said they'll strengthen their commitment in Russia and the CIS, which has a vast but mostly underdeveloped tourism potential.

Russian timber and U.S. technology

A group of small family-owned sawmills in the Pacific Northwest has entered into a joint venture to log the vast forests of eastern Russia, hoping to secure supplies as U.S. logging declines.

The Global Forestry Management Group (GFMG), made up of ten small, independent forest-products companies in Oregon, Washington and California, is shipping $3 million in heavy logging equipment to the Khabarovsk region of Eastern Russia. The equipment is part of a $9 million investment by the U.S. mills. They announced a joint venture late last month with two Russian partners based in Khabarovsk — Exprales and SovGavan Lespromkhoz.

The two private Russian companies were formed to develop a forest-products industry in the Khabarovsk region, north of the Russian border with China, said Mike Haglund, an attorney representing the Portland-based GFMG. The joint venture includes the construction of a log export facility at Sovetskaya Gaven, a former Russian naval base, and the leasing of about one million acres of Russian timberlands. Eventually, the venture could involve the investment of $40 million to $70 million, Haglund said in an interview.

All of the U.S. mills depend heavily on logging supplies from federal timberlands in the Pacific Northwest, where harvesting has been curtailed to protect endangered species such as the northern spotted owl. The Americans hope Russian forests will eventually provide a new source of either logs or rough-sawed lumber that can be turned into finished lumber products in the U.S. mills, said Haglund.

The first goal of the GFMG venture is to establish a working logging industry that initially will sell timber to markets in China, Japan, and Korea to raise capital, said Haglund. Money from those sales will then be invested in the construction of modern mills in Russia, which could produce rough-sawed lumber for export to the United States. There it would be turned into finished lumber.

Mercedes helps Russia produce jeeps

Mercedes-Benz and the Ulyanovsk automobile factory expect to agree next month on a $450 million joint venture to produce jeeps, minitrucks and minivans, officials of the two companies say.

Under the deal, two automobile factories would be set up at UAZ, as the Ulyanovsk plant is commonly known, where the plant currently produces military-style jeeps. One factory would assemble vehicles; the second would eventually produce engines, UAZ deputy general director Vladimir Antonov said in an interview Wednesday.

The joint venture, located 700 kilometers east of Moscow, would produce three types of vehicles: four-wheel-drive off-road vehicles;

minitrucks; and a variety of minibuses, including ambulances and mobile intensive-care units, Antonov said.

The total value of the project would amount to 700 million Deutsche marks ($450 million), according to Mercedes-Benz's Moscow press spokeswoman, Emma Vasyilkova.

Bottling franchises for Russian Coke

The international motors and marketing group, Inchcape, said it was extending links with the U.S. soft-drinks giant Coca-Cola Co. by investing in bottling franchises in six of the twelve largest cities in the Russian Federation. The new Russian franchises cover an area south and east of Moscow with a population approaching 50 million, including Nizny Novgorod and Volgograd.

Only in April, it opened a $35 million plant in Moscow to produce its Coke, Fanta, and Sprite brands. Added to a factory in St. Petersburg, that took investment to more than $100 million in activities that already employ 3,000 people in the country. As a first step in the investment topping F25 million ($38.3 million) over three years, Inchcape is buying 11 percent of the Volzhsky brewery and soft-drinks business in Volgograd. Inchcape shares added 3 pence to 460 in early trading on news of the Russian deal.

Hyundai's Russian TVs

The Russian firm IVK has signed a $1.3 million contract with Korean firm Hyundai to assemble 10,000 color televisions by the end of the year at the Kvant electronics factory in the Moscow region, Interfax reported Thursday. Earlier this month, IVK signed a deal with U.S. firm Intel to assemble computers, retailing at under $2,000, based on the company's Pentium chip at Kvant.

Mobile radiotelephone network in Moscow

France Telecom Mobile International announced that it had purchased an 11 percent stake in the joint-stock company Mobilnaya TeleSistema (MTC), which operates a digital mobile radiotelephone network in Moscow. MTC has a license to run the GSM-standard network in the capital for ten years. In July the company started operating the first segment of the network. Sources at MTC say it has already invested $28 million in the project. By 1997, investments may total $100 million and will be aimed at boosting the MTC's capacity.

Samsonites in Russia

Astrum International, which owns Samsonite and American Tourister, signed an agreement to begin production of their famous-name luggage in Russia. Astrum will invest around $13 million in Dokofa Ltd., located outside of Tula, for refitting part of the factory with western equipment, providing luggage molds and designs, and worker retraining. Dokofa will help Samsonite and American Tourister market their goods here in Russia.

Production, scheduled to begin this summer, will aim for both Russian and international markets.

SPI Pharmaceutical trades shares

In what Mayor Anatoly Sobchak hailed as a historic transaction, California-based SPI Pharmaceutical is trading its own shares for a stake in Oktyabr, Russia's oldest pharmaceutical company. SPI Chairman and former Yugoslav Prime Minister Milan Panic said he hoped to eventually take a 70-percent controlling interest in Oktyabr — a run-down, three-factory complex founded in 1714 by Tsar Peter the Great and one of Russia's largest pharmaceutical firms — which would produce SPI-brand medicines for the Russian and European markets.

Summary

The fact that so many large businesses are interested in Russia should be telling you something. You know that their decisions are based on sound research and advice — they don't take major risks. Furthermore, statistics show that numerous smaller ventures comprise the majority of investments, even though these don't generally make the news headlines.

The next chapter provides you with helpful contacts for information and financing — whether your business is large or small.

Chapter 13

Helpful Resources

Полезные советы

Sources of help and information

If you are interested in doing business in Russia, a number of organizations can help you get started. You can access, through these organizations, all kinds of information about not just Russia, but all of the Newly Independent States (NIS).

One-stop assistance

If you represent a U.S. business interested in doing business in Russia or other former Soviet Union states, your first source of information is the Business Information Service for the Newly Independent States (BISNIS). BISNIS is a service provided by the U.S. Department of Commerce. Through BISNIS, you can find out current information on commercial opportunities, sources of financing, up-to-date lists of trade officials and enterprise contacts, and U.S. government programs for support in trade and investment. BISNIS offers the following services and publications.

International trade specialists. Experts on trade and market development are available to answer your questions and provide information on U.S. government programs, NIS contacts, market data, trade leads, current legislation, and trade regulations.

BISNIS Bulletin. The *BISNIS Bulletin* is a regular publication that provides current information about commercial developments and trade opportunities in the NIS. The booklet also covers government negotiations between the United States and the NIS, tax regulations, legal developments, marketing data, tariff rates, calendar of trade events, financing information, market research updates, and U.S. government and other international agency programs providing assistance.

BISNIS Search for Partners. This newsletter focuses on helping U.S. businesses find opportunities in states of the former Soviet Union. The publication describes enterprises and businesses in the NIS that are seeking U.S. trade and investment partners. A comprehensive profile of each business, its activities, its needs, and contact information is given so that U.S. businesses can directly contact the NIS businesses. The opportunities described are provided solely as an informational service and do not represent an endorsement by the U.S. Department of Commerce. You will need to practice due diligence to verify the information before you make an investment.

Flashfax BISNIS Bank. Flashfax is a 24-hour, automated information bank of current trade leads and information that is provided to you immediately via fax. All you need is a touch-tone phone to access hundreds of documents. The documents are divided amongst three menus:

- Menu 1 lists trade and investment opportunities and trade promotional information in the NIS.
- Menu 2 lists industry and country-specific information and financing alternatives, including topics such as trade statistics, economic overviews by country, and sources of finance.
- Menu 3 lists those BISNIS periodic publications that can also be obtained by fax.

Flashfax is free and easy to use, however, there is a limit of three documents per call. Use a touch-tone phone and follow the step-by-step ordering instructions. The recording will ask you for the document order number and your fax number. The menu is updated once a week. To get copies of menus 1, 2, and 3, call the Flashfax number below and order documents 0001, 0002, and 0003.

Information center and reference library. BISNIS maintains a library that is open to the U.S. business community and is located at the BISNIS office in Washington, D.C. The library includes current trade directories, newsletters, market research, and other publications on doing business in the NIS. A current listing of enterprise activities in the NIS is also maintained. BISNIS can also provide you with up-to-date information about nearly all of the programs in this chapter. For more information, contact:

BISNIS

International Trade Administration
U.S. Department of Commerce
Room 7413
Washington, DC 20230
(202) 482-4655
FAX (202) 482-2293
(202) 482-3145 (Flashfax)

U.S. and Foreign Commercial Service Offices

The U.S. and Foreign Commercial Service (US & FCS) was established in 1980 to help American exporters compete more effectively in the world marketplace. Commercial officers and consultants overseas collect market information and make contacts with agents, distributors, key buyers, and government officials.

Since 1993, the US & FCS has increased activities in Russia in an effort to enhance trade promotion and market development in the region. Offices are located in Moscow, St. Petersburg, Vladivostok, and Khabarovsk. Contact the International Trade Administration (ITA) of the U.S. Department of Commerce at the address above for current addresses and phone numbers.

American Business Centers

As part of US & FCS's expanded effort to help American businesspeople in Russia, the US & FCS has provided for the establishment of nine American Business Centers (ABCs) in Russia. The ABCs provide you with a professional working environment and the services you need to do business.

The services include:

- Offices and conference rooms
- International phone and fax
- Computer equipment
- Secretarial assistance

- Business appointment scheduling
- Interpretation and translation
- Photocopying
- Business counseling
- Market research
- Exhibition space

The nine centers in Russia that are underway or already open are located in these cities:

- Chelyabinsk
- Khabarovsk
- Nizhnevartovsk
- Nizhni Novgorod
- Novosibirsk
- St. Petersburg
- Vladivostok
- Volgograd
- Yekaterinburg

For more information about using the ABC services, contact:

U.S. and Foreign Commercial Service
(202) 482-4655, ext. 21

American Institute of Business and Economics

The American Institute of Business and Economics can help you provide training in Western business practices to your Russian partners and employees. For more information, contact:

American Institute of Business and Economics
Moscow State University
Main Building, Room A-416
Moscow, Russia
939-10-70
FAX 932-88-94

American Institute of Business and Economics
216 Bliss Lane
Great Falls, VA 22066
(703) 759-2507
FAX (703) 759-3389

Council for Trade and Economic Cooperation

The Council for Trade and Economic Cooperation (CIS USA) is a very good contact for you to find out more about going to Russia. CIS USA is a nongovernmental organization of CIS and U.S. business circles and is the legal successor to the American-Soviet Trade and Economic Council. Membership consists of 400 industrial enterprises, banks, joint ventures, and trading companies.

The organization's work is focused on identification and promotion of concrete cooperation projects with U.S. corporations. They will prepare customized market research, feasibility studies, and similar made-to-order research you may need. Various committees cover all kinds of business areas from service industries to investments, including agribusiness, transport, law, and banking. Mr. Arkady I. Volsky is the group's chairman of the board of directors. You can get in touch with them by phone or fax at:

Council for Trade and Economic Cooperation
095-243-54-70
FAX 095-230-24-67

Of course, this is a contact for major, large-scale projects. However, a number of consultants — foreign, Russian, and mixed — are available for lesser projects.

Financial assistance

Several independent organizations and U.S. government agencies are providing financing to U.S. businesses interested in doing business in Russia and other areas of the NIS. Some of the organizations and agencies you can contact are listed below.

Export-Import Bank

The Export-Import Bank, referred to as Eximbank, is an independent U.S. government agency. The agency provides support to U.S. exporters through the following services:

- Short and medium-term export credit insurance
- Medium and long-term loan guarantees
- Medium and long-term direct and intermediary loans
- Working capital guarantees
- Project financing

Eximbank offers support for Russia, Belarus, Kazakhstan, Ukraine, Uzbekistan, and Turkmenistan.

The Oil and Gas Framework Agreement, signed between the United States and Russia, provides financing through Eximbank for Russia's purchase of at least $2 billion of U.S. oil, gas, and petrochemical equipment and services to help revitalize existing oil and gas production and facilities. Russian oil and gas producers apply to Eximbank for final commitments. U.S. suppliers should contact the Russian oil and gas producers directly. For more information about Eximbank's financing programs, contact:

International Business Development Group
Export-Import Bank of the United States
811 Vermont Avenue, NW
Washington, DC 20571
(202) 565-3900 (General information)
(800) 565-EXIM (Export Finance 24-Hour Hotline)

Overseas Private Investment Corporation

The Overseas Private Investment Corporation (OPIC) promotes U.S. private investments in developing countries through four basic programs consisting of:

- Financing of investments through direct loans and loan guarantees;
- Insuring investments against a broad range of political risks;
- Providing a variety of investor services; and
- Assisting with project development.

OPIC's programs are designed to reduce the risks associated with overseas investments. For more information, contact:

Overseas Private Investment Corporation
1100 New York Avenue
Washington, DC 20527
(202) 336-8400

U.S. Trade and Development Agency

The U.S. Trade and Development Agency (TDA) is an independent U.S. government agency that provides funds for U.S. businesses to carry out feasibility studies. The funding is provided in the form of nonreimbursable grants, which can be used for studies to determine the technical, economic, and financial feasibility of major projects. The detailed data can be used to make decisions on how to proceed with project implementation.

While historically TDA projects have been public-sector undertakings by government ministries or agencies, TDA is now funding both public and private-sector projects involving major infrastructure and industrial ventures, including joint ventures in which U.S. companies plan to take equity. For more information, contact:

U.S. Trade and Development Agency
1621 North Kent Street, Room 309
Rosslyn, VA 22209
(703) 875-4357

U.S. Department of Agriculture

The U.S. Department of Agriculture (USDA) offers credit guarantees to help facilitate purchases of U.S. agricultural commodities by former Soviet Union states. The USDA's Commodity Credit Corporation (CCC) administers the credit guarantee program, GSM-102. GSM-102 is designed to increase the willingness of private banks to extend credit to foreign buyers for purchase of U.S. agricultural exports. Under the plan, the U.S. government guarantees to reimburse U.S. banks or other financial institutions if a foreign buyer's bank defaults on payments. For more information, contact:

Export Credits – Program Development Division
Foreign Agricultural Service
U.S. Department of Agriculture
Ag Box 1034
Washington, DC 20250
(202) 720-5319

U.S. Small Business Administration

The U.S. Small Business Administration (SBA) can help you develop export markets through financial and business development assistance. Although the SBA does not have any programs that specifically target Russia or the NIS, you can obtain SBA financing through its three main guarantee programs:

- Regular Business Loan Guarantee
- Export Revolving Line of Credit
- International Trade Loan Guarantee

For more information, contact:

Office of International Trade
U.S. Small Business Administration
409 Third Street SW, 8th Floor
Washington, DC 20416
(202) 205-6720
(800) 827-5722 (SBA Answer Desk)

United States Agency for International Development

The United States Agency for International Development (USAID) is encouraging U.S. private-sector involvement to help carry out several initiatives directed specifically at helping the former Soviet Union states. USAID finances technical and humanitarian assistance projects by choosing proposals that respond to requests for proposals (RFPs) and requests for applications (RFAs), which are publicized in the *Commerce Business Daily*. To subscribe, contact:

Superintendent of Documents
Commerce Business Daily
(202) 783-3238

The World Bank Group

In the more than 40 years of its existence, the World Bank has provided more than $200 billion in financial and technical assistance for developing countries to stimulate economic growth and stability. The bank has targeted a $600 million rehabilitation loan for the Russian government to finance imports to help stabilize the economy and assist Russia's economic reform. The loan will provide funding in the sectors of health, agriculture, transportation, and energy.

Opportunities from the World Bank are open to foreign companies, as well as U.S. businesses. The World Bank Group is comprised of the International Development Agency, the International Bank for Reconstruction and Development (IBRD), the International Finance Corporation (IFC), and the Multilateral Investment Guarantee Agency (MIGA).

Each of these entities administers different types of programs, ranging from government guaranteed loans to investment guarantees against risks of currency transfer, expropriation, war, civil disturbance, and breach of contract by the host government.

For more information on World Bank opportunities and how the bank operates, request document number 6835 from Flashfax or contact BISNIS at the address and phone number given at the beginning of this chapter.

The European Bank for Reconstruction and Development

The European Bank for Reconstruction and Development (EBRD) is a financial institution that makes loans and investments in the countries of Central and Eastern Europe.

EBRD will support projects in those countries committed to multiparty democracy and pluralism. The bank offers assistance in the form of advice, loans, equity investments, and debt guarantees and will finance the types of projects that will do the following:

- Help develop the private sector;
- Foster privatization;
- Increase direct foreign investment;
- Create and strengthen financial institutions;
- Restructure the industrial base;
- Build a modern infrastructure;
- Promote small and medium-sized enterprises; and
- Improve the environment.

To request private-sector development financing, you will need to submit a comprehensive business plan, as well as other project information.

For more information, request Flashfax document number, 6840 or contact BISNIS. BISNIS can provide more information on EBRD and put you in contact with EBRD representatives.

The Eurasia Foundation

Financed by the U.S. Agency for International Development, the Eurasia Foundation is a new, privately managed, grant-making organization. The foundation will make grants to American organizations with partners in Russia or the NIS, as well as directly to Russian and other NIS organizations.

The program's focus will be on:

- Private-sector development, including management training, economics education, curriculum development, policy advice, and information systems;

- Public-sector reform, including public administration, public policy advice, and development of a nongovernmental sector; and
- Media and communications, including support and development for print, broadcast, and electronic media.

The foundation mostly will make grants to nonprofit institutions. However, it will consider some for-profit projects fitting within the stated goals. If you are interested in Eurasia Foundation's programs, you can make a grant application by letter of inquiry.

To learn more about the application process, order Flashfax document number 6875, or contact the foundation directly.

Program Office
Eurasia Foundation
1527 New Hampshire Avenue, NW
Washington, DC 20036

Russian-American Enterprise Fund

The Russian-American Enterprise Fund, a nonprofit organization, has been established to stimulate the start up and expansion of small and medium-sized businesses in the Russian Federation. Funding of $300 million dollars will be provided by USAID over a four-to-five year period. The Russian Fund will take equity positions in and make loans to promising Russian enterprises with the goal of fostering economic development, democracy building, and environmental reforms. Guidelines are not yet established. For more information about this program, contact BISNIS or order Flashfax document number 6880.

Helpful publications

In addition to the publications previously mentioned in this chapter, several other sources can provide you with useful information about Russia and doing business in general.

Russian Information Services

Russian Information Services offers an extensive selection of publications about Russia, with items ranging from cookbooks to travel guides, maps, Russian literature, language dictionaries, and periodicals.

Access, their biannual catalogue of information resources, can be obtained by contacting:

Russian Information Services
89 Main Street, Suite 2
Montpelier, VT 05602
(802) 223-4955
FAX (802) 223-6105

Biznews Russia

To become familiar with what is going on and to find sources for assistance, subscribe to *Biznews Russia,* a biweekly newsletter covering the business information in today's Russia.

Biznews Russia
P.O. Box 761
McMinnville, OR 97128
(800) 409-3555

The Oasis Press/PSI Research

The Oasis Press publishes more than 90 titles in the subject area of business reference books. More than one million businesses nationwide use these solutions-oriented books. Two books you may find helpful are listed below.

Export Now. This book will prepare you to enter the export market by clearly explaining the basics and articulating the specific requirements for export licensing, preparation of documents, payment methods, packaging, and shipping. *Export Now* also includes advice on evaluating foreign representatives, planning international marketing strategies, and discovering official U.S. policy for various countries and regions.

The Successful Business Plan: Secrets & Strategies. If you need to seek financing, this book will help you have what bankers and venture capitalists want to see before funding a project. The book is a start-to-finish guide that provides insider tips to writing a business plan.

For more information about these and other publications, contact:

The Oasis Press
(800) 228-2275

Contact the authors

The authors welcome your questions and comments. If you would like more information, you can contact:

Robert M. Johnstone, P.C., Lawyers
1215 North Adams
P.O. Box 626
McMinnville, OR 97128-0626

(503) 472-9555
(800) 409-3555 (Nationwide)
FAX (503) 472-9550

Chapter 14

Conclusion

Заключение

The Russian dream

Russia is a country that has eleven time zones, thus it can literally be said that the sun never sets on Russian enterprise. Therefore, a conclusion for a book of this title is inappropriate. The country is rebuilding after 70 years of ruinous Socialist and Communist policies. Russians now live in a state of constant change and not always change for the better. Change, as we have indicated in the preceding chapters, is taking place at a breathtaking speed and, at the same time, paradoxically many things seem to remain unchanged.

Today, Russia is also going through internal crises attributed to change. One of these crises pertains to the change of the "Russian dream" of the ideal life style. The Russian dream can be equated to the "American dream," but it is different. The Russian dream had at its roots the Bible and the works of Socialist writers who described Utopian civilization. For many years, the people have known that the Russian dream was illusionary, but still it was there as the only dream for the people. The people at least thought they knew where they were going — even if they doubted they would ever get there.

An analysis of the emergence of the market economy in Russia is that it is not a goal to the Russian people as we perceive goals. The change to a market economy cannot be a goal for 150 million people. The change to a market economy is rather a strategy that is supposed to lead or bring the Russian people to a conclusion, whereby it will be possible to realize the dream. The Russian people want to know where they are going — they are less concerned about the method of getting to their destination. They look for leadership to tell them where they are going. For the 70 years preceding the fall of Communism, Russians were told they were "building a new collective society."

Today, Russians are told that societies are built by building individual successes rather than by collective success, reversing the teachings of an entire lifetime. Russians aren't familiar with the concept and the idea of "building capitalism." Russian leadership today, instead of depropagandizing people, is much involved in destructive political machinations. Before his death, the famous Russian film director Sergei Bondarchuk, who directed the Russian film, *War and Peace*, made a succinct observation. As a member of the Supreme Soviet for many years under Brezhnev, Bondarchuk told Tankred Golenpolsky:

> *The difference between us and them ('them' refers to newly elected Russian Parliamentarians) is that when we were elected, we knew that we were to be in the Supreme Soviet for a decade or so, and because of that we did not hurry in getting all sorts of 'perks' that come with being a member of Parliament. These new Parliamentarians, who are elected for four years without the stability of office, appear in many cases to be trying to hoard in their first year of office as much or more than their predecessors had attained in a decade.*

Perhaps this observation accounts for some present-day corruption in Russia. Certainly, foreign investors through their activity have contributed to the corruption in government. Foreign investors have often planted the seeds of greed in the minds of Russian government officials — who are seeking individual profit without regard to the best interests of the people they were elected to serve — to the detriment of the free enterprise that will create wealth in Russia.

In discussions with foreigners who are working within Russia, one often hears complaints. However, when confronted with the response, "Well, if it's so bad, why don't you just leave and go," no reasonable answer has been forthcoming. But, when these complainers stay, they can prevent new competitors from coming into the vast marketplace.

Summary

This book, upon initial review, might be more appropriately entitled "first steps in doing business in Russia." However, after reflecting upon this entire project and the transitions of the manuscript through the editing process, we, as the authors, are left with the conclusion that this work is worthwhile reading even for those veterans who have done business in the Russian market for a considerable time. The value of this book is that it stresses the importance of a bicultural attitude in approaching business relations.

One of the points made in this book is that although you may be an excellent businessperson, you may nevertheless fail or not do as well simply because of not understanding the local psychology. In relationships between individuals of different countries, patience and understanding are essential. In doing business in Russia, you must understand, first of all, the values of your Russian counterpart.

When you arrive at a mutuality of values, only then can your goals as business participants be decided upon. Once values and goals have been established, then you can implement particular business strategies successfully.

To force strategies based upon models tried in the West, without adequate consideration from a bicultural viewpoint, is perilous and predictably unproductive in terms of any long-range business success.

Another point you should keep in mind to ensure business success is the fact that Russia's laws concerning business are still evolving. Although the new *Civil Code* went into effect in January 1995, the government already anticipates further refinements and changes to the code.

Make sure to seek qualified advice about any project you are contemplating throughout all phases of your project's development.

Throughout the lives of the authors, relationships between the United States and Russia have progressed from a frigid state to a warming that has caused each society to embrace the other in the recognition of the great similarities and opportunities. Yet, each side is well advised to ponder the unique cultural differences.

The authors most sincerely hope that our children will be able to learn and understand each other from a bicultural viewpoint better than we did. We hope, as most likely do all of our readers, to have helped prepare a better garden in which the seeds of our children's productivity will be better able to flourish. This is the purpose of this book, which, because of the dynamic state of development in Russia, can have no real conclusion written at this time.

Glossary

Словарь

black funds. Funds used in a business that are not shown on the bookkeeping and are kept hidden from the tax agencies.

closed-type joint stock company. Russian form of business organization similar to a closely held corporation, in which stock is held by a small group of people and not publicly traded.

cooperative. Legal form of business organization allowed under the new *Civil Code* for Russian participants only. No Western equivalent exists for cooperatives, which may be either producing or consuming cooperatives. The cooperatives are a remnant of the former Soviet command economy and are akin to the collective farms.

DACHAS. Suburban houses/country homes.

decree. Law executing a ruling issued by the government. It differs from a law act worded by the DUMA and from the OOKAZ (order) sent down by the President.

DUMA. The lower house of the Parliament.

export of capital. The process of using capital and savings to conduct business abroad.

GOSKOMSTAT. State Committee on Statistics.

instruction. A departmental document explaining the rights and powers of various state agencies in applying and interpreting the law. "Instructions" have the tendency to interpret law exclusively in the interest of the agency.

joint venture. A Russian joint venture refers to a business or partnership that involves a Russian and a foreigner — that is, not a Russian with another Russian.

kommandite partnership. Russian legal form of business organization that is similar to a Western-style limited partnership.

militia. Police.

municipal enterprise. State-owned enterprise set up by the local or regional administration.

NE PONIMAYU. A phrase meaning, "I don't understand."

order. An instruction ruled by the local administration or agency.

PETROVKA 38. The criminal police headquarters.

private limited company. Russian form of business organization similar to a limited liability company.

privatization. The turning or selling of a state-owned enterprise to private owners.

public limited company (public corporation). Russian legal form of business organization, essentially the same as a public corporation in Western business practice.

RAKUSHKA. Russian garage or stall for automobile.

right to rend. The right to take for rent a plot of land or a building with a permit to resell as such to third parties.

state-owned enterprise. Unitary enterprise owned by federal or local administration as provided by the new *Civil Code*.

stock-jobbing. The repeated selling and reselling of shares purchased at low prices and sold immediately at inflated prices without any actual investment taking place that strengthens the business.

UCHASTKOVY. Russian word for police officer who supervises a certain territory or "beat."

ZA RODINU. A toast meaning, "To the motherland."

Appendix
Приложение

Small and medium-sized businesses poll

In June and July 1994, Russian sociologists polled representatives of small and medium-sized businesses (SME). The survey embraced more than 800 enterprises operating in Moscow, Tula, the Tula region, Volgograd, and Syktyvkar. The survey covered businesses of twelve major industries and within the services sector. The survey did not analyze the situation in agribusiness.

The average number of workers employed by the surveyed enterprises does not exceed 200 people. The survey also covered a relatively small group of enterprises where the number of workers surpasses the conventional margin of official statistics. This is done to keep sight of those businesses that have a direct relation to SMB.

According to the same poll in 1993, 34 percent of the businesses planned to increase capital investment, while 20 percent were going to curtail their investment. The 1994 poll showed 37 percent of businesspeople plan to boost investment, and only eight percent spoke against it. Others planned either to sustain the current level — or were unable to answer this question. Table 23 on the next page shows these business' answers to questions about the biggest problems confronting small and medium-sized businesses.

Table 23: Problems of Small and Medium-Sized Businesses (by percent)

Business	Funding invest-ment	Crediting circulating assets	Personnel Selection	Marketing	Delay in banking settlements	Unstable legislation	Search for premises	Mutual debts
Consumer goods production	12.1	6.9	8.9	12.1	10.9	14.9	5.2	14.1
Production of machinery	7.2	4.3	10.1	15.9	11.6	13.0	2.9	20.3
Trade	10.0	7.6	9.4	15.6	11.1	17.5	5.6	9.1
Mediation services	9.9	8.9	9.9	12.3	13.0	15.4	4.5	10.3
Everyday services	10.2	5.2	14.2	7.7	7.4	16.3	8.3	5.2
Transportation	7.6	5.1	9.3	9.3	19.5	15.3	3.4	14.4
Information, intellec-tual services	12.8	8.0	15.2	4.0	11.2	14.4	10.4	8.8
Industrial construction	12.2	3.3	9.8	6.5	12.2	12.2	3.3	17.1
Housing construction	12.8	7.7	9.6	3.8	9.0	12.2	5.8	21.8
Engineering, innovative activity	12.1	6.1	15.2	6.1	15.2	13.6	9.1	12.1
Rank	5	7	6	2	3	1	8	4

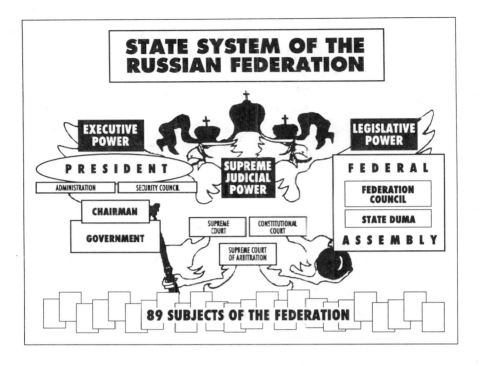

Russian Government Structure

This chart shows the three major branches of power in the Russian Federation — legislative, executive, and judicial — depicted on the wings of the two-headed eagle, Russia's state emblem.

The judicial power depicted in the center symbolizes a sound legal basis for legislative and executive power, which are equally important. Russia's sovereignty, independence, and democracy is based on these triune state structures.

The eagle's wing-span signifies the Russian state's sovereignty over all its territory, thus guaranteeing its integrity and inviolability.

Neither element of the mighty structure dominates. Although independent, both chambers of the Federal Council depicted on the right, 'legislative' wing, operate in close contact.

The executive power depicted in the left wing is represented by the President and the government.

Most importantly, Russia's statehood is based on a union of 89 subjects of the Russian Federation.

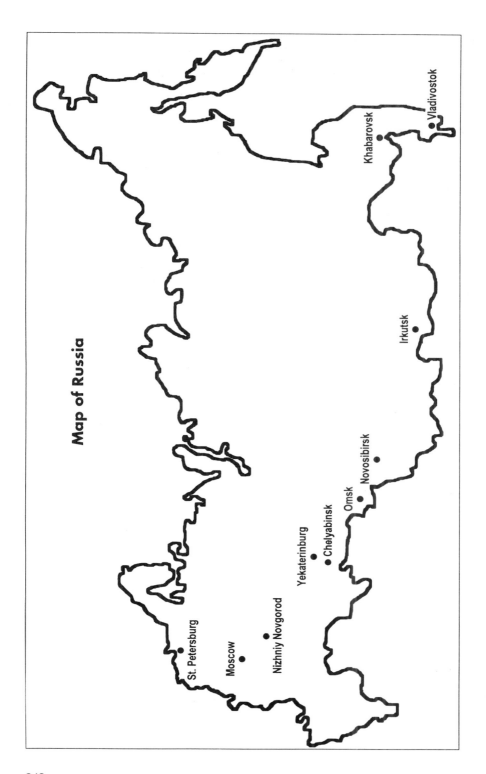

Map of Russia

Vladivostok

Khabarovsk

Irkutsk

Novosibirsk

Omsk

Chelyabinsk

Yekaterinburg

Nizhniy Novgorod

Moscow

St. Petersburg

Index
Указатель

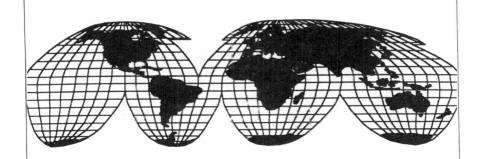

Introducing

PSI Research/EXECARDS® most
powerful source of business communications

*The International
Thank You card*

EXECARDS bridge the
language barrier and
build positive business
relationships.

Show your appreciation and gratitude with
a Thank You card that speaks the language
of your customer.

To see the complete line of EXECARDS call
or FAX our customer service department for
a *free* color catalog.

**Call 800-228-2275
FAX 503-476-1479**

 EXECARDS

PSI Research/EXECARDS 300 North Valley Drive • Grants Pass, OR 97526

Please, where is a telephone booth?

1-b

Save me!

1-d

I have not been met.

Please help me meet an official in the
airport/train station who speaks English.

1-a

Help!

1-c

Вызовите, пожалуйста, милицию.
Я иностранец. Меня ограбили.

Покажите, пожалуйста, где
находится милиция.

2-b

2-a

Покажите, пожалуйста, где
находится ближайший туалет.

Мне плохо/Я ранен. Вызовите,
пожалуйста, скорую помощь.

2-d

2-c

3-a

Please, help me hail a taxi.

3-b

Please, show me the metro station entrance.

3-c

Please, help me contact the U.S. Embassy.

3-d

Help me get home, please.

_____

_____

(address)

Покажите, пожалуйста, вход в метро.

Помогите, пожалуйста, взять такси.

3-a

Помогите, пожалуйста, мне
добраться до
Американсково Посольство

3-b

Помогите, пожалуйста, мне
добраться домой.

3-d